Art at Auction
1973-74

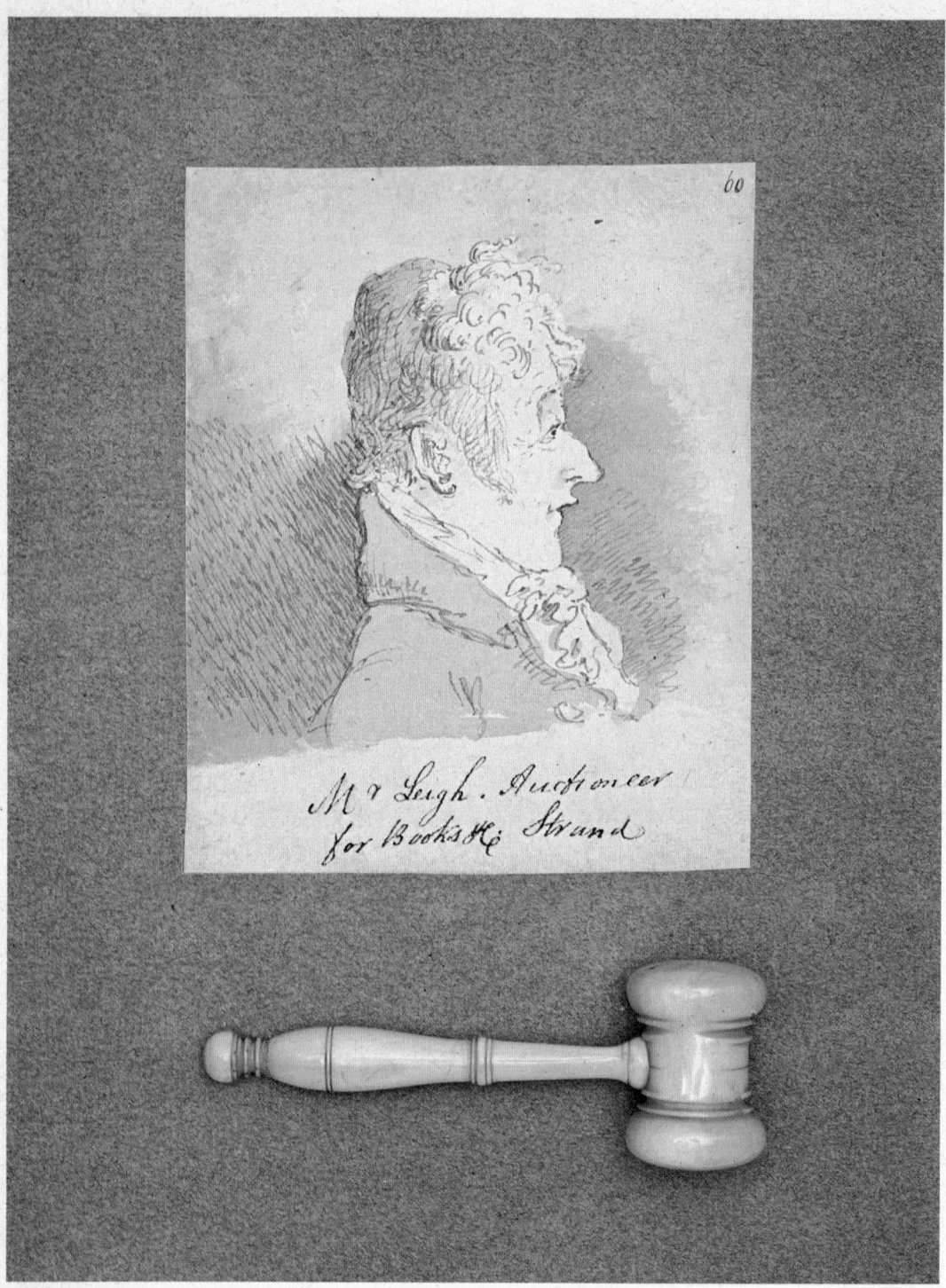

JOHN NIXON
Mr Leigh, auctioneer for books &c Strand
Pen and grey ink, grey and blue wash.
Inscribed. 4¾in by 3⅞in
Christie's £294 ($705). 4.VI.74
George Leigh was from 1774 a partner in S. Baker and G. Leigh, book auctioneers of York Street and the Strand. The firm became Leigh and Sotheby when his nephew John joined him in 1780

The auctioneer's hammer in use at Sotheby between 1744 and 1837

See note on George Leigh on page 4

Art at Auction

The Year at Sotheby Parke Bernet

1973-74

Two hundred and fortieth season

Sotheby Parke Bernet Publications

Sotheby Parke Bernet Publications Ltd
36 Dover Street, London W1

© Sotheby Parke Bernet Publications Ltd, 1974

All rights reserved including the right to reproduce
this book or portions thereof in any form
First published in 1974

Edited by Annamaria Edelstein,
assisted by Joan Sarll (UK) and Letitia Roberts (USA)

ISBN 0 85667 016 2

Printed and bound in Great Britain by W. S. Cowell Limited

GEORGE LEIGH

While Samuel Baker was 'the father of our tribe' Dibdin calls George Leigh 'the Raffaelle of Auctioneers' and goes on to say 'His voice was soft and he had a sort of jerk in its *cadenza* – somewhere between the affettuoso and adajio. Now and then his hammer came down with a sharp and startling thump; but in general it moved mechanically, and dropt in a sort of 'dying dying fall''.

Richard Gough in 1812 referring to Leigh: 'This genuine disciple of the elder Sam (Baker) is still at the head of his profession, assisted by a younger Sam (Sotheby); and of the Auctioneers of Books may not improperly be styled *facile princeps*. His pleasant disposition, his skill and his integrity are as well known as his *snuff-box*, described by Mr. Dibdin as having a not less imposing air than the remarkable periwig of Sir Fopling of old, which, according to the piquant note of Dr. Warburton, usually made its entrance upon the stage in a Sedan chair, brought in by two chairmen, with infinite satisfaction to the audience.
When a high price book is balancing between £15 and £20, it is a fearful sign of its reaching an additional sum if Mr. Leigh should lay down the hammer and delve into this said crumple horn shaped snuff box'.

The last of the three generations of the Sotheby family, Samuel Leigh Sotheby who died in 1861 at the age of 55 was obviously named after our courteous subject.

See illustration on frontispiece

Contents

9 Old Master Pictures

16 *Elizabethan Portraits* by Jack B. Gold

34 *Guardi: Nice Distinctions* by James Byam Shaw, CBE

44 Old Master Drawings

50 *The Jack Dick Collection of English Sporting Paintings: Parts I and II* by N. C. Selway

60 English Pictures, Drawings and Sculpture

76 *The Sale of the Allen Funt Collection of Paintings by Sir Lawrence Alma-Tadema* by Russell Ash

95 European Pictures

100 Impressionist and Modern Pictures, Drawings and Sculpture

132 Russian Pictures

134 Ballet

136 *The Robert C. Scull Auction* by John Tancock

146 Contemporary Pictures

154 Topographical Pictures

160 Canadian Pictures

162 American Pictures

175 Prints

189 *Photography as Art* by Graham Ovenden

197 Manuscripts and Printed Books

227 Works of Art

244 Icons

248 *'Typically Russian Enamel'* by Robert C. Woolley

257 Russian Works of Art

261 Objects of Vertu

The original and historically important orrery made by John Rowley and named after his patron the 4th Earl of Orrery. The instrument shows the motions of the earth and the moon relative to the sun at the centre of the system. The complicated mechanism with epicyclic gearing is contained within the cylindrical black lacquered base decorated with gold painted birds and flowers and fitted with brass carrying handles, diameter 77cm
London £29,000 ($69,600). 24.VI.74
From the collection of the Rt Hon Earl of Cork and Orrery. Now in the Science Museum, London
John Rowley, later Master of Mechanics to George I, took his inspiration for constructing this, the original orrery, from an instrument made by Tompion and Graham which is now in the Museum of the History of Science at Oxford.
According to the writings of Sir Richard Steele, the contemporary essayist, Rowley's machine was acquired by his patron, the 4th Earl of Orrery and named after him in 1713 by Sir Richard who wished to do honour to the maker and supposed inventor of such an ingenious and complicated machine

Contents *continued*

- 266 Portrait Miniatures
- 269 Arms and Armour
- 277 Silver and Metalwork
- 293 *'Benvenuto Cellini' and the nineteenth-century Collector and Goldsmith* by John Culme
- 297 Pewter
- 299 Coins and Medals
- 301 *Coin Sales* by T. G. Eden
- 305 Clocks, Watches and Scientific Instruments
- 313 Antiquities, Islamic, Tibetan, Nepalese and Primitive Works of Art
- 326 *French Furniture in the Saleroom and outside:* 1800–1914 by Sir Francis Watson, KCVO, FBA
- 339 Furniture, Decorations and Textiles
- 369 Musical Instruments
- 373 Ceramics
- 374 *The Medici Bowl from Seton College* by Joseph Kuntz
- 399 Chinese Ceramics and Works of Art
- 427 Japanese Ceramics and Works of Art
- 436 *The Harari Collection of Inro* by Neil Davey
- 439 Glass and Paperweights
- 443 Art Nouveau and Art Deco
- 447 *The Bugattis* by Malcolm Haslam
- 456 Jewellery
- 467 *Sir William Dobell at the Sydney Opera House*
- 469 Wine sales
- 471 Natural History
- 472 Acknowledgements
- 475 Index

For the sake of consistency all exchange rates have been estimated at $2.40 to the £1 despite fluctuations.

Pictures, Drawings and Sculpture

  9 OLD MASTER PICTURES
 44 OLD MASTER DRAWINGS
 60 ENGLISH PICTURES, DRAWINGS AND SCULPTURE
 95 EUROPEAN PICTURES
100 IMPRESSIONIST AND MODERN PICTURES, DRAWINGS AND SCULPTURE
132 RUSSIAN PICTURES
134 BALLET
146 CONTEMPORARY PICTURES
154 TOPOGRAPHICAL PICTURES
160 CANADIAN PICTURES
162 AMERICAN PICTURES

PIETER BRUEGHEL THE YOUNGER
The Triumph of Death
On panel, 20in by 34½in
London £41,000 ($98,400). 10.VII.74
From the collection of Sir Sacheverell Sitwell, Bt

PIETRO DI DOMENICO DA MONTEPULCIANO
Polyptych: *Madonna and Child enthroned with angels, SS Michael, Stephen, Lawrence and Cosmas*
Central panel 51in by 21⅝in, side panels 45in by 13in
Florence L 70,000,000 (£46,205; $110,106). 10.IV.74

Opposite page
GIOVANNI DI PAOLO
Christ on the Cross
On panel, 45in by 34¾in
London £60,000 ($144,000). 12.XII.73
From the collection of Mr J. J. Visser of The Hague

OLD MASTER PICTURES 11

HANS MALER
Portrait of Barbara Kilingerin
On panel, inscribed *M* with the sitter's name and age, 20, dated 1530, 17½in by 14¼in
London £36,000 ($86,400). 10.VII.74

OLD MASTER PICTURES 13

JOOS VAN CLEVE
The Holy Family
On panel, 23¼in by 17½in
London £22,000 ($52,800). 10.VII.74
Formerly in the collection of Count Andrassy, Budapest

14 OLD MASTER PICTURES

GIOVANNI ANTONIO CANALE, called CANALETTO
The Bucintoro at the Molo on Ascension Day
59½in by 53¾in
London £280,000 ($672,000). 12.XII.73

OLD MASTER PICTURES 15

CLAUDE GELEE, called CLAUDE LORRAIN
Landscape with Mercury and Argus
Signed, 23½in by 29in
London £105,000 ($252,000). 27.III.74
From the collection of George Harwood Esq

16 ELIZABETHAN PORTRAITS

ENGLISH SCHOOL
Portrait of Sir Francis Knollys, KG
(After restoration of original face)
On panel, inscribed with the age of the sitter, 72, 29½in by 25in
London £550 ($1,320). 30.1.74
Now the property of the National Trust, Greys Court, Henley

Elizabethan Portraits

By Jack B. Gold

Between the time of Van Dyck's first visit to London and the quatercentenary celebrations of Shakespeare's birth ten years ago, hardly anyone regarded the stiff portraits of the Tudor period as works of art. The Renaissance had been slow to take a hold in England, and although literature and music were affected early in the sixteenth century, continental fashions in the visual arts were delayed for another hundred years. After Henry VIII's death the English court became increasingly insular, partly for political reasons but also for want of foreign consorts to the succeeding Tudor monarchs, his three children. Edward VI died too young to marry; Mary's husband, Philip of Spain, spent only a few years in England and had little influence on the arts, and although Elizabeth encouraged a series of foreign suitors, and adopted various continental fashions in dress, she preserved the country from artistic as well as political involvements abroad. Painting especially remained essentially gothic for decades after Titian and Tintoretto had perfected a style as far removed from English taste as the Impressionists first seemed to the traditionalists of Paris and London three hundred years later.

The chief patron of artists in the Middle Ages had been the Church. After the Reformation had banned sacred pictures almost the only remaining outlets for artists were the secular decorations erected for royal celebrations, and in the second half of the sixteenth century painting portraits. Previously these had seldom been painted at all except in the form of kneeling donors at the foot of altarpieces, but now every builder of a new house wanted portraits of himself and his contemporaries to hang on his panelled walls. The demand for painters used to this sort of work could only be met by importing artists from abroad, mostly from the Low Countries and Germany; of these Holbein was by far the most important, though his influence was not as long lasting as might be expected. His followers in this country all succumbed to the demands of English taste, though some preserved his sharp eye for character but after a few years their work seemed to owe more to the engraved brass effigies in parish churches than to the cartoons of their master.

These Tudor portraits have proved very vulnerable and a large proportion of them must have perished. The strong oak panels on which they are painted are actually more prone to decay than canvas. They have had to endure the hazards of dry rot, woodworm, warping and twisting through changes of atmosphere, and often long years of banishment to the attics of country houses during their centuries of neglect. Those that have survived have mostly suffered further from the ravages of ignorant restorers. Very few remain intact. Their surfaces have been scoured by over-cleaning, their clothes and armour have been ignorantly repainted, their faces altered to fit prevailing fashions of beauty and inscriptions of names and dates added in accordance with inaccurate traditions or just wishful thinking. Collectors should be expert in genealogy, heraldry, armour and dress fashions; then with the help of a dendrologist to date the timber of the panels, their mistakes can be reduced.

The renewal of interest in Tudor portraits began with the exhibition held at Stratford-on-

Avon and later at the National Portrait Gallery to celebrate the four hundredth anniversary of Shakespeare's birth. They have been followed by a spate of popular biographies, films and television serials followed by exhibitions of their costumes, and the opening of increasing numbers of Tudor country houses to the public. Some serious general studies and learned catalogues of particular collections have also appeared. Previously very few picture connoisseurs had been interested in the period and the dispersal of the splendid Elizabethan portrait collections from Ditchley and Wroxton Abbey between the wars provoked very little excitement. Good portraits of the period could still be bought very cheaply until the mid-1960s when prices began to rise and the flow of Elizabethans through the salerooms increased accordingly, though prices seldom reached four figures till the 1970s. They are now in short supply and very much more expensive; the attics seem to have been cleared.

It is a difficult period to catalogue. Elizabethan artists were still treated like mediaeval artisans, and paid accordingly. They had no social status before the Stuart dynasty, their names are seldom recorded nor their paintings signed, so that attributions remain speculative. Most of their works can be divided into recognisable groups, though there is fierce disagreement even about these. What does seem certain is that nearly all portraits were co-operatively produced by various specialists working together in the same studio, one or other concentrating on drapery, jewellery, armour or heraldry, and of course headed by the face-painter whose name, if identified, is given the credit for the completed result. Dating is complicated by alterations made in the sitters' lifetime like enlarging a ruff to catch up with fashion, or the addition of garters or coronets. The identity of a sitter can often be deduced from dates and ages inscribed on backgrounds, as well as by the provenance of the portrait, but inscriptions must be contemporary to be trustworthy. The most reliable identification of a sitter whose face is unfamiliar is a Lumley label, a painted addition to the portraits of his contemporaries collected by the 7th Lord Lumley in the form of a *trompe-l'oeil* crumpled scrap of paper fixed with sealing wax on which the name of the person is inscribed. The National Gallery removed one such from the background of Holbein's Duchess of Milan.

Portraits of sovereigns are always in demand, but in Queen Elizabeth's time those of her leading subjects were almost as keenly sought after. Many replicas might be painted at the same time so that it is often impossible to differentiate between originals and replicas. The 'pricked' cartoons from which the outlines of portraits were drawn made repetitions easy, and by reversing the drawing the same pinholes could be used to make the sitter look the opposite way. Patrons seldom posed in the modern sense, and the same cartoon was often re-used at intervals throughout the life of some celebrities. Most of the innumerable portraits of Burleigh and Leicester keep the same outlines over many years of repetition with variations only in their clothing. A familiar image with appropriate insignia rather than a true likeness was what was required, and very few elderly sitters would have tolerated accurate representations of themselves. Burleigh's official portraits remained unchanged over several decades, and the aging Queen's image actually went into reverse and was more youthful in Hilliard's last miniatures than the first, and at the end of her life this lead was followed by many painters 'in large', notably by the Fleming Marcus Gheeraerts the younger.

Elizabethan portraits must therefore be judged by standards different from those of later periods. They are essentially formal, and their obvious merit usually lies in the sparkling decorative detail rather than their human interest, but those painted under the influence of Hilliard by his English associates have an extra quality not found in any of their immigrant rivals' work. Their sitters are transformed by the same native genius which infused the English

ENGLISH SCHOOL
Portrait of Lettice Knollys
On panel, inscribed, *circa* 1600, 18¾in by 14¼in
London £550 ($1,230). 30.1.74

Left: before restoration
Above: restored. The reduction in width is caused by the trimming of the split in the panel

poetry of the period. Hilliard in his miniatures gives his young women a lyrical sweetness, and his men a knightly gallantry without equal in English art of any period. Some of the full scale portraits attributed to those English born contemporaries whom he influenced such as William Segar, George Gower, Robert Peak and John Bettes the younger seem similarly inspired. It is by the measure of their native poetic qualities that Elizabethan portraits should ultimately be judged.

Towards the end of the past season, when Tudor portraits have been in short supply Sotheby's sold two notable collections. One confined to members of the Knollys family had passed by unbroken inheritance to the anonymous vendor and the other, an assembly of miscellaneous notables, had been acquired during the present century by the late Major and Mrs Eric Bullivant. The Knollys portraits were of particular interest as that family does not seem to have been painted as often as most others of comparable importance at court. There is no portrait of the celebrated Sir Francis Knollys, the Lord Treasurer, in the National Portrait Gallery. Lady Knollys, his wife, painted as a stout old lady with her little dog on a table beside her, was a first cousin of Queen Elizabeth and her Flemish-style portrait was the pick of the collection, but the head of Lettice her daughter (illustrated above), who was successively wife of Walter, Earl of Essex and Robert, Earl of Leicester, is specially interesting as most of her reputed portraits are of doubtful authenticity. This one was inscribed 'Lettice Knollys, Countess of Essex now Lady Dowager of the Earl of Leicester', which supports a contemporary identification, and it does convey some of the competing charm which caused the Queen to describe her as a 'she wolf' and banish her from court. In the portrait of Sir Francis, her father, the head had unfortunately been entirely overpainted in a thick twentieth-century manner, but a very good earlier copy of the portrait was available and, with the help of the recumbent effigy on his tomb, a more accurate restoration has since been possible (see p 16). This portrait and another in the sale of his eldest son William, who was created Earl of Banbury, are now back in the family's original home, Greys Court, Henley, now the property of the National Trust.

The Bullivant collection seems to have been assembled for decorative rather than historical interest, although it contained some celebrities. The portraits, mostly framed in similar black and gold seventeenth-century style mouldings, were nearly all about the same size, and even had a certain similarity of style, their hands particularly having the same grey shadows. All appeared to be in perfect condition but it would have been ingenuous to suppose they could be unrestored. They had in fact all been 'cradled' in crossed wooden supports after the panels on which they were painted had been shaved to cigar box thickness, which makes it possible to correct twisted joints and flatten irregular surfaces. It had been an extremely expert operation, and the restoration of any damage was very hard to detect, though there were some tell-tale inaccuracies to alert the wary. Bidding for the collection was very keen, and three portraits were bought for the nation. Walter Devereux, 1st Earl of Essex, father of Queen Elizabeth's favourite and first husband of Lettice Knollys, went to the National Portrait Gallery, but his faithless wife, who was included in the previous collection, has not joined him and her second husband who was already there. The newly created young Earl is wearing a suit of very fine black and damascened German tilting armour and is in the style of the Flemish-born Antonis Mor. He is holding a baton with an exquisite miniature royal coat-of-arms on the tip, and his own arms, with their many quarterings, are an essential decorative feature of the design (p 21). The Gallery also added another portrait of his son Robert to the collection.

£29,000, the highest price of the sale and an auction record for any Tudor portrait, was paid on behalf of the Tate Gallery for a delicately detailed late Elizabethan costume painting called Lady Mary Howard (p 21). The intricately embroidered bodice, and starched lace ruff are of exceptional quality, but the pretty face has a curiously modern look. A large and very much patched version of the well-known 'Tudor Succession' group of Henry VIII with his descendants at Sudeley Castle will certainly provide problems, if its complete restoration is attempted. Its interest lies mostly in the changes made after an interval of about thirty years between the painting of the original and the copy. Queen Elizabeth appears much younger in the later version of her final guise of the semi-divine and ageless Virgin, but the attendant deities of Peace and Plenty are rendered in a stiff and awkward manner by a copyist unused to the continental mannerist style of the originals. The unobtrusive addition of the head and shoulders of a young man in a low archway on the left of the picture may be a clue to the second painter's identity.

Heraldry is often a help in identifying sitters but, like inscriptions, it is not always trustworthy. Walter Devereux's obviously contemporary coat-of-arms surmounted by his new coronet as Earl of Essex leaves no doubt as to his identity, and an anonymous lady's portrait bearing the arms of Okeover of Okeover Hall, Derbyshire, indicated her married name, the size of her ruff indicated her date, and Burke's *Landed Gentry* gave the name of the wife living in that decade. Further confirmation was available when somebody pointed out that one of her jewels was an oak-apple between two leaves. In contrast to these two examples the version of the Knollys coat-of-arms, with its elephant crest, which appeared on most of the portraits of the previous collection, had been added much later, and indicated the owner of the picture rather than the family of the sitter.

MARCUS GHEERAERTS THE YOUNGER
Portrait of a Lady, said to be Lady Mary Howard
On panel, inscribed with the age of the sitter, 23, and dated 1592, 44½in by 33¼in £29,000 ($69,600)

Attributed to WILLIAM SEGAR
Walter, Earl of Essex
On panel, inscribed and dated 1572, 42in by 34in £2,800 ($6,720)

The paintings illustrated above were in the collection of the late Mr and Mrs Eric Bullivant sold in London on 8th May 1974

None of the pictures in either sale was in its original frame. Panel portraits, usually described as 'tables' in contemporary inventories, were not necessarily framed at all, but late Tudor and early Jacobean portraits were usually very simply enclosed in plain mitred oak mouldings painted black and only rarely decorated. Occasionally they were embellished with a filigree pattern in gold leaf, or inscribed all round with a motto, but seldom with names or dates. The early seventeenth-century view of a rich Flemish picture collection included in the National Gallery 150th anniversary exhibition, shows no carved frames, but within a few years they became fashionable both sides of the Channel.

The Elizabethan style scarcely outlasted the Queen herself: James I's reign brought great changes. His court was less isolated than his predecessor's and painting, along with architecture began to join up with continental taste, as both his sons bought European works of art. For the first decade or so some splendid formal costume pieces were still produced in the old style, but they soon became less rigid and more three-dimensional. Hilliard lived on, but his work and that of his followers no longer seems 'twin born with poetry' as that of his youth. By the end of the reign the transitional period of Jacobean art was almost over and with the arrival of Van Dyck the surviving painters of the old tradition turned to the provinces, where taste was slower to change. England had rejoined the mainstream of European art and in Charles I's London, Elizabethan portraits seemed absurdly archaic. They remained so until their rediscovery in the reign of Elizabeth II.

22 OLD MASTER PICTURES

CLAUDE GELEE,
called CLAUDE LORRAIN
*Landscape with Rebecca
taking leave of her father*
23¼in by 31in
London £50,000 ($120,000).
12.XII.73

Opposite page above
PIETER BRUEGHEL THE YOUNGER
A peasant wedding
On panel, signed and dated 1630,
29in by 49in
London £90,000 ($216,000).
12.XII.73

JAN FRANS VAN BLOEMEN, called ORIZONTE
One of a pair of *Southern landscapes*
38in by 56in
New York $29,000 (£12,083). 18.VI.74

HENDRICK AVERCAMP
A winter scene with skaters on a frozen river
On panel, signed with monogram and dated 1609, 11½in by 17in
London £44,000 ($105,600). 10.VII.74
Formerly in the collection of Baron H. Thyssen-Bornemisza, Schloss Rohoncz

24 OLD MASTER PICTURES

SALOMON VAN RUYSDAEL
A river scene with a château
On panel, signed and dated 1665, 15¾in by 21¾in
London £35,000 ($84,000). 27.III.74
From the collection of Ronald A. Cookson Esq, OBE

JAN BOTH
Italian landscape with sportsmen
Signed, 37½in by 61in
London £27,000 ($64,800). 10.VII.74
Formerly in the collection of Viscount Hambleden

OLD MASTER PICTURES 25

JAN SIBERECHTS
Interior of an art-collector's house
22in by 25¼in
London £66,000 ($158,400).
12.XII.73

JACQUES BLANCHARD
Charity
41¾in by 54¼in
London £23,500 ($56,400).
27.III.74
From the Goodwood
Collection

26 OLD MASTER PICTURES

OSIAS BEERT THE ELDER
A still life
On metal, 13½in by 19½in
New York $30,000 (£12,500).
6.XII.73

CLARA PEETERS
A still life of cheeses
On panel, 17½in by 25in
London £7,000 ($16,800)
8.V.74

OLD MASTER PICTURES 27

LOUISE MOILLON
A still life of fruit
On panel, signed, 28in by 41in
New York $120,000 (£50,000).
6.XII.73

JAN DAVIDSZ. DE HEEM
Flowers and fruit
Signed and dated in a cartouche:
J D De Heem 1675, 25¼in by 31½in
London £26,000 ($62,400).
10.VII.74
From the collection of
Sir John Eden, Bt

28 OLD MASTER PICTURES

THE MASTER OF THE MANSI MAGDALEN
The Virgin and Child with St Anne
On panel, 29½in by 20¾in
London £31,000 ($74,400). 27.III.74
From the collection of Chevalier Etienne de Geradon

OLD MASTER PICTURES 29

DOMENIKOS THEOTOKOPOULOS called EL GRECO
Christ blessing
Probably painted *circa* 1580, 37½in by 26¼in
London £51,000 ($122,400). 10.VII.74

30 OLD MASTER PICTURES

Left and opposite page
PAOLO CALIARI, called
PAOLO VERONESE
An astronomer and *A patriarch*
A pair, each 81in by 46in
London £155,000 ($372,000).
12.XII.73
Formerly in the collection of
Robert Goelet Esq

32 OLD MASTER PICTURES

FRANCESCO GUARDI
The Scala dei Giganti at the Doge's Palace, Venice
On panel, 8in by 6½in
London £30,000 ($72,000). 27.III.74
From the collection of Dr J. R. J. Angus

GIOVANNI ANTONIO CANALE, called CANALETTO
Above: Venice, the Piazzetta and
Below: Venice, the Piazza San Marco
A pair painted *circa* 1740, each 9in by 15¾in
London £130,000 ($312,000). 27.III.74
From the collection of Mrs Charles Gifford

Fig 1 FRANCESCO GUARDI *Piazza San Marco, looking towards the Basilica* (Collection of the Duke of Hamilton)

Fig 2 FRANCESCO GUARDI *The Lagoon with the Fondamenta Nuove on the left* (Formerly sold at Sotheby's)

Guardi: Nice Distinctions

By James Byam Shaw

I do not know who was the inventor of the code that is printed, as a precaution against the incursions of the law, in the front of every catalogue issued by Sotheby's, to explain the extent of responsibility accepted by the firm (and the owners concerned) in auction sales: I mean the code that explains the varying forms in which the artist's name is given, to indicate degrees of reliability in the attribution – the use of the full name for a firm attribution; of the family name preceded by only an initial for a possible but uncertain attribution; and of the family name alone for a very doubtful one. It is a system of long standing, both at Sotheby's and Christie's, which was perfectly understood in the art trade in the old days; but since the law regarding 'false pretences' was redefined and extended (against expert advice) some years ago, to cover the sale of works of art at auction – where the old principle of *Caveat Emptor* is in my view justifiable, and the protection of a foolish and ignorant buyer is both undeserved and impracticable – it has been used by other firms of auctioneers, and clearly stated in print. In any case it is a very useful formula, which sometimes enables the learned cataloguer (and the cataloguers in our great auction houses must nowadays be learned indeed) to convey as much in the form of the name as an academic art historian could convey in a dozen pages of argument. Yet it is I imagine not always easy to apply to the satisfaction of the proprietor who wishes to sell his picture, or even of the cataloguer himself, who has to consider the interests both of the proprietor and of his firm, as well as his own reputation as a connoisseur, and to express his opinion in this simple fashion. I intend in the present essay to consider the application of the formula to the case of a single artist, Francesco Guardi, whose works – genuine, doubtful or admittedly suspect – must be among the most difficult to classify so succinctly.

Everyone with some knowledge of Venetian art of the eighteenth century, and some experience of the market in England, where Guardi's work has been so long appreciated and was once so richly represented in the old private collections, probably has a dream-vision of a painting by Francesco that would be likely to cause a stir of excitement among the connoisseurs, and more particularly the gentlemen of the trade, on its appearance in the saleroom. I say 'in the saleroom', because the requirements on such an occasion are subtly different from what one would expect of the same picture on a drawing-room wall or in a great public gallery. The frame, for one thing, may be a poor one, or at least an unsuitable one, a replacement, say by the owner's grandfather, to suit the fashion of the time. And for another thing, in such circumstances the picture may be the more desirable for a thick coat of much discoloured varnish, which disguises the true colour – turning the brilliance of the Venetian sky into the dusty grey-green-blue of an old Cambridge oarsman's cap – but not the quality of the brushwork underneath. This varnish will of course eventually be removed under the careful touch of an experienced modern restorer, but it is in the meantime a sort of guarantee that the surface has not been disturbed by the rough cleaning methods of two or three generations ago[1]. The dream-picture then would be a picture in what is called (not very appropriately) 'virgin condition'. What might be the other *desiderata*? It would be a famous and familiar Venetian view – a view perhaps of Piazza San Marco, looking towards the Basilica, with the shadow falling from the left half across the Piazza, from the sun in the West, as Guardi nearly always painted it in this view. That is the subject of a very large number of Guardi's most beautiful paintings[2]; it is perhaps the view most desired by every tourist, not only in Guardi's time but also today, for it is less changed since the eighteenth century than any famous view in any famous city in Europe[3]; and it would be peopled, not by flocks of obtrusive pigeons and Germans in *Lederhosen*, or those less serious birds of passage in singlets and jeans, but by the elegant society of Venice. There might be a group of Procurators in their splendid robes, a gentleman with his hat under his arm conversing with two ladies, and one or two very up to date ladies with their hair dressed high – for fine feathers rather than the tricorne (for it will surely be a painting of Guardi's most brilliant period, of the 1770s or 1780s); here and there, perhaps, a father leading his son by the hand, a pair of ragamuffin boys, and a dog or two; and if any of all these are tourists, they would be Grand Tourists, 'people of importance', English, French, Russian or German[4]. Such a painting was sold at Sotheby's from the Caldwell collection on 24th April 1939 – in those happier days when such a masterpiece could be obtained for a few thousand pounds of good money – and is now in the Duke of Hamilton's collection. In that picture (which I remember well) were all the virtues of Guardi's art: true observation of the Venetian sky, with a little cloud, streaky over the horizon, light and fleeting above; lace-like delicacy in the architecture of St Mark's; transparent shadow; and the best characteristics of his figure-painting – occasional ragged touches of black in the dresses, and exquisite flicks of white to suggest the headdress of a lady, a lace sleeve, a hand holding a fan, a tiny pointed shoe, or the powder of a gentleman's wig. All muted at the time of the sale by the old varnish, not lost, but still awaiting the full revelation (Fig 1).

This is 'Francesco Guardi' without question. Such pictures were no doubt painted for the important people, and on them Francesco expended all his subtle talent, his most exquisite touch. With the Grand Tourists, these views of the Piazza were most in demand; but for them

---

1 Or less than that. I have a sad memory of seeing a beautiful little Guardi in this condition being cleaned by an old restorer (a charming old man, working not half a mile from Bond Street, about forty years ago) who took up a handful of rough salt to remove the varnish. I protested, rather feebly (for it was not my picture): 'Surely, Mr...., you will destroy the fine glazing of the shadows under the bridge.' To which he replied, that if he did, he could easily put it back again.

2 There are no less than twenty-three paintings of almost exactly the same view reproduced in Morassi's recent corpus of Guardi (1973, cat. nos. 314 – 318 and 320 – 337). Of all these only five are lit by the morning sun from the East or South, with shadows from the right hand side, and most of them are early in date. There are barely half a dozen views taken in the opposite direction, from San Marco towards the church of San Giminiano on the West side of the Piazza (which was demolished in the Napoleonic era).

3 As can be seen by comparison with the photograph reproduced on pp 66 – 67 of Terisio Pignatti's recent guide to Venice. Only a few chimney-stacks are now missing. It is evident that the proportions of the Campanile (rebuilt *come era, dove era* after its collapse in 1902) were invariably romanticised by Guardi into a more slender and elegant construction. Was it not a just criticism?

4 All these little figures appear, with variations, again and again in the paintings of this view and elsewhere, and were generally derived from the artist's summary pen and wash sketches, single figures and groups, often thrown together on a single sheet. The gentleman with his hat under his arm, talking to the two ladies, is ubiquitous: we find him with several others of the figures I have described, in a very characteristic signed drawing in the Metropolitan Museum (Byam Shaw, *The Drawings of Francesco Guardi*, 1951, pl 50), and there he is unmistakably in about a dozen of the paintings, all of the late period.

too he would contrive a brilliant impression of one of the great Venetian ceremonies or festivals – Piazza San Marco transformed by temporary architecture for the Feast of the Assumption; or the Doge's state barge, the Bucintoro, rowing out to the Lido to 'wed the Adriatic' with a ring on the same occasion; or the Regatta on the Grand Canal. There were other favourite views: the Doge's Palace seen across the water from San Giorgio Maggiore; or San Giorgio seen from the opposite side; the entrance to the Grand Canal with the Dogana or the church of the Salute; the Rialto bridge. There is a set of four of these famous subjects – San Giorgio, the Salute, the Dogana and the Rialto – in the Wallace Collection in London, as fine as any ever painted and not as well known as they should be; and two more, no less beautiful, in the National Gallery, bequeathed by the Misses Cohen. These were for the *forestieri* souvenirs of a delightful visit, and hundreds of them must have been carried off to England and France, particularly, in Guardi's time and afterwards, whenever the European wars allowed the Grand Tours to begin again. Very few seem to have remained in Venice. The Venetians needed no souvenirs; and from Guardi I suspect they preferred to buy those romantic compositions, most of them of small dimensions – put together sometimes from Venetian architecture arbitrarily arranged, sometimes from memories of Antiquity, or imaginary Gothic ruins, arches and bridges by the lagoon – the so-called *capricci,* peopled by peasants and fisherfolk, or by the elegant Venetians of Guardi's time.

These *capricci,* which displayed the required artistic virtue of *invenzione* – though in fact they are remarkably repetitive in motif – were painted I imagine for the artist's own pleasure, as well as for Venetian patrons, particularly in his later years; they are in general of a more level standard of execution than the views, which, in the eyes of the contemporary connoisseur, hardly deserved a place in the category of true art. There are many of the views of Venice which are noticeably inferior to the best – to the kind of picture I have attempted to describe; lacking the perfection of idiom, the ultimate brilliance of handling. Nor can the deficiencies always be attributed to poor condition, though careless cleaning can be as disastrous to the delicate texture of a Guardi as it so notoriously is to that of a Terborch, a De Hoogh, a Vermeer – or a George Stubbs. In Guardi's figures particularly, there is an undeniable variation in quality; and again, that cannot be said to be entirely a matter of date. It is true that he reached that highest level of delicacy and charm, in handling and colour, only in his work of the 1770s and 80s; and the larger figures which he favoured in his earlier view paintings, when he was attempting to imitate the more fashionable Canaletto, from the middle 1750s through the first half at least of the 1760s, are indeed more coarsely – or say broadly – painted, in the manner of Carlevarijs and Canaletto, his predecessors in the art of the *vedutista*. But it is not to such figures (of which the two great Venetian views at Waddesdon, or the earlier of the two views of the Piazza in the National Gallery, provide good examples) that I am referring: I mean rather those elongated pin-headed gondoliers and bargemen, often with one arm stiffly outstretched like a finger-post, in the pair of lagoon views in the Fitzwilliam Museum, Cambridge (Morassi, 1973, cat. nos. 639, 658), or the series of six views of the Grand Canal and the Fondamenta Nuove in the collection of the Duke of Buccleuch[5]; these are quite unlike the larger, Canalettian figures of the relatively early Waddesdon paintings (dateable for topographical reasons after 1755, perhaps *circa* 1760), and equally unlike the familiar Guardi figures

5 All reproduced (with some good details) and catalogued by Morassi (cat. nos. 514, 549, 553, 561, 615 and 620) though not indexed. They are mostly said by Morassi to be very early: but he has to admit that the *View of the Rialto* (M. 549) is not before 1754, when the campanile of San Bartolommeo was rebuilt in the form shown here. I agree with Michael Levey in believing that the whole set must be of the same date.

of the 1770s and 80s. Now some of this group of pictures are very fine in their way, with beautiful skies and (in the lagoon scenes) a subtle rendering of the still, shallow water[6]; and furthermore a good many of them, including all six of the Duke of Buccleuch's, are signed by Francesco, and the signatures are surely unimpeachable[7].

It would be flying in the face of the evidence to catalogue these as anything but 'Francesco Guardi'. And yet, in some of them, the strangeness of the figures, and also the variation in quality, must strike any careful observer. Francesco had, so far as we know, no school, such as the great Renaissance artists had. But he had a younger brother, Nicolò, of whom we know nothing except that he was a painter, and he also had a son, Giacomo, of whom we know a good deal, not much to his credit so far as artistic talent is concerned. Both presumably worked in the studio, which must have been a typical Venetian family affair in the tradition of the studios of Tintoretto and Bassano – a sort of firm or factory, of which the eldest Guardi brother, Antonio (1698-1760), was the leader until he died, and was succeeded by Francesco. Nicolò was born in 1715, and lived until 1786; thus he may well have assisted Francesco, to a limited extent, when be began painting views of Venice in the 1750s. Giacomo was born in 1764, and may equally well have been his father's assistant from about 1780 or soon afterwards. It is no more than guess-work to suggest (as I have done elsewhere[8]) that is was Nicolò who painted those strange figures in some of the beautiful lagoon scenes and other early views; all one is justified in saying is, that may have been the case. But Giacomo must surely be responsible for some of the weaker passages in the later views. He certainly went on producing drawings of Venice in his father's manner (Fig 3), and often signed them, long after his father's death, until he died himself in 1835; in fact, certain rather inferior, repetitive drawings, which can be confidently attributed to Giacomo (for his style is known), are even inscribed with Francesco's name but in Giacomo's handwriting – not perhaps as fraudulent a practice as it might appear today, for they were no doubt repetitions of his father's compositions[9]. He, at least, must occasionally have ventured a little more on his own, in paintings which owed little but the general idea to Francesco – something for the more popular tourist market, the less exacting collector, but still from the Guardi studio in Francesco's lifetime, and sold (presumably with Francesco's approval) as by 'Guardi'. Such, as I see it, is probably the origin of the numerous second-rate pictures that might conveniently and justifiably be catalogued as 'F. Guardi'. And to this category should probably be added paintings that might once have qualified for the higher grade, but whose present condition is such as to blur the distinction.

We are left with the problem of the really poor examples of what may be called 'Guardiesque', including paintings of palpably suspect origin. There is no doubt whatever that a great many forgeries of Guardi's paintings, some of them very skilful, have been produced since the beginning of the present century, as the demand for his work has gradually increased. Professor Morassi, at the end of his recent corpus (1973), has reproduced half a dozen, and has some interesting remarks on the subject (pp 293 – 296); and I have myself a file of photographs of pictures attributed to Guardi, which I would guarantee are not as old as I am. But I have

6 A particularly good example, of the lagoon with the Fondamenta Nuove on the left (of which there is a variant in the Duke of Buccleuch's series) was sold at Sotheby's on 18th November 1959 (Morassi cat. no. 617) (here reproduced, Fig 2).
7 Francesco Guardi seems in fact to have signed frequently when he was 'making his way' as a view painter; but hardly ever in his later, most characteristic period.
8 *Burlington Magazine,* vol XCVII, 1955, p 16.
9 See my book, *The Drawings of Francesco Guardi,* 1951, pp 50 – 51.

Fig 3 GIACOMO GUARDI *Piazza San Marco, looking towards the Basilica* (Formerly at Colnaghi's)

also a (much larger) file of photographs of drawings which are certainly imitations or forgeries of the present century; and since I own a small collection of these drawings it is perhaps wise to confine my illustrations to these. In any case the deception is easier to detect in the reproduction of a drawing than in that of a painting.

The commonest of these forgeries are by the hand responsible for a drawing of *The Ascent of Count Zambeccari's Balloon from the Giudecca* – a subject both drawn and painted by Guardi himself[10]. But since I have already reproduced this forgery and commented upon it in my book on Guardi's drawings published in 1951, I will refer here to another, larger example by the same hand, which is also in my own little Chamber of Horrors. It is on eighteenth-century paper[11], and it is discoloured, spotted and abraded, probably by deliberate exposure. The drawing is of course a Guardi composition, a view of the Fabbriche Nuove, above the Rialto bridge, from across the Grand Canal – a typical gay Venetian scene, with men drying sails on a barge in the right foreground, gondolas jostling a passenger barge in the centre of the canal, a swarm of other gondolas and barges moored along the far side, and in the distance the

10 Exhibited at the British Museum, *Forgeries and Deceptive Copies,* 1961, and again at the Minneapolis Institute of Arts, *Fakes and Forgeries,* a year ago.
11 Not watermarked; but this draughtsman evidently had a good supply of paper of Guardi's time. I have seen several of his drawings on paper watermarked with three crescent moons diminishing in size, a mark that appears on the paper of many genuine drawings by Guardi, Tiepolo and other Venetian contemporaries.

Fig 4 Modern forgery of Guardi in the possession of the author

Fig 6 FRANCESCO GUARDI *Fishing boats in the Lagoon* (Formerly sold at Sotheby's; contrast with figure 5)

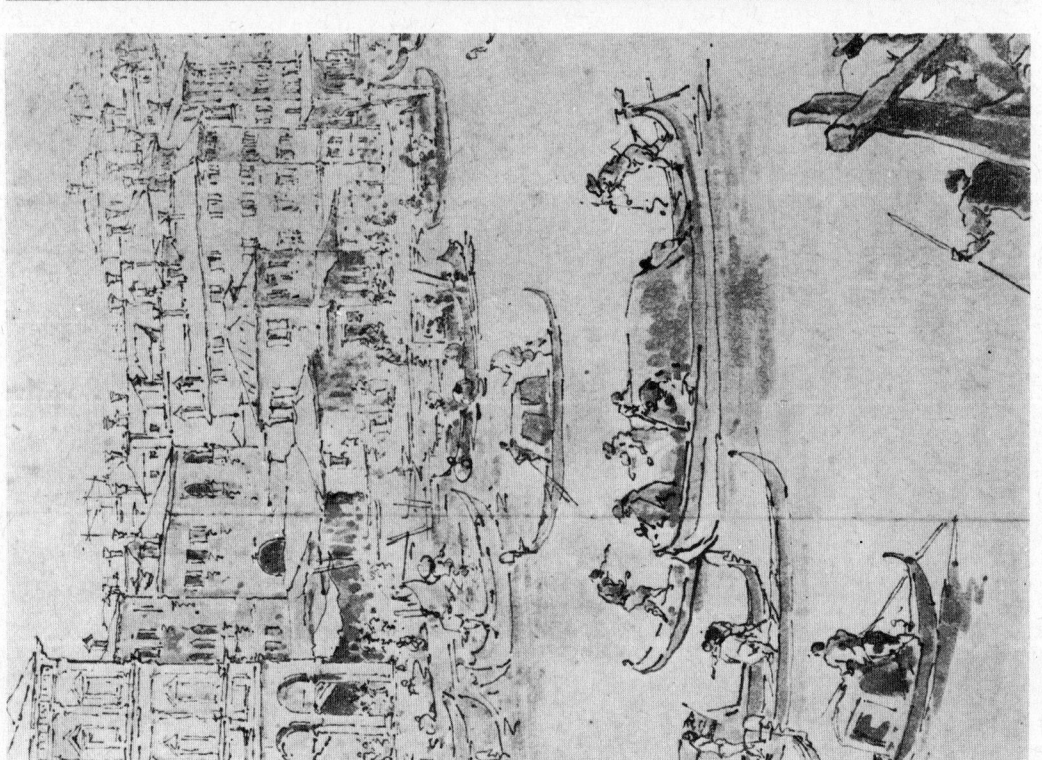

Fig 5 Modern forgery of Guardi, detail of figure 4

Burchiello, the canal omnibus (Fig 4). All this is copied almost exactly from a painting by Francesco in the Brera Gallery at Milan; but whereas the painting is one of Guardi's comparatively early views, not later than the early 1760s, with plebeian figures that have little of the characteristic flourish and sparkle of his developed style, our draughtsman has attempted to imitate in his figures the mannerism of Guardi's late drawings, when (if I may quote a description which I wrote many years ago) 'his pen seems to flutter over the paper like a winged insect . . . and produces by its very inconstancy a magical effect of light and air'. To imitate so personal an idiom, so impressionist a style, no doubt seems an easier task to set oneself than to attempt to reproduce the classic linear perfection of a Leonardo or a Dürer; but it has its pitfalls. If we turn our eyes in the present example from the figures in the foreground, which might pass muster to a casual glance, and scrutinise more carefully the middle and far distance, we see how the draughtsman tires of his deliberate tricks of penmanship; how the rendering of the figures degenerates into a series of ludicrous corkscrew scribbles, less like the fluttering of a winged insect than the wriggling of a worm; and how the Venetian architecture is drawn not as Guardi himself drew it, suggesting so well its strange appearance of instability, but with a kind of indecision that betrays the imitator's hand. (Fig 5. Contrast with the fine original of a similar subject here reproduced as Figure 6.) One observes particularly in the contours of the buildings – for instance along the top of the roof of the Fabbriche Nuove – how his pen rests at intervals, forming a sort of full stop in the line, and then proceeds again, leaving a little gap. This is very characteristic of our draughtsman. It was also characteristic of him to repeat the same composition several times[12]. I cannot name this practitioner, but I know many other imitations of Guardi by his hand, and it has been suggested that he was the Milanese artist Ponga, who worked in the early decades of this century – in any case he found his model for the drawing here discussed in the principal public gallery of Milan[13]. Some of his productions have been sold for high prices at auction, and good examples have found their way into great museums, into the Albertina, the Art Institute of Chicago, the Museum Boymans-van Beuningen at Rotterdam and the British Museum; acquired long ago, in some cases as authentic drawings by Francesco Guardi, but now generally recognised for what they are. We have all, probably, been bitten once[14].

By the kindness of Mr Paul Wallraf, who gave me the information and the photograph, I am able to reproduce a clever imitation of Guardi by a Venetian artist whose name, De Can, may be quoted, since I understand that he sells (or used to sell, for I am not sure if he is still alive) his drawings at modest prices, as his own work (Fig 7). What happens to them afterwards is not his concern. I have seen another version of this very drawing, evidently by his hand again, which was bought in a shop in Venice by an optimistic English visitor – it was labelled quite correctly 'Venetian School', with no name or date attached. And there are many more about, by other, different hands, in the market and in private collections, all imitations whether fraudulently intended or not, which can be sorted into groups according to style.

The reader will have had enough of this subject; but it is important that prospective buyers

12 I have a photograph of another version of the drawing here reproduced.
13 And see below, note 14.
14 The drawing reproduced here as Fig 4 was acquired by the late Lord Mount Temple in Italy in 1912; another, based on the companion painting in the Brera, is in the Lisbon Museum. Mlle. de Mendonça was kind enough to inform me that this was bought *'dans le bric à brac'* at Oporto. Another, of the Salute, was sold at Amsterdam from the J. P. Richter collection in May 1913. These, and the Albertina and Chicago drawings, are all on very large double sheets of old paper, folded down the middle.

Fig 7 DE CAN, in the manner of GUARDI *The Arcade of the Doge's Palace* (In the possession of Mr Paul Wallraf)

should realise that so many imitations exist, and are occasionally included in respectable sale catalogues under the simple denomination 'Guardi', without the first name or initial. Those who are unaware of the catalogue conventions may think that imitations and forgeries are unduly dignified by this description; but on the other hand the distinction even between these two categories is not always easy, and it is unfair, and sometimes dangerous, to condemn a painting or drawing as a forgery unless one is absolutely sure. It seems to me that for those who take the trouble to read the preamble printed in the catalogue the warning is sufficient: works so described are, in the opinion of the auctioneers, 'of the school, or by one of the followers of the artist, or in his style, and of uncertain date' – so almost certainly not by the artist's own hand, and possibly late imitations or forgeries. And the moral of *that* is – *Caveat Emptor,* as I suggested before.

SEBASTIANO DEL PIOMBO
The Virgin and Child
Black chalk heightened with white chalk, 25.5 cm by 18.7 cm
London £16,000 ($38,400). 27.VI.74

FRANCESCO GOYA
A Maja
Black chalk. Signed. Datable between 1824-8, 19.2 cm by 14.7 cm
London £28,000 ($67,200). 13.XII.73

46 OLD MASTER DRAWINGS

REMBRANDT HARMENSZ. VAN RIJN
The rest on the flight into Egypt
Pen and brown ink and wash.
Dated by Rembrandt scholars
circa 1655, 17.4 cm by 23.4 cm
London £29,000 ($69,600).
27.VI.74

JEAN-AUGUSTE-DOMINIQUE INGRES
The ailing Scipio receives his son who is sent to him by Antiochus
Graphite and brown wash.
Signed, 24.2 cm by 37.3 cm
London £20,000 ($48,000).
27.VI.74
A study for the (destroyed) painting which Ingres submitted at the age of twenty for the Prix de Rome

ATTRIBUTED TO FRANÇOIS QUESNEL
Portrait said to be Christine of Lorraine, Grand Duchess of Tuscany
Coloured chalks, 30 cm by 21 cm
London £2,600 ($6,240). 27.VI.74
Now in the Nationalmuseum, Stockholm

SIR PETER PAUL RUBENS
Samson and the lion
Pen and brown ink and wash, 13.5 cm by 9.5 cm
London £3,000 ($7,200). 13.XII.73
An early work which can be dated before Rubens departed for Italy in 1600

ANNIBALE CARRACCI
Head of a boy wearing a flat cap
Red chalk heightened with white. Datable *circa* 1585, 22 cm by 18.5 cm
London £4,200 ($10.080). 27.VI.74

Left AGOSTINO CARRACCI
The Last Supper
Pen and brown ink and brown wash. Datable before 1596, 26.5 cm by 35.5 cm.
Florence L.5,000,000 (£3,300; $7,685). 10.IV.74
A study for a small painting on copper decorating the altar tabernacle of the Certosa in Ferrara

Opposite page below
ANTOINE WATERLOO
Wooded landscape with weir and two waterwheels
Drawn with the brush in black and grey wash, 44.2 cm by 56.1 cm
London £4,400 ($10,560). 13.XII.73
One of the series of large drawings which Waterloo executed during his journey to Germany. He is known to have travelled as far as Danzig

OLD MASTER DRAWINGS 49

JAN VAN DER STRAET called
STRADANUS
Three hunters stalking deer
Pen and brown ink. Datable
before 1578, 19.8 cm by
28.1 cm.
London £1,600 ($3,840).
27.VI.74
A study in reverse for one of
the engravings executed by
Philip Galle for the series
Hunting Parties which were
dedicated to Cosimo
de'Medici

Fig 1   GEORGE STUBBS, ARA
Goldfinder
On panel signed and dated 1774, 31½in by 39½in
London £225,000 ($540,000). 31.X.73
Sold at auction in London on 17th June 1966 for £75,600

The Jack Dick Collection of English Sporting Paintings Parts I and II

By N. C. Selway

By any standards the collection of sporting paintings gathered by Jack Dick between the years of 1963 and 1969 was a remarkable achievement. Only a man of immense drive with unlimited enthusiasm and resources could have put together, in such a short space of time, this complete representation of the sporting painter's art.

In 1963, as a successful breeder of Aberdeen Angus, he started to take an interest in paintings of cattle and soon discovered that a far wider and more attractive field lay close at hand. Before long he was widely known to the art dealers of London and New York as a man who would brook no resistance to his demands for their finest sporting paintings, and, in the saleroom, as a bidder ready to join in, if necessary, by transatlantic link-up. Nor was his attention confined solely to dealers and salerooms, and soon no collection was safe from his predatory eye. If he wanted a painting he meant to have it. Little account would be taken of intercontinental time changes and another collector might well receive a call in the small hours of the morning demanding to know whether he was ready yet to part with some prized possession, and, in due course, the private plane would be at La Guardia airport ready to transport the possible seller in the right direction.

It was collecting on the grand scale and, contrary to sometimes expressed opinion, inspired by a genuine love for this school of painting; very soon Jack Dick acquired a sound knowledge of his chosen subject.

A visit to Black Watch Farms at Wappinger Falls, up the Hudson River in New York, was always a worthwhile experience. Pedigree horses and cattle in the fields around the house and, inside, every room from cellar to attic utilised for the collection. Soon more wall space and a bigger house became available when Dick decided to sell his business and move to Greenwich, Connecticut. Sadly, with the move, his luck turned and he ran into financial difficulties. Perforce no more additions to the collection were made after 1969 and in 1973 it was decided to put all of his paintings on the market, the first of four sales to take place in October 1973.

Jack Dick's death early in 1974 came as a shock. It is pleasant to think that he lived long enough to witness and enjoy the success of the first sale on October 31st when it quickly became apparent that very high prices would be fetched.

As was anticipated before the sale, the Stubbs painting of *Goldfinder* (Fig 1), a dark bay

Fig 8 JOHN FERNELEY, SNR
Charlemagne
Signed and dated Melton Mowbray 1829, 28in by 36in
London £16,000 ($38,400). 26.VI.74

stallion, with a mare and rather leggy foal in a typical lake and parkland setting, fetched the top price of £225,000, which compared not unfavourably with the £75,600 it had fetched in the saleroom in 1966.

The Swaine family by Devis (Fig 2), more a conversation piece perhaps than a sporting painting, fetched £136,000, by far the highest price ever paid for a work by this artist. The picture could in fact claim to have a sporting pedigree since it had once been admired in the Arthur Gilbey collection of fishing paintings, and it figures as an illustration in Shaw Sparrow's *Angling in British Art*.

Several of a fine group of paintings by J. F. Herring Senior sold exceptionally well and there was considerable competition for *Vespa* (Fig 3), Oaks winner in 1833, with her owner Sir Mark Wood, and trainer, which finally went for £62,000. Another Herring which caught the eye was of *The Sorby family* of Button Hall, Sheffield, out for the day with the gun, and taking it the easy way. This attractive woodland scene made £36,000.

The Mail change was a favourite subject of Herring's – he had once been a stage-coach driver – and there are different versions of this picture. This, the most important, fetched £70,000 (Fig 4). To a coaching enthusiast the scene is full of romance as the distant mail approaches and the fresh horse team prick their ears at the familiar sound. The change of horses with a well-drilled team will take no more than a minute. No time could be wasted as the Royal Mail ran to the tightest schedule.

The pick of John Ferneley Senior's paintings was perhaps *Velocipede* (Fig 5), a handsome chestnut racehorse, winner of the 1828 St Leger, with trainer and jockey, and also a distinguished provenance from the racing world. Not over-priced at £25,000. *Gayhurst*, another fine

Fig 5   JOHN FERNELEY, SNR
Velocipede
Signed and dated *Melton Mowbray 1829*, 34in by 44in
London £25,000 ($60,000). 31.x.73

racehorse and jockey, this time on Newmarket Heath, made £22,000, and a charming study of *Brood mares*, with a King Charles spaniel in the foreground of a wooded landscape, brought £19,000. *Lord Howe's grey hunter*, with his groom, in a Leicestershire setting and a Ferneley wintry sky, fetched £23,000.

Portraits by Ben Marshall are always much sought after and *Mr Wastall with his jockey, trainer and groom* (see p 61) proved no exception. This small painting of a racehorse conversation between members of the sporting fraternity fetched the high price of £47,000. *Mameluke*, by the same artist, the Derby winner of 1827, with a distant view of Epsom Downs, fetched £40,000, and a realistically aggressive looking *Shetland pony with two Welsh ponies*, all capable of winning rosettes at a Ponies of Britain show, brought £22,000.

Trafalgar Square by James Pollard, as seen before the erection of the Nelson Column, and depicting the traffic problems of the day, went for £54,000 – a record price for the artist, and a possible yardstick of inflationary pressures since 1966, when it last appeared in the saleroom and made £12,500.

Approach to Christmas, the original of perhaps the most popular of Pollard's coaching prints, sold for £38,000, and a little gem of *The Norwich Mail* for £15,000. This was an interesting painting, commissioned by Sir Thomas Neave to mark the occasion of his former coachman's employment as a Royal Mail coachman, and Mr Damorin is seen driving past the lodge gates of Dagnam Park in fine style.

A small fishing painting by the same artist, *Trolling for pike on the river Lea*, brought £10,000. Fishing on the Lea was Pollard's favourite pastime and most of his scenes portray a stretch of water not far from Waltham Abbey. He was also a frequenter of the racecourse

54 THE JACK DICK COLLECTION

Fig 2 ARTHUR DEVIS
A family of anglers: the Swaine family of Laverington Hall, in the Isle of Ely
Signed and dated 1749, 25in by 40½in
London £136,000 ($326,400). 31.x.73
Sold in New York in 1968 for £40,000

THE JACK DICK COLLECTION 55

Fig 3 JOHN FREDERICK HERRING, SNR
Vespa
Signed and dated 1833, 28in by 36in
London £62,000 ($148,800). 31.x.73

and his four paintings of *Epsom races* which fetched £85,000 bring to life vividly the racing world of those days – *Settling day at Tattersalls* (Fig 6) is said to include amongst the galaxy of racing men many of the then leading characters of the Turf.

Other paintings which took the eye in the first sale were a charming small painting, by Charles Towne, of a *Spaniel* busily engaged in treeing a stoat, which made £3,200, and an agreeable James Ward of a *White sand pony* and some friendly donkeys, all about to engage in some industrial project in a sandpit, which sold for £11,500.

A set of four large *Hunting scenes* by James Barenger – £23,000 – were remarkable principally for the skill with which Barenger portrays the excitement of the hounds when released from kennels and their enthusiastic demolition of any obstacle in their way; notable also, a set of Reinagle *Shooting* paintings of wild rural countryside and threatening skies, dated 1849, which were well worth the £18,000 they made.

The first sale totalled £1,247,900. By the time of the second sale on 26th June there had been, in the interim, various kinds of crises including a change of government and a promise of a wealth tax, and there was considerable speculation as to how things would go. The weakness of the stockmarket in recent months had hardly been encouraging. In the event prices were in line with gloomy forecasts. Some of the paintings on offer were of inferior quality to those in the first sale, but the understandable absence of many private buyers surely must be ascribed to the economic climate. Paintings of real quality still made good prices; nine pictures, however, remained unsold. *Hyde Park Corner* by James Pollard (Fig 7) sold for £33,000. This is the original painting for one of the set of well-known engravings entitled *Scenes on the Road or A Trip to Epsom and Back* and depicts the scene on Derby Day as the bloods are setting off and traffic begins to build up. The Chelsea pensioner on the kerb is obviously airing his views on the topic of the day. Others in this set show increasing chaos on the road after indulgence in stimulants and much of the driving appears to be without the required degree of care and attention. By the same artist *The race for the Derby Stakes* and *The finish of the Goodwood Cup*, both engraved pictures signed and dated 1833, made an enchanting pair and fetched £14,000 and £13,500 respectively.

Once more great interest was taken in a small conversation piece by Ben Marshall. Similar in size to *Mr Wastall's group* in the first sale and entitled *Three worthies of the turf* (see p 61), it had been commissioned by the Duke of Grafton of the day, presumably as a token of esteem to three old friends. Marshall had died before the sketch was finished but his Grace had 'advanced a considerable sum to the Artist' and therefore is was collected and later donated to the family of John Hilton who appears in the group. It fetched £25,000 compared with the £12,000 it had made in the saleroom in 1969.

A fine Cooper Henderson, *Rule o' th' Road*, with the Royal Mail asserting its authority over other road users made £6,500. Cooper Henderson, with his own distinctive charm, portrays a rather later period of coaching history than Pollard which can best be described as Early Victorian. Correct down to the smallest detail his pictures are alive with the spirit of coaching in its fastest days just before the advent of railways.

Most of Henry Alken's work in the two sales portrayed various aspects of the hunting field which no artist captures more successfully. As a change from hunting pink his version of the *Derby* delighted the eye with the colourful silks of the jockeys and showed the field bunched together soon after the start of what would appear to be a rather slowly run race. This panorama of Epsom Downs on a lovely day was bought for £12,000.

Ferneley's *Mr Holyoake, Squire Osbaldeston, and Sir Harry Goodricke* taking a fence together when out with the Quorn fetched £22,000. This superb hunting painting completely captures the *joie de vivre* of the chase and fetched the best price for the artist's work in the sale. *Charlemagne*, a proud Arabian stallion surveying a desert scene, complete with pyramids, made £16,000 (Fig 8).

The finish of the 1840 St Leger between Launcelot and Maroon by Herring caught the eye perhaps because of the unusual effect of the two horses depicted carrying the same colours of yellow jacket and black cap, in this case those of the Marquess of Westminster who owned both horses. In 1966 when this picture was last in the saleroom it had fetched £6,300 – it now made £26,000.

Another fine Herring of *Don Antonio* on Newmarket Heath, with two rather soberly clad gentlemen in the foreground helping themselves to a pinch of snuff, went for £15,000.

The Squire's favourite hunters by John Boultbee, which had once adorned the elegant Park Avenue apartment of the late Jay Rousuck – no higher compliment to the quality of a sporting painting – went for £6,000, and a fine shooting painting *Awaiting the flush* by Barenger, who excels once again with the dogs, brought £9,500.

Examples of James Seymour's work, other than single horses, rarely appear and when they do invariably create interest. *Lord Craven coursing at Ashdown Park*, with a vignette of ghostly Ashdown House at the foot of the Berkshire Downs, was a good purchase at £9,900. The gross total of the second sale was £588,900.

Fig 4 JOHN FREDERICK HERRING, SNR
Coach horses awaiting the change on the Great North Road between Newark and Lincoln
Signed and dated 1838, 48in by 73in
London £70,000 ($168,000). 31.x.73
Sold in London in 1967 for £5,700

Fig 7 JAMES POLLARD
Hyde Park Corner
Signed and dated 1838, 12¼in by 20in
London £33,000 ($79,200). 26.VI.74

THE JACK DICK COLLECTION 59

Fig 6 JAMES POLLARD
The Epsom races; The betting post; Preparing to start; The race over; Settling day at Tattersalls (illustrated)
A set of four, the first three signed and dated respectively 1834, 1835, 1835, each 12in by 18½in
London £85,000 ($204,000). 31.x.73

JEREMIAH DAVIDSON
The Morton family
Signed and dated 1740,
94in by 111in
London £4,000 ($9,600).
17.VII.74
From the collection of the
Rt Hon the Earl of Morton
Now in the Scottish
National Portrait Gallery,
Edinburgh

WILLIAM MARLOW
St Peter's, Rome
35½in by 50in
London £18,000 ($43,200).
20.III.74
From the collection of the
Rev Brendan Blundell

BEN MARSHALL
Three worthies of the turf
18¾in by 15in
London £25,000 ($60,000). 26.VI.74
Sold at Sotheby's on 29.VIII.69 for £12,000

BEN MARSHALL
Mr Wastall with his jockey, Frank Buckle
18in by 14½in
London £47,000 ($112,800). 31.X.73
Sold in London in 1968 for £8,000

These two paintings were in the Jack Dick Collection of sporting pictures and are discussed in the article on p51

THOMAS HUDSON
Portrait of a gentleman
80in by 58½in
London £14,000 ($33,600). 28.XI.73
From the collection of Peter Morris Esq

SIR JOSHUA REYNOLDS, PRA
Portrait of Mrs Freeman
50in by 40in
New York $20,000 (£8,333). 18.VI.74
From the collection of the late Thérèse Lownes Noble

ARTHUR DEVIS
The Cholmondeley children around a table in a baroque interior
39in by 49in
London £32,000 ($76,800). 17.VII.74
From the collection of the late Mr and Mrs Eric Bullivant

JAMES SEYMOUR
Racehorses exercising on Newmarket Heath
36in by 45in
London £38,000 ($91,200). 31.X.73
From the collection of Mr and Mrs Jack R. Dick
Formerly in the collections of the 2nd Duke of Westminster and Lady Ursula Vernon
Sold at Sotheby's on 23rd March 1966 for £2,600

Vol II, No 14: *In the Boschetto at Portici*
Pencil and grey wash, titled and dated *August 23*, 7in by 9⅜in

JOHN ROBERT COZENS
Three drawings from the seven sketch-books of drawings made by Cozens on his journey to Italy in 1782-83. The journey was organised by William Beckford, and from Beckford's letters and Cozens' drawings, most of which are inscribed with the place and day of their execution, the journey can be reconstructed in detail.
London £120,000 ($345,600). 29.XI.73 (Seven sketch-books sold as single lot) From the collection of His Grace the Duke of Hamilton and Brandon. Formerly in the collection of William Beckford

Vol IV, No 24: *Astroni, the crater of a volcano, the King's hunting place*
Pencil and grey wash, titled and dated *November 11*, 7in by 9½in

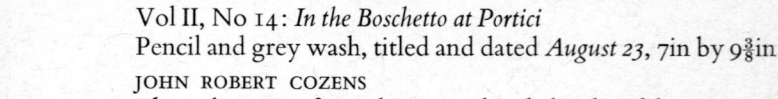

Vol VI, No 22: *Between Florence and Bologna, a Villa*

JOHN ROBERT COZENS
On the Galleria di Sopra, above Lake Albano
Watercolour, signed and dated 1778, 14½in by 20½in
London £38,000 ($91,200). 29.XI.73
From the collection of the late Sir Augustus Daniel

66 ENGLISH PICTURES

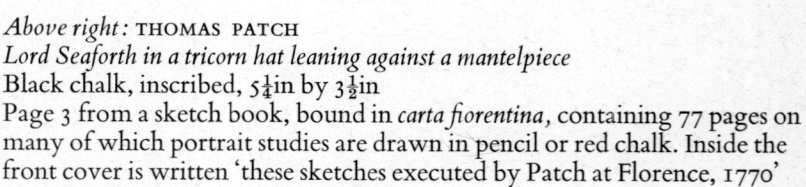

Above right: THOMAS PATCH
Lord Seaforth in a tricorn hat leaning against a mantelpiece
Black chalk, inscribed, 5¼in by 3½in
Page 3 from a sketch book, bound in *carta fiorentina*, containing 77 pages on many of which portrait studies are drawn in pencil or red chalk. Inside the front cover is written 'these sketches executed by Patch at Florence, 1770'
London £14,000 ($33,600). 21.III.74

Left: WILLIAM BLAKE
From 'Jerusalem, the Emanation of the Giant Albion', 1804, two trial proofs drawn upon in pen and ink and coloured by Blake
Above The spectre: Bath who is legions
Plate 41, 5¼in by 6¾in £13,000 ($31,200)
Below Vala and Jerusalem: leaning against the pillars
Plate 32, 6¾in by 6¾in £12,000 ($28,800)
Sold in London on 21st March 1974
From the collection of the late Kerison Preston

ENGLISH DRAWINGS 67

JOSEPH MALLORD WILLIAM TURNER, RA
Wharfedale from the Chiven, a view of Farnley Hall from above Otley
Watercolour, signed, executed circa 1816, 11in by 15½in
London £12,000 ($28,800). 18.VII.74

68 ENGLISH DRAWINGS

THOMAS ROWLANDSON
York races
Signed, inscribed and dated 1802, 4¾in by 7¾in
London £1,600 ($3,840). 18.VII.74

JOHN JOSEPH COTMAN
Postwick Grove
Watercolour heightened with bodycolour, signed and dated 1875, 18½in by 36½in
London £3,500 ($8,400). 18.VII.74
From the collection of Mrs J. S. Cotman

THOMAS WHITCOMBE
The battle of Trafalgar: the Victory sailing into the French line accompanied by the Euryalus
Signed, 34in by 56½in
London £11,000 ($26,400). 20.III.74
From the collection of the Royal United Services Institute for Defence Studies

SAMUEL SCOTT
Men-of-war and other shipping
Signed, 36¼in by 68½in
New York $44,000 (£18,333) 1.VI.74
From the collection of Louise C. Morgan

JOHN MELHUISH STRUDWICK
Saint Cecilia
37¾in by 25in
London £15,000 ($36,000). 9.IV.74
From the collection of the late Kerison Preston

EDWARD WILLIAM COOKE, RA
The Van Kook and other Dutch fishing smacks trawling off shore
Signed and dated 1863, 36in by 54½in
London £6,800 ($16,320). 9.IV.74

ALBERT JOSEPH MOORE, ARWS
Portrait of a girl
Signed with device, 10in by 10in
London £6,200 ($14,880). 9.IV.74
From the collection of Miss M. E. Allen

DANTE GABRIEL ROSSETTI
Regina cordium, a portrait of Elizabeth Siddal
Red and black chalk, signed with monogram and dated 1860, 7¾in by 7¼in
London £7,000 ($16,800). 9.IV.74
From the collection of the late Kerison Preston

RICHARD ANSDELL, RA
Addax
Signed *Rich. Ansdell* and dated 1842, 30in by 50in
Los Angeles $19,000 (£7,917). 27.V.74
From the collection of George G. Frelinghuysen Esq
Formerly in the collection of the Earl of Derby

WILLIAM HUGGINS OF LIVERPOOL
The tigers' lair
On board, signed and dated 1861, 17½in by 24in
London £6,500 ($15,600). 9.IV.74

76 THE ALLEN FUNT COLLECTION

Fig 6 SIR LAWRENCE ALMA-TADEMA, RA
A coign of vantage
On panel, signed and inscribed *Op* CCCXXXIII, painted in 1895, 25$\frac{3}{16}$in by 17$\frac{1}{2}$in
London £20,000 ($48,000). 6.XI.73

The Sale of The Allen Funt Collection of Paintings by Sir Lawrence Alma-Tadema

By Russell Ash

The sale of thirty-five paintings by an artist of the eminence of Alma-Tadema is a rare enough event. In the case of the Funt Sale, it provided at one and the same time an important exhibition of the painter's work – the first in England for sixty years – neatly representing every phase of his development from 1864 to 1910, as well as an interesting insight into the relative popularity of his different subjects, as reflected by the wide variation in the prices they fetched.

The circumstances of the sale, which were not fully reported by the British Press, deserve some attention. The collection was assembled over a period of approximately six years by Mr Allen Funt, the American television personality and the genius behind the successful programme, *Candid Camera*. Mr Funt is also the producer of such cinematic gems as *What do you say to a naked lady?* (United Artists, 1970). It might be maintained, in fact, that Mr Funt's talents lie in particular in the use of novelty and surprise as an artistic device. His collecting of Alma-Tadema's work was certainly in keeping with these innovatory shock tactics. To many, the Funt collection was a costly joke and a precursor of the late 60s/early 70s fad for *kitsch*. To the *New York Times* it was 'the best of the worst'. Mr Funt thought differently. His was a remarkably single-minded and sustained challenge to the numerous critics of Alma-Tadema's art, and one which not only pleased him intellectually, but, ultimately was to reward him financially.

In 1967, as Mr Funt recalls, he was looking for something to hang on the walls of a room which he had decorated in Victorian style, when Alma-Tadema's work was first shown to him. 'I didn't even know the name', he later admitted, 'until a dealer in London asked me one day if I wanted to see a picture by the worst painter who ever lived'. He was intrigued, expecting the picture to be 'a monster'. He was shown *The voice of spring* (Fig 1: Funt 35), a charming and idyllic work which appealed to Mr Funt. He bought it, and this was the start of his collection of thirty-five Alma-Tademas.

It would be a better story if Mr Funt had been far enough ahead of the field to buy his Tademas for next-to-nothing, like those 'cranks' who bought Pre-Raphaelites in the 40s, but he did not. In all, the collection cost him over a quarter of a million dollars and he got almost no bargains. The reason is that by the time his interest was aroused, the market was already beginning to rise.

Fig 2 SIR LAWRENCE ALMA-TADEMA, RA
Spring
Signed and inscribed *Op* CCCXXVI,
painted in 1894, 70¼in by 31½in
Los Angeles $55,000 (£22,000). 28.11.72
From the collection of the late
Victor Emmanuel Wenzel von Metternich

Tadema had been enormously popular in America during his lifetime. *A reading from Homer* (now in the Philadelphia Museum of Art) was, at $30,000, the highest priced painting of the 1903 season, and several of the works acquired by Mr Funt in the 1960s were already American residents before Tadema's death in 1912. Tadema lived long enough, however, to see the beginning of the decline in popularity of his paintings. The memorial exhibition of his works at the Royal Academy in 1913 was poorly attended – a mere 17,000 visitors, in sharp contrast to the 105,000 who queued to see that of Landseer, who died at the height of his fame. For nearly fifty years, Tadema received scant attention. Writing about him in *The Listener* in 1954, Philip Carr had to explain that despite his odd name, Alma-Tadema was not a woman. By then, many public collections, appalled to find Tademas rubbing frames with their venerable Old Masters, off-loaded them in a depressed market. In 1954, Exeter City Art Gallery did comparatively well in getting 130 guineas for a typical work, *The year's at the spring, all's right with the world,* and *In a rose garden* (Funt 24) exited from the Lady Lever Art Gallery for £241.10s. *Spring* (Fig 2), arguably Tadema's finest painting, had made £900 in 1945, and in doing so became the most highly priced Tadema for a quarter of a century. (It was sold by Sotheby Parke Bernet, Los Angeles in 1972 for $55,000). Many first-rate works changed hands for less than £100, and as late as 1960, two outstanding paintings, *The roses of Heliogabalus* (Fig 3: Funt 23), commissioned in 1888 for £4,000, was bought in at £105, and *The finding of Moses* (Fig 4: Funt 31), painted in 1904 for £5,250, for £252.

Market conditions and a general reappraisal of 'Victoriana' in the early 1960s made the time right for a Tadema revival, which was boosted by the first serious studies of his work for fifty years, and by the exhibition of twenty-six of his paintings at the Robert Isaacson Gallery, New York, in 1962. Prices soon rose to £500, and by 1963 the £2,000 threshold was passed with *Antony and Cleopatra* (Fig 5: Funt 21).

By 1969, *A parting kiss* (Funt 19) made £4,600, and prices continued to rise steadily over the subsequent four years. (The Funt Sale itself would suggest that by 1973 an average price would be about £7,000 – but more pertinent than this theoretical average is the fact that the sale encompassed works fetching from £900 to £30,000. This is a range which clearly indicates that, as far as collectors are concerned, an historical subject from Tadema's later period is considered to be worth over thirty times as much as a portrait subject of the same period, or an historical work from his earlier period.)

So it was that as the Tadema market was recovering, Mr Funt entered upon the scene, letting it be known that he was interested in purchasing any Tadema which might be offered to him. He summed up his motives thus:

'How did it happen, I wondered, that I should have selected a painter without advice or guidance and come up with the work of a man who ranked last of all the artists of his time? I jumped to the defence. I swore I'd find someone worse no matter how long it took me. Soon I found myself with a homeful of Alma-Tadema paintings and a warm feeling of sympathy for this painter who received rather critical treatment. I have now discovered many better painters in his time and many worse. Because I had received my share of brickbats from the critics, I enjoyed sympathising with Alma-Tadema'.

This affinity led to the assembly of the largest collection of Alma-Tademas ever owned by one man – probably (since he painted on commission and always sold his works so readily) including Alma-Tadema himself. Had Mr Funt ultimately bequeathed them to some public art gallery, it would have been the world's greatest Alma-Tadema collection, not only in terms of size, but also in scope and quality, comprising twenty-nine paintings which Tadema regarded as sufficiently important to assign to them opus numbers, five other works, and one study.

But tragedy struck. Mr Funt's accountant, Seymour Goldes, was, in 1972, discovered to have embezzled $1,200,000 of Mr Funt's money, and subsequently committed suicide. Mr Funt was left, in his own words, with 'everything a rich man has – except cash.' The only assets he could turn to were his paintings, and so, after a swan-song exhibition at the Metropolitan Museum of Art (where they were described by a critic as 'refreshing camp') they were offered for sale at Sotheby's Belgravia.

Fig 3 SIR LAWRENCE ALMA-TADEMA, RA
The roses of Heliogabalus
Signed and inscribed *Op* CCLXXXIII, painted in 1888, 52in by 84½in
London £28,000 ($67,300). 6.XI.73

The sale was to bring Mr Funt $425,000 – and, apparently, no regrets. Apart from his framed collection of replicas of all thirty-five paintings, printed at a cost of $90 each, he had, he remarked philosophically, 'had the joy of owning them. It was fun to immerse myself in them. But it's time for something else'.

What novel field, we may speculate, will Mr Funt's courageous gaze turn toward in future years?

The sale, apart from its impressiveness as an outstanding collection of Tadema's work, was important for two reasons. It provided those members of the public who attended the preview with the first opportunity since 1913 to see Tademas *en masse*. Few public collections in Great Britain have more than a couple of works, and the Tate Gallery, with five, exhibits only one, lends two to Leighton House, and hides the others. Secondly, whether by serendipity or design, the Funt Collection was highly representative of Tadema's career, including paintings spanning over fifty years of the artist's life, and depicting him in all his periods and moods.

The earliest, the watercolour *Fredegonda at the deathbed of Praetextatus* (Funt 1), dates from Tadema's interest in Merovingian history, which occupied him in the late 1850s and early

Fig 4 SIR LAWRENCE ALMA-TADEMA, RA
The finding of Moses
Signed and inscribed *Op* CCCLXXVII, painted in 1904, 54⅛in by 84in
London £30,000 ($72,000). 6.XI.73

1860s. (Tadema, born in Friesland in 1836, studied at Antwerp and worked in Brussels and Paris before making London his home by 1870.) This work, unlike his oils of the same period, is pleasantly light. Most of his early paintings are sombre and heavy, and many have characteristic deep Pompeian red backgrounds. By the 1870s, Tadema had begun to emerge from the shadows – a move which was accompanied by his rapid rise to fame. His dark, early pictures were relatively as little in demand in his day as now, and his gloomy *A collector of pictures* (Funt 9) or *The nurse* (Funt 12) contrast sharply with such dazzlingly bright works as *A coign of vantage* (Fig 6: Funt 27) or *Expectations* (Funt 22). This move from dark to light is well chronicled in the Funt pictures. There is a transitional period where his characters move from murky interiors onto terraces and into doorways, before finally seating themselves on marble benches beside the Mediterranean in light so brilliant that they have to shield their eyes.

A recurrent theme of Tadema's, the lone figure, or a couple of figures, seated on a marble bench, often with the sunlit sea in the background, seems as fresh and appealing today as when it left his easel. Three typical examples in the sale (Funt 18, 22 & 35) reached from £7,500 to £13,200.

Fig 1 SIR LAWRENCE ALMA-TADEMA, RA
The voice of spring
On panel, signed and inscribed *Op* CCCXCVII, painted in 1910, 19⅛in by 45¼in
London £9,500 ($22,800).6.XI.73

Fig 7 SIR LAWRENCE ALMA-TADEMA, RA
Amo te, ama me
On panel, signed and inscribed *Op* CCXXXIV, painted in 1881, 6⅞in by 15in
London £7,500 ($18,000). 6.XI.73

Fig 5 SIR LAWRENCE ALMA-TADEMA, RA
Antony and Cleopatra
On panel, signed and inscribed *Op* CCXLVI, painted in 1883, 25¾in by 36¼in
London £18,000 ($43,200). 6.XI.73

    Tadema was also master of historical *genre*. He never dealt with an epic or mythological scene, but was in his element when dealing with an everyday event – Caracalla does not ride in triumph after a victory against the Alemanni; he visits the baths named after him. Antony and Cleopatra are snapped on the point of meeting (Fig 5). Heliogabalus presides at a banquet (Fig 3). Even Pharoah's daughter is not depicted in the act of discovering Moses – he is already found and *The finding of Moses* (Fig 4: Funt 31) shows his being carried to the palace in his cradle. Tadema's narrative pictures are, in short, unconcerned with action, which he was almost incapable of portraying. They are carefully posed, equipped with archaeologically perfect props, and are technically brilliant, but are quite devoid of movement and the story line is as tenuous as Tadema discovered, through experience, his clients demanded.

    Of the paintings in the Funt Sale, the top ten prices were gained by five historical themes and five bright and exotically sentimental subjects, all dating from the 1880s to the later years of his career. Of these, the top price (a world record for a Tadema) was paid for *The finding of Moses* (£30,000), and all went for over £7,500. The lowest prices were paid for pictures painted before 1870, ten of which achieved less than £2,000. (The only anomaly is the only Christian subject Tadema is known to have painted – *Orante* (Funt 32) – painted in 1907, which at £900 was the cheapest work in the sale. Interestingly, the companion painting, *Bacchante* (Funt 33) fetched £2,300, which suggests that Tadema's representations of pagan vice are more appealing even today than any further examples of Christian virtue might have been!)

These prices also show the difficulty of providing estimates in sales of this kind. Only ten of the thirty-five paintings went for prices in the range estimated – a success rate of only 28%, while nine (26%), mostly early works, went for below the estimate and sixteen (46%), largely late paintings, were sold for above the estimated ceiling price – clearly a reflection of the competitive nature of the bidding for Tadema's most characteristic mid- to late-period works. The two most expensive works in the sale, *The roses of Heliogabalus* and *The finding of Moses* are also the largest, and yet it is also of interest to note the relative popularity of Tadema's smaller paintings. Many of his works, in fact, are virtually miniatures – tiny pictures so crowded with figures that Tadema took an egotistical delight in providing his visitors with a magnifying glass with which to examine the detail. It is surprising to find that, *pro rata*, these small pictures are quite as desirable as his larger works. *Amo te, ama me* (Fig 7: Funt 18) a small painting sold for £7,500 is valued at £70 per square inch, while the large *The finding of Moses*, although at £30,000 the top price in the sale, seems almost undervalued at a mere £6.50 per square inch.

Finally, it must be mentioned that all these prices show that Tadema, despite his resurrection, is still relatively underpriced if one takes into account the rate of inflation since his day. To achieve comparable prices we must look forward to the £100,000 Alma-Tadema.

BIBLIOGRAPHY
Russell Ash, *Alma Tadema*, Shire Publications, 1973.
Metropolitan Museum of Art *Victorians in Togas: Paintings by Sir Lawrence Alma-Tadema from the Collection of Allen Funt* (1973)
Sotheby's Belgravia *Alma-Tadema* (Catalogue of the sale of the Allen Funt Collection, 1973)

SIR ALFRED MUNNINGS, PRA
'Going out at Kempton'
Painted in 1939, 19in by 30in
New York $96,000 (£40,000). 17.IV.74
From the collection of the late Samuel B. Eckert

SIR ALFRED MUNNINGS, PRA
The path to the orchard
Signed and dated 1908, 29½in by 42in
London £32,000 ($76,800). 19.VI.74

ROBERT BEVAN
The cab yard, St John's Wood, evening
Painted *circa* 1910, 24¾in by 30in
London £17,000 ($40,800). 13.III.74
From the collection of the late Mrs F. A. Girling

AUGUSTUS JOHN, OM, RA
Dorelia
Black chalk, signed, 13¼in by 9½in
London £1,700 ($4,080). 13.III.74

MARK GERTLER *Self-Portrait*
Pencil, signed and dated '09, 10in by 7¾in
London £1,800 ($4,320). 13.III.74
From the collection of the late Kerrison Preston Esq
Below left EDWARD BURRA *Le bal, No. 6*
Pencil and watercolour, heightened with bodycolour, signed and dated *Nov.* 1928, 26in by 18¾in
London £8,200 ($19,680). 19.VI.74
From the collection of Professor N. B. B. Symons
Formerly in the collection of Augustus John, OM, RA

PHILIP WILSON STEER, OM *Girl on a sofa (Rose Pettigrew)*
Signed and dated '91, 21¾in by 23½in
London £11,500 ($27,600). 21.XI.73
From the collection of D. Samuel Esq

ENGLISH PICTURES 89

Left
HENRY MOORE, OM, CH
Study for sculpture: seated figures
Pen and ink, watercolour and crayon, signed and dated '44, 21½in by 14½in
New York $26,000 (£10,833). 2.V.74
From the collection of the Norton Simon Foundation

Below left
PAUL NASH
Pyramids in the sea
Black chalk, pen and ink and blue-grey wash, signed, inscribed on the mount. Executed in 1911, 12¾in by 11½in
London £3,000 ($7,200). 21.XI.73
From the collection of Mrs J. R. Grimsdale

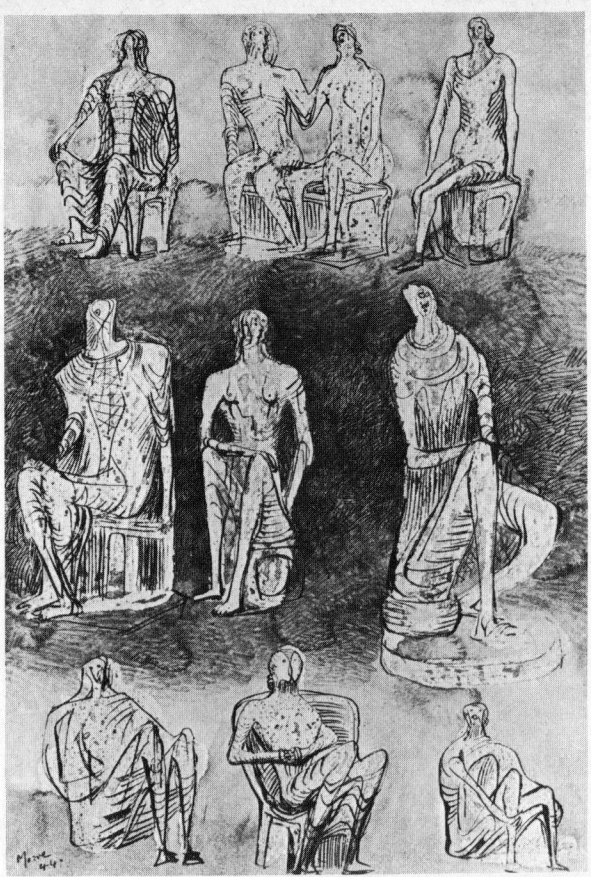

Below right
PAUL NASH
The three, 1911
Pen and ink, coloured chalks and wash, signed with monogram, 15¼in by 10¾in
London £2,700 ($6,480). 19.VI.74
From the collection of the Lord Croft

90 ENGLISH PICTURES

LUCIAN FREUD
Portrait of a man
Painted *circa* 1957-58, 23½in by 23½in
London £15,000 ($36,000). 19.VI.74
From the collection of George Pulay Esq

WALTER RICHARD SICKERT, ARA
The new home
Signed, painted in 1908, 19in by 15⅝in
London £18,500 ($44,400). 13.III.74
From the collection of the late Mrs F. A. Girling

BEN NICHOLSON
Blue Trevose
Oil on board, signed, titled and dated *Dec.* 1957
on the reverse, 46¾in by 29¾in
New York $105,000 (£43,750). I.V.74
From the collection of Arnold H. Maremont Esq

ENGLISH SCULPTURE 93

HENRY MOORE, OM, CH
Madonna and Child
Bronze, a maquette from an edition of seven, signed, 1943, height 6in
London £15,000 ($36,000). 19.VI.74
From the collection of Alexander Lampert Esq

HENRY MOORE, OM, CH
Maquette for Family Group
Bronze on a marble base, from an edition of seven, signed, 1945, height 5in
London £17,500 ($42,000). 19.VI.74
From the collection of Lady Hendy

HENRY MOORE, OM, CH
Girl seated against square wall
Bronze, dark gold patina, one of an edition of twelve, inscribed *B*,
executed in 1957-58, height 40in
New York $90,000 (£37,500). 17.x.73
From the collection of Mrs Cécile Narcoux Baillargeon

EUROPEAN EIGHTEENTH-CENTURY PICTURES 95

ISAAK OUWATER
A view of the gates and wall of a fortified town
Signed and dated 1780, 18in by 22in
London £8,800 ($21,120).
14.XI.73

ISAAK OUWATER
A view of the moat and a town gate at Utrecht
Signed and indistinctly dated, 18in by 22in
London £9,000 ($21,600).
14.XI.73

PIERRE GAUTHEROT
The meeting between Napoleon I, Emperor of the French and Alexander I, Tsar and Emperor of the Russias
Signed, inscribed and dated 1812, 69½in by 85½in
London £7,500 ($18,000).
14.XI.73
From the collection of the Officers of the Royal Marines

CARLO BOSSOLI
The Palace of the Tartars at Bahçe, Turkey
Watercolour heightened with bodycolour, signed and dated 1854 and inscribed on the reverse, 43in by 61in
London £3,000 ($7,200).
13.VI.74
From the collection of Mrs David Talbot-Rice

EUROPEAN EIGHTEENTH- AND NINETEENTH-CENTURY PICTURES 97

GIOVANNI COSTA
A scirocco day on the seacoast near Rome
Painted between 1853 and 1859, 34in by 76in
London £15,000 ($36,000). 14.XI.73
From the collection of David Stopford Brooke Esq

JACOB PHILIPPE HACKAERT
A distant view of St Peter's Rome from the banks of the Tiber
Signed and dated 1770, 30in by 35¼in
London £9,500 ($22,800). 14.XI.73
From the collection of Mrs R. Harkness

98 EUROPEAN NINETEENTH-CENTURY PICTURES

JOSEPH NIGG
Still life of summer flowers and fruit
Signed and dated 1818, on panel, 31¾in by 25in
London £15,000 ($36,000). 12.VI.74

FERDINAND GEORG WALDMÜLLER
A view of the Dachstein, Austria
Signed and dated 1833, on panel, 12in by 10¼in
London £24,000 ($57,600). 6.III.74

FERDINAND GEORG
WALDMÜLLER
The gypsy family
Signed and dated 1838, on
panel, 24in by 29½in
London £35,000 ($84,000).
6.III.74
From the collection of
Mrs. M. A. Potter

IVAN AIVASOVSKY
Fishing village at sunset
Signed and dated 1880, 47in by 73½in
New York $7,500 (£3,125). 17.IV.74

HERMANUS KOEKKOEK, SNR
A Dutch river scene
Signed, canvas laid on panel, 14in by 22¼in
London £12,800 ($30,720). 14.XI.73

100 IMPRESSIONIST AND MODERN PICTURES

HENRI DE TOULOUSE-LAUTREC
Au Cirque Fernando, ecuyère sur un cheval blanc
Pastel and gouache on board. Signed.
Painted in 1888, 23½in by 31¼in
London £210,000 ($504,000). 2.IV.74

IMPRESSIONIST AND MODERN PICTURES 101

VINCENT VAN GOGH
Le parc de l'Institut Saint Paul à Saint Rémy
Black chalk, reed pen and ink. Drawn in 1889, 18½in by 24in
London £67,000 ($160,800). 2.IV.74
From the collection of the Norton Simon Foundation, Beverly Hills

EUGENE BOUDIN
Plage à Trouville
On panel. Signed and dated *Trouville* 7-84, 8¼in by 16⅝in
New York $105,000 (£43,750). 17.x.73. From the collection of the late Edwin C. Vogel

CAMILLE PISSARRO
L'Ecluse à Pontoise
Signed. Painted *circa* 1869, 23in by 28¼in
London £106,000 ($254,400). 2.IV.74

Opposite page below
JOHAN BARTHOLD JONGKIND
Nôtre Dame de Paris, prise du Pont de L'Archevêché
Signed, dated and inscribed *Paris* 1849, 13in by 23¾in
New York $80,000 (£33,333). 28.XI.73
From the collection of Arthur Sachs and Marian François-Poncet of Paris

HENRI DE TOULOUSE–LAUTREC
Yvette Guilbert
Gouache and charcoal. Signed with the monogram. Executed in 1893,
21½in by 15in
London £53,000 ($127,200). 2.IV.74

HONORE DAUMIER
Avant l'audience – L'avocat et son client
Watercolour, gouache and pencil, 7in by 8½in
London £60,000 ($144,000). 2.IV.74

106 IMPRESSIONIST AND MODERN PICTURES

CAMILLE PISSARRO
Femme cassant du bois
Gouache. Stamped with the initials (Lugt 613e). Executed *circa* 1890,
23¼in by 18¼in
London £45,000 ($108,000). 2.IV.74
From the collection of the Norton Simon Foundation, Beverly Hills

EDGAR DEGAS
Salle de danse
Pastel and charcoal. Signed. Executed *circa* 1878, 19¼in by 12½in
London £142,000 ($340,800). 2.IV.74

ALFRED SISLEY
L'inondation à Port-Marly
Signed and dated '76, 19¾in by 24in
London £111,000 ($266,400). 2.IV.74

IMPRESSIONIST AND MODERN PICTURES 109

PIERRE AUGUSTE RENOIR
Jeune fille au chapeau de paille
Signed. Painted in 1884, 22in by 18¼in
New York $525,000 (£218,750). 17.X.73
From the collection of the late Edwin C. Vogel of New York

110   MODERN SCULPTURE

HENRI MATISSE
Nu couché I
Bronze.
Signed with the initials. Executed in 1907. Length 19½in
New York $360,000 (£150,000). 17.x.73

PABLO PICASSO
Jeune homme au bouquet
Gouache on board. Signed; also signed later and dated 1904 *ou* 5 on the reverse, 27¼in by 21⅜in
New York $720,000 (£300,000). 17.X.73
From the collection of Bernice McIlhenny Wintersteen of Pennsylvania

112　IMPRESSIONIST AND MODERN PICTURES

PABLO PICASSO
Tête de femme
Watercolour. Signed on the reverse. Painted *circa* 1908, 23¾in by 18¾in
New York $190,000 (£79,166). 17.x.73
From the collection of Bernice McIlhenny Wintersteen of Pennsylvania

PABLO PICASSO
Femme assise
Signed. Painted in 1909, 31½in by 25½in
London £340,000 ($816,000). 5.XII.73

GINO SEVERINI
Crash
Signed. Painted in 1915, 36¼in by 28¾in
New York $175,000 (£72,916). 1.v.74
From the collection of Arnold H. Maremont

FERNAND LEGER
Composition
Signed and dated '24, 52in by 39¾in
New York $265,000 (£110,418). 2.v.74

PABLO PICASSO
La coiffure
Inscribed and dated *Dinard* 1922 on the stretcher, 8⅝in by 6¼in
New York $250,000 (£104,166). 17.x.73
From the collection of Bernice McIlhenny Wintersteen of Pennsylvania

PABLO PICASSO
Buste devant la fenêtre
Signed. Painted *circa* 1941-42, 39¼in by 31¾in
New York $375,000 (£156,250). 17.x.73
From the collection of Bernice McIlhenny Wintersteen of Pennsylvania

118 IMPRESSIONIST AND MODERN PICTURES

EGON SCHIELE
Frau mit blauen Strümpfen
Gouache. Signed and dated 1912, 17¼in by 12½in
London £25,000 ($60,000). 3.IV.74

EMIL NOLDE
Porträt einer Dame (Rotbraunes und blaues Haar)
Watercolour. Signed. Executed *circa* 1920–25, 18¾in by 13¾in
New York $38,000 (£15,833). 2.v.74
From the collection of the Norton Simon, Inc, Museum of Art, Beverly Hills

PAUL KLEE
Rotgrüne und violett-gelbe Rhythmen
On board, signed and dated 1920 38; signed, titled and dated 1920 38
on the reverse, 14¾in by 13¼in
London £76,000 ($182,400). 3.VII.74

MAX ERNST
Cactus
Pencil frottage. Signed. Drawn in 1925, 17in by 10in
London £19,000 ($45,600). 3.IV.74

FRANCIS PICABIA
La ville de New York aperçue à travers le corps
Watercolour and pencil. Signed, titled and dated 1912,
21¾in by 29½in
New York $67,500 (£28,125). 2.v.74

MAX ERNST
Couple étroitement enlacé dans les flammes
Signed. Painted in 1927, 31½in by 39¼in
New York $230,000 (£95,833). 2.v.74

124 MODERN SCULPTURE

CONSTANTIN BRANCUSI
La negresse blonde II
Polished bronze; has two bases of marble and limestone. Signed and dated 1926. Height without base $15\frac{1}{4}$in
New York $750,000 (£312,500). 1.v.74
From the collection of Arnold H. Maremont

IMPRESSIONIST AND MODERN PICTURES 125

JOAN MIRO
Femme nue
On board. Signed, dated 8.32., and titled on the reverse,
13in by 7¾in
New York $110,000 (£45,833). 2.V.74
From the collection of the late R. Sturgis Ingersoll
of Philadelphia

SALVADOR DALI
Resurrection of the flesh
Signed and dated 1945, 36¼in by 28¾in
New York $245,000 (£108,083). 2.v.74

IMPRESSIONIST AND MODERN PICTURES 127

ALBERTO GIACOMETTI
Annette
Signed and dated 1954, 25¼in by 21⅛in
New York $160,000 (£66,667) 1.v.74
From the collection of Arnold H. Maremont

128 MODERN SCULPTURE

MARC CHAGALL
Panier de fleurs
Signed. Painted *circa* 1925, 21½in by 32in
New York $250,000 (£104,167). 17.x.73

Opposite page
MARINO MARINI
Cavaliere
Bronze. Stamped with the monogram. Executed in 1949 (an edition of three casts). Height 73½in
New York $160,000 (£66,667). 2.v.74
From the collection of the late R. Sturgis Ingersoll Esq of Philadelphia

130 IMPRESSIONIST AND MODERN PICTURES

NICOLAS DE STAËL
Fleurs grises
Signed. Painted in 1952, 51½in by 35½in
New York $150,000 (£62,500). 28.XI.73
From the Estate of the late Barbara McFadden Willcox

JEAN DUBUFFET
Paysage du Pas-de-Calais III
Signed and dated '63; signed, titled and dated *août* '63 on
the reverse, 63¾in by 102¾in
New York $110,000 (£45,833). 2.V.74

132 RUSSIAN PICTURES

VASSILY ERMILOV
Suprematist composition
Painted wooden relief on panel, executed *circa* 1919-21, 18¾in by 18¾in
London £3,200 ($7,680). 4.VII.74

EL LISSITZKY
Proun 5A
Charcoal, indian ink and gouache, signed on the mount, executed in 1919, 11¼in by 10¾in
London £10,000 ($24,000). 4.VII.74
Formerly in the collection of Sophie Lissitzky-Küppers

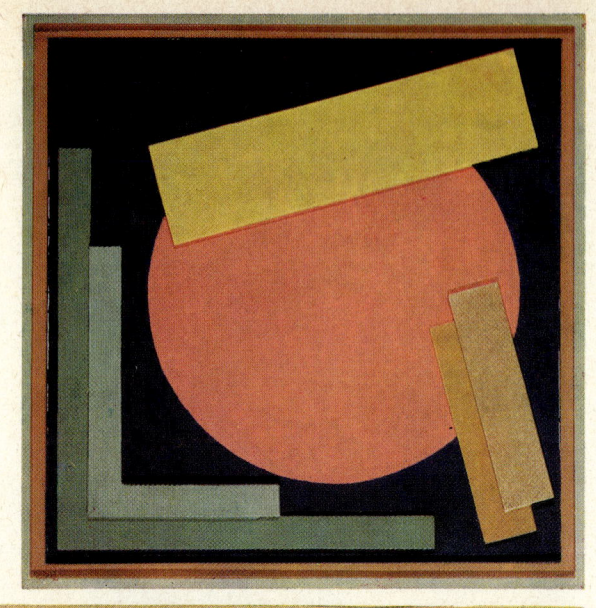

KASIMIR MALEVICH
Suprematist composition
Pencil, drawn *circa* 1915-16, 10in by 8¾in
London £2,500 ($6,000). 4.VII.74

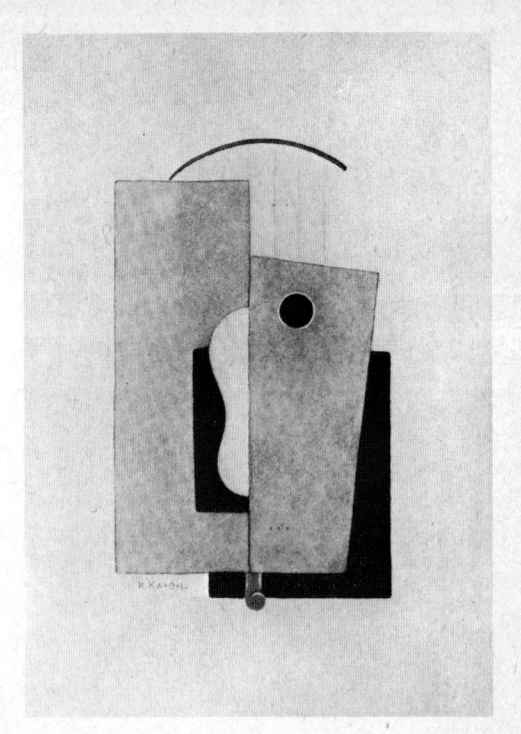

IVAN KLIUN
Constructivist composition
Watercolour, signed, executed *circa* 1920,
11¼in by 7¾in
London £2,600 ($6,240). 4.VII.74

ALEXANDRA EXTER
Abstract composition
Gouache, executed *circa* 1916, 26in by 22in
London £2,200 ($5,280). 4.VII.74
From the collection of Mr and Mrs Clifford Davis of
West Simsbury, Connecticut

KASIMIR MALEVICH
Suprematism (34 lithographs)
Book lithographed by the Vitebsk Art Workshops
1920
London £3,100 ($7,440). 4.VII.74
The lithography was presumably executed under
the direction of Lissitzky, who was at this time in
charge of the Vitebsk workshops

134 BALLET

LEON BAKST
Modern dress
Pencil, brush and indian ink watercolour and gouache, signed and dated 1910, 12¾in by 11½in
London £6,800 ($16,320). 30.V.74

LEON BAKST – *Schéhérazade*
Design for Boulgakoff's costume as the Sultan
Pencil, gouache, watercolour and gold paint, signed and dated 1910, 13¾in by 8½in
London £4,700 ($11,280). 30.V.74
Schéhérazade – music by Rimsky-Korsakov, scenario by Bakst, choreography by Fokine, decor and costumes by Bakst – was first performed by the Diaghilev Ballet at the Paris Opera, on 4th June 1910

WILLEM DE KOONING
Police Gazette
Oil, enamel and charcoal on canvas, signed and dated 1955 on the reverse, 43¼in by 50¼in
New York $180,000 (£75,000). 18.x.73

The Robert C. Scull Auction

By John Tancock

Sales of contemporary art have hitherto been somewhat risky affairs. Auctions restricted to the disposal of objects that have already achieved a certain status in the market by virtue of age, rarity or conspicuous quality are relatively predictable. Sales in which contemporary works of art predominate, on the other hand, tend to be full of surprises since the market value of the artist's work is still in the process of being established. It can be devastating for an artist and for his patrons if his work is auctioned prematurely since his critical reputation might not have reached the stage where the resale value approaches the original price, minimal as this might have been.

The Robert C. Scull auction, on the other hand, which took place on the evening of October 18th, 1973, was a source of major satisfaction for the seller who saw his judgement as to what constituted the most significant art of the previous two decades supported by the international crowd of collectors and dealers who attended the sale in droves and for not a few of the artists, at least those who did not resent the fact that part of the enormous profits realised did not accrue to them directly. Of all the collectors who attached themselves to the rise of Pop art in the 1960s Mr Scull lived most constantly in the limelight. The pleasures of anonymity were alien to his outgoing personality. Both he and his wife socialised with the artists and were portrayed by them. Andy Warhol painted *Ethel Scull 36 times*, George Segal embalmed them in plaster, Alfred Leslie depicted Robert Scull on a gigantic scale and Milet Andrejevic exposed him in *Time reveals the truth*. Robert Scull entered the highly political art-world of the 1960s and became part of its fabric, its most conspicuous patron. His was a collection formed in public (although not a public collection), one groomed for stardom and destined for success from the very beginning. He was like a film-producer who sees the star potential in a bit-player lingering over a soda on Sunset Strip. In 1962 Pop art was far from being the great success it has since become, on the contrary, it was greeted with considerable hostility. One commentator, in a passage of invective since placed in historical perspective, referred to the invasion of the art-galleries 'by the pin-headed and contemptible style of gum-chewers, bobby-soxers, and, worse, delinquents'[1]. Twelve years later, even on the occasion of the exhibition of Pop art at the Whitney Museum of American Art, the feeling of unease on the part of an influential sector of critical opinion had still not subsided. To the art

---

[1] Max Kozloff 'Pop Culture, Metaphysical Disgust, and the New Vulgarians', *Art International,* March 1962, reprinted *Renderings Critical Essays on a Century of Modern Art* (Simon and Schuster, New York, 1968), p 221. In his postscript the author gives two reasons for his negative reaction to Pop art. 'One was a prejudice against closed, hard-contoured form, still nurtured by the Abstract Expressionist experience. The other, shared by numerous others in the climate of hostility, was a horror of the vulgar, a disgust with American commercial culture, such that it was inconceivable to admit it into the aesthetic and humanistic realm supposedly represented by the galleries.'

FRANZ KLINE
Orange and black wall
Painted in 1959, 66½in by 144in
New York $125,000 (£52,083). 18.x.73

critic of *The New York Times*, the movement was 'an indigestible lump in the throat of high culture . . . far more important as an episode in the sociology of culture than as a form of artistic expression'[2].

Unperturbed, then or now, by the misgivings of these critics, Robert Scull bought whatever excited him and soon formed one of the most comprehensive collections of American art of the 1950s and 1960s, rivalled perhaps only by that of Peter Ludwig in Cologne. But Scull was not only a collector, he was also an advocate for the art he admired and owned and worked hard to ensure that it was given exposure in the most prestigious exhibitions and publications. Prestige, of course, tends to impart value and in retrospect it now seems almost inevitable that his collecting enterprise would culminate in a sale, one, in the words of Mr Scull, that would 'prove to the world that American art has found its place in history . . . with buyers, with people who believe in it'[3].

It was not the first time that Mr Scull had committed a group of works from his collection to auction. Important paintings by Franz Kline, Willem de Kooning, Barnett Newman, Mark Rothko and Clyfford Still were included in a sale on 13th October, 1965 although not everything was sold, two works by de Kooning, *Police Gazette* and *Spike's folly I*, and Larry Rivers' *Vocabulary lesson III (parts of the body)*, remaining to be sold in 1973. Auctions which included major contemporary works were somewhat intermittent after that until 18th November, 1970 when six more items from the Scull collection were included in a sale although, once again, not everything sold; Mark Rothko's *No. 16-1960* and Jasper Johns' *Two flags* were both bought-in for what might appear to be relatively substantial prices[4], but

---

2 Hilton Kramer 'A Perfect Middlebrow Amalgam' *The New York Times,* Sunday, 14th April, 1974, p 23
3 Dorothy Seiberling 'Scull's Angles: Going Once, Going Twice . . .' *New York Magazine,* 17th September, 1973, p 58
4 Rothko's *No. 16-1960* was bought in for $85,000 and Jasper Johns' *Two flags* for $105,000

ANDY WARHOL
Flowers
Painted in 1964, 82in by 162in
New York $135,000 (£56,250). 18.x.73

Mr Scull was as astute in his reading of the market as he was in his initial choice of artists. He preferred to wait until the market caught up with the values he ascribed to their works and this finally occurred on 18th October, 1973.

Prior to the sale Mr Scull had been investigating various ways in which he might divest himself of part of his collection, most of which was of necessity stored in warehouses and rarely seen. There were protracted negotiations with the Neue Pinakothek Munich, which wanted to buy a substantial part of the collection but the project fell through because the necessary state funds were required to finance the Olympic Games. The Metropolitan Museum of Art in New York was another potential recipient but a combination of circumstances – notably spectacular purchases in other areas and expensive building plans – prevented any serious negotiations from developing. It was at this point that the decision was made to turn to Sotheby Parke Bernet and, in consultation with the relevant experts, a selection was made that covered the whole range of the collection, from well-established figures of the 1950s – Barnett Newman, Willem de Kooning, Jasper Johns and Robert Rauschenberg – to younger artists of promise such as Dan Christensen, Walter de Maria and Peter Young. 'I put the sale together as if I were making an exhibition,' Mr Scull said, 'tried to give it balance, see that things worked with each other. The catalogue is all I'll have to show for the collection, so I wanted it to be a good reminder of another era of my art life'[5]. This it turned out to be but few would have anticipated the vast interest it excited once in circulation. Articles appeared in publications as diverse as *The Christian Science Monitor*, where Mr Scull was called a 'modern Medici', and *Andy Warhol's Interview* where it was announced that the Sculls were hiring bodyguards. The television networks gave the event ample coverage and the normally rather sedate New York galleries of Sotheby Parke Bernet were invaded by a team of cameramen and interviewers producing a documentary film tracing the

[5] Ibid

JASPER JOHNS
Double white map
Encaustic and collage on canvas, painted in 1965, 90in by 70in
New York $240,000 (£100,000). 18.x.73

JASPER JOHNS
Painted bronze – Ale cans
Bronze, no. 1 of an edition of 2, the other cast belongs to the artist, height 7½in
New York $90,000 (£37,500). 18.x.73

development of the sale from the initial idea to the drama of the final night. The sale could well have been something of an anticlimax after all this publicity but two demonstrations outside the galleries on Madison Avenue – one by Women in the Arts who objected to the fact that there was only one work by a woman (Lee Bontecou) in the sale and another by the Taxi Rank and File Coalition carrying placards saying 'Robbing Cabbies Is His Living Buying Artists Is His Game' – made it clear to the potential buyers and spectators struggling to get in that the auction itself might prove to be an unusual event. The beginning went quietly; works by Lee Bontecou, John Chamberlain and Dan Christensen fetching good if not spectacular prices. The first real excitement of the evening came with the sale of Willem de Kooning's *Police Gazette* (bought in for $37,000 in 1965) for $180,000, establishing a record for de Kooning and for a work by an Abstract Expressionist artist. There were many other astonishing prices, records being set for works by Barnett Newman ($155,000 for *White fire II*), Franz Kline ($125,000 for *Orange and black wall* and $90,000 for *Wotan*), Robert Rauschenberg ($90,000 for *Double feature*), Larry Poons ($26,000 for *Wildcat arrival*), James Rosenquist ($45,000 for *Early in the morning*), Cy Twombly ($40,000 for '*A*'), Lucas Samaras

($20,000 for *Box No.* 1) and Andy Warhol ($135,000 for *Flowers*). Most laden with records was the work of Jasper Johns. *Double white map* sold for $240,000 the highest known price for a work of Jasper Johns, it doubled the auction record for a living American artist previously held by Georgia O'Keeffe's *Poppies* sold for $120,000 on 14th March 1973, and missing by $20,000 the highest price for an American painting, held by Eastman Johnson's copy of Emanuel Leutze's *Washington crossing the Delaware* (See p168). *Painted bronze* sold for

Opposite page
ROBERT RAUSCHENBERG
Double feature
Combine painting on canvas, painted in 1959, 90¾in by 52in
New York $90,000 (£37,500). 18.x.73

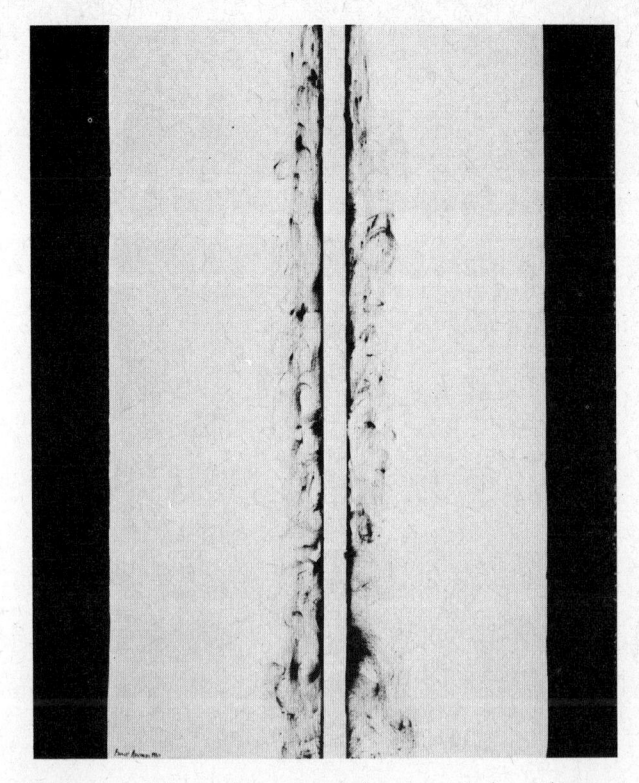

Right
BARNETT NEWMAN
White fire II
Signed and dated 1960, 96in by 76in
New York $155,000 (£64,583). 18.x.73

$90,000 and established an auction record for a Johns sculpture and for a work by a living American sculptor; the previous record was Claes Oldenburg's *Stove* which sold for $45,000 at Sotheby Parke Bernet in 1970.

To the general public, of course, even more astonishing than the prices paid was the astronomical increase in value that had occurred between the time when Mr Scull purchased the works of art and the night they were sold. It is now common knowledge, for example, that the $90,000 *Ale cans* were originally purchased for $960 and that the $240,000 *Double white map* cost $10,200. After the results were announced Mr Scull became the target for a great deal of hostile criticism, the substance of most of it being that he was a speculator who lived off the artists, buying low and selling high. 'Profit Without Honor' was the title of a particularly vicious article on the sale in *New York Magazine*[6]. A case can be made – although one difficult to legislate or enforce – for artists' rights in the resale of their works. Far less defensible is the criticism of collectors for having exercised discrimination and chosen well, whether this was done independently or in consultation with outside advisers. No collection is formed in a vacuum and Mr Scull's was no exception. He sought the advice of perspicacious dealers like Leo Castelli and Richard Bellamy and bought what he did because of its intrinsic quality, not because it was a safe investment. Indeed fifteen years ago most people would have said that the purchase of Jasper Johns' *Painted bronze* for $960 was the exact reverse.

Where Mr Scull was unusually lucky was in the coinciding of his personal taste with a more general trend of the market. With New York becoming a leading centre of the art-world and American painting of the 1950s and 1960s commanding considerable attention at

6 Barbara Rose 'Profit Without Honor' *New York Magazine*, 5th November, 1973, p 80

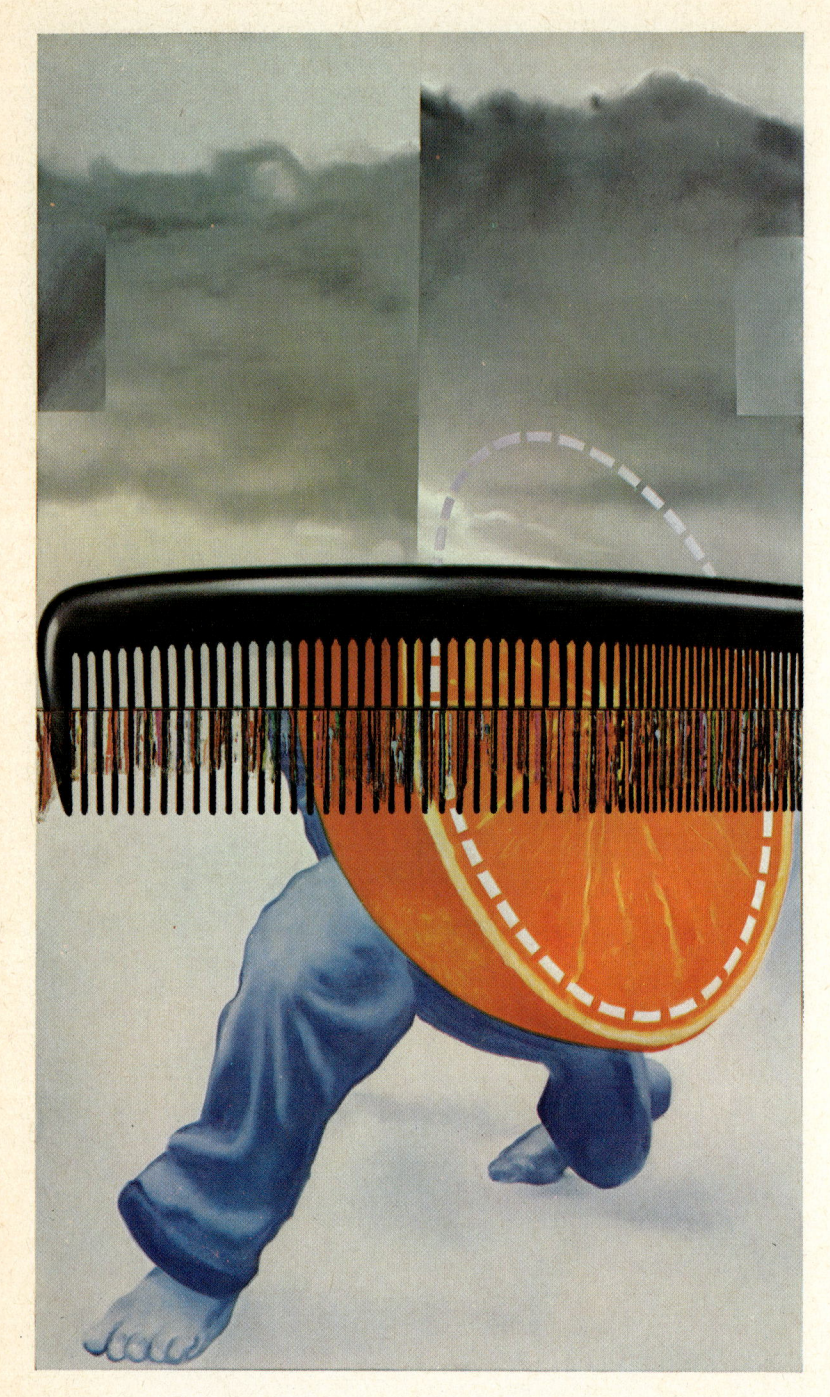

JAMES ROSENQUIST
Early in the morning
Signed and dated 1963, 95in by 56in
New York $45,000 (£18,750). 18.x.73

an international level, prices rose far more rapidly than could ever have been anticipated. The timing of the Scull sale was crucial, responding to the needs of the collecting public in an uncanny way. At the same time it provided a yardstick against which all future sales of contemporary art will be measured, both in terms of the quality of the material sold and the overall success of the sale.

THE ROBERT C. SCULL AUCTION 145

LUCAS SAMARAS
Box no. 1
Mixed media, executed in 1962, 9in by 16in by 17in
New York $20,000 (£8,333). 18.x.73

CY TWOMBLY
'*A*'
Oil and pencil on canvas, signed and dated 1956, 50in by 62⅝in
New York $40,000 (£16,666). 18.x.73

146   CONTEMPORARY PAINTINGS

ARSHILE GORKY
Housatonic
Black ink and crayon on paper, signed and dated '43, 18in by 23½in
New York $55,000 (£22,917). 3.v.74
From the collection of the Norton Simon, Inc, Museum of Art, Beverley Hills

ROBERT RAUSCHENBERG
Express
Oil on canvas with silkscreen, painted in 1963, 72in by 120in
New York $150,000 (£62,500). 3.v.74

148 CONTEMPORARY PAINTINGS

CONTEMPORARY PAINTINGS 149

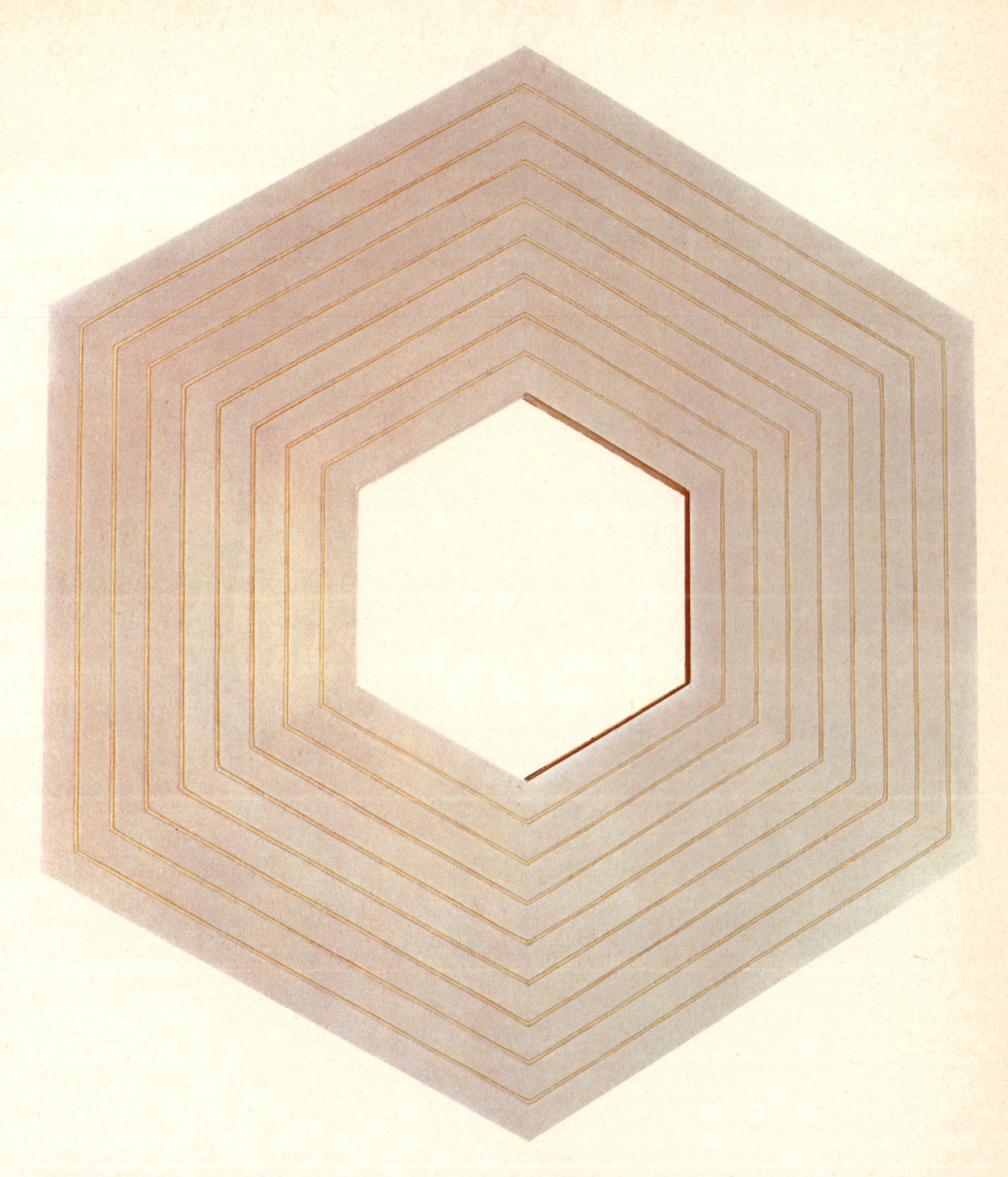

Opposite page
LUCIO FONTANA
Concetto spaziale – La fine di Dio
Signed, 70in by 49in
London £28,000 ($67,200). 3.IV.74

FRANK STELLA
Sidney Guberman
Metallic paint on canvas, painted in 1963, 77in by 89½in
New York $67,500 (£28,125). 3.V.74

150 CONTEMPORARY PAINTINGS

CY TWOMBLY
Bolsena
Oil and pencil on canvas, 78½in by 94¼in
London £21,000 ($50,400). 3.IV.74

DAVID HOCKNEY
Building, Pershing Square, Los Angeles
Acrylic on canvas, signed, titled and dated February–March 1964 on the reverse, 58in by 58in
London £24,000 ($57,600). 3.IV.74
From the collection of R. Chapman Esq

TOM WESSELMAN
Great American nude no.73
Signed, titled and dated 1965 on the stretcher, 72in by 89in
London £18,000 ($43,200). 3.IV.74

RICHARD LINDNER
Moon over Alabama
Signed and dated 1963, 80in by 40in
New York $135,000 (£56,250). 3.V.74

THOMAS W. BOWLER
Table Bay, Cape Good Hope, 1854
Pen and ink and watercolour, heightened with white, signed in ink, 9in by 29⅜in
Johannesburg R19,000 (£11,692; $28,061). 25.IX.73
From the collection of L. Poulton Esq

JOHN SKINNER PROUT
Sydney Harbour
Watercolour, signed, 10⅞in by 15¼in
London £1,300 ($3,120). 1.XI.73

CAPTAIN ROBERT SMITH
Above: View of Mount Erskine and Pulo Ticoose Bay, Prince of Wales Island
27¼in by 39in
London £2,900 ($6,960). 28.XI.73
Below: View of Suffolk House, Prince of Wales Island, 27¼in by 39in
London £3,600 ($8,640). 28.XI.73
Suffolk House was the Governor's residence
Both pictures from the collection of David Graham Esq

H. C. HAGEDORN
Panoramic view of Rio de Janeiro and its harbour
Watercolour and bodycolour, signed, 27½in by 82½in
London £2,900 ($6,960). 14.V.74

CURRIER AND IVES
The American national game of baseball. Grand match for the championship at the Elysian Fields, Hoboken, N.J.
Hand-coloured lithograph printed with tint stone, published by Currier and Ives, New York, 1866, 19¾in by 29⅞in
New York $7,000 (£2,917). 16.XI.73

MAJ-GEN HORATIO GORDON ROBLEY
Portrait of Tomika Te Mutu, Chief Ngaiterangi Tribe
Watercolour, signed, the sitter's name in the bottom margin, size of sheet 10½in by 9½in
London £750 ($1,800). 1.XI.73
From the T. E. Donne Collection

JOHN BARR CLARKE HOYTE
Milford Sound
Watercolour, heightened with white, signed and dated 1871, 13in by 23¾in
London £750 ($1,800). 1.XI.73

THOMAS BAINES, FRGS
Surf boats off the jetty, Algoa Bay
Oil on paper, laid down on canvas, signed, inscribed *Grahamstown*, dated Sept. 8, 18 . . . (48?), 18in by 25¾in
Johannesburg R12,000 (£7,385; $17,724). 25.IX.73
From the collection of Dr John MacGillivray

TOPOGRAPHICAL PICTURES 159

ANTON VAN WOUW
Bad news
Bronze, signed, inscribed *S.A. Joh-burg, 1907*, foundry mark G. *Nisini-Fusi, Roma*, height 11in
Johannesburg R14,000 (£8,615; $20,676). 25.IX.73

JACOB HENDRIK PIERNEEF
The old Dutch Reformed church – Tulbagh, now the Museum
Oil, signed and dated 1927, 20in by 25in
Johannesburg R9,000 (£5,538; $13,291). 25.IX.73
From the collection of Mrs A. M. Preller

160 CANADIAN PICTURES

CORNELIUS KRIEGHOFF
Indian hunters camping
Signed, 13in by 18in
Toronto $22,000 (£9,031).
23.X.73

PAUL KANE
French river rapids
14¾in by 21¾in
Toronto $11,000 (£4,515).
23.X.73

CANADIAN PICTURES 161

EMILY CARR
British Columbia forest
Oil on paper, signed, 34¼in by 23¼in
Toronto $22,000 (£9,031). 13.V.74

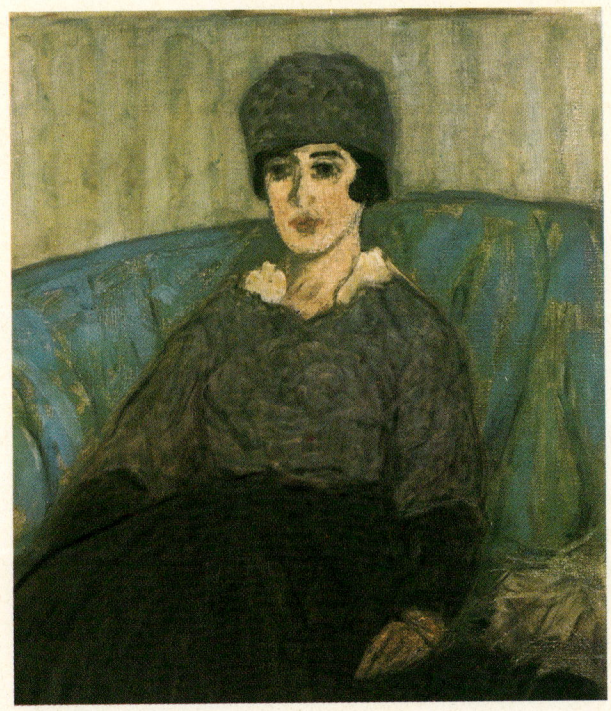

JAMES WILSON MORRICE
Blanche
Signed, 24in by 19½in
Toronto $25,000 (£10,262). 23.X.73

FREDERIC EDWIN CHURCH, NA
Cotopaxi
Signed and dated 1855, 31in by 47in
New York $90,000 (£37,500). 25.x.73
From the collection of Sanford Agnew Esq

The decade of the 1850s was the most formative of the Hudson River School, and, during that period, Church stood out among his contemporaries as the leader of the American landscapists. In the company of Cyrus Field, he made an extended trip to Columbia, Ecuador and Panama in 1853. In 1855 Church painted the first of his views of Cotopaxi.
This picture was at one time in the collection of William T. Blodgett, a New York manufacturer and one of Church's most important patrons.

THOMAS MORAN, NA
Canyon mists: Zoroaster Peak (Grand Canyon, Arizona)
Signed and dated *May* 1914, and with the artist's thumbprint, 30¼in by 25¼in
New York $80,000 (£33,333). 25.X.73

Left and opposite page above
AMMI PHILLIPS
A lady and a gentleman
A pair of portraits. Painted
circa 1826–1828, 30in by 24in
New York $32,500 (£13,542).
14.XI.73
From the Edith Gregor Halpert
Folk Art Collection

Below
WILLIAM M. HARNETT
The social club
Signed and dated 1879,
13¼in by 20¼in
New York $57,500 (£23,958).
25.X.73

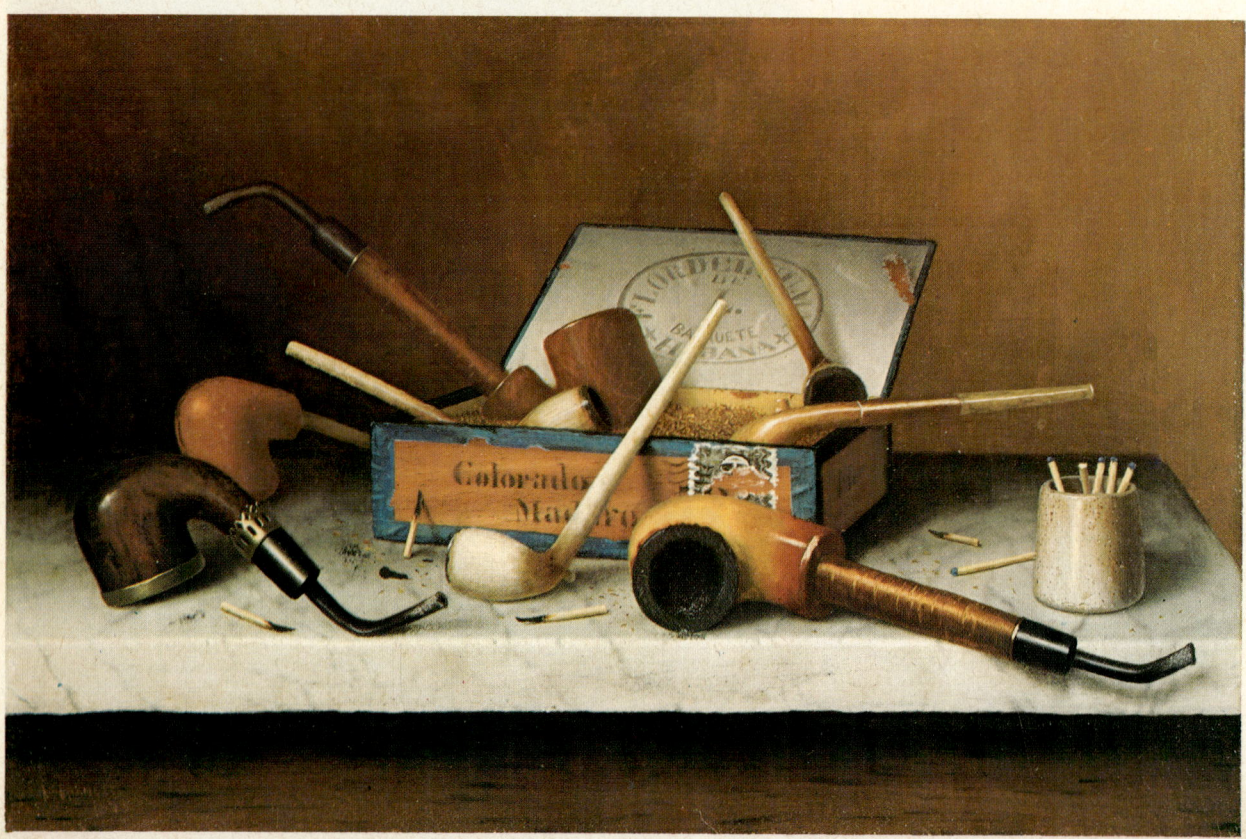

Below
WILLIAM M. HARNETT
Still life with New York Herald *and Butler's* Hudibras
Signed and dated 1880,
11in by 15in
New York $30,000 (£12,500).
23.V.74

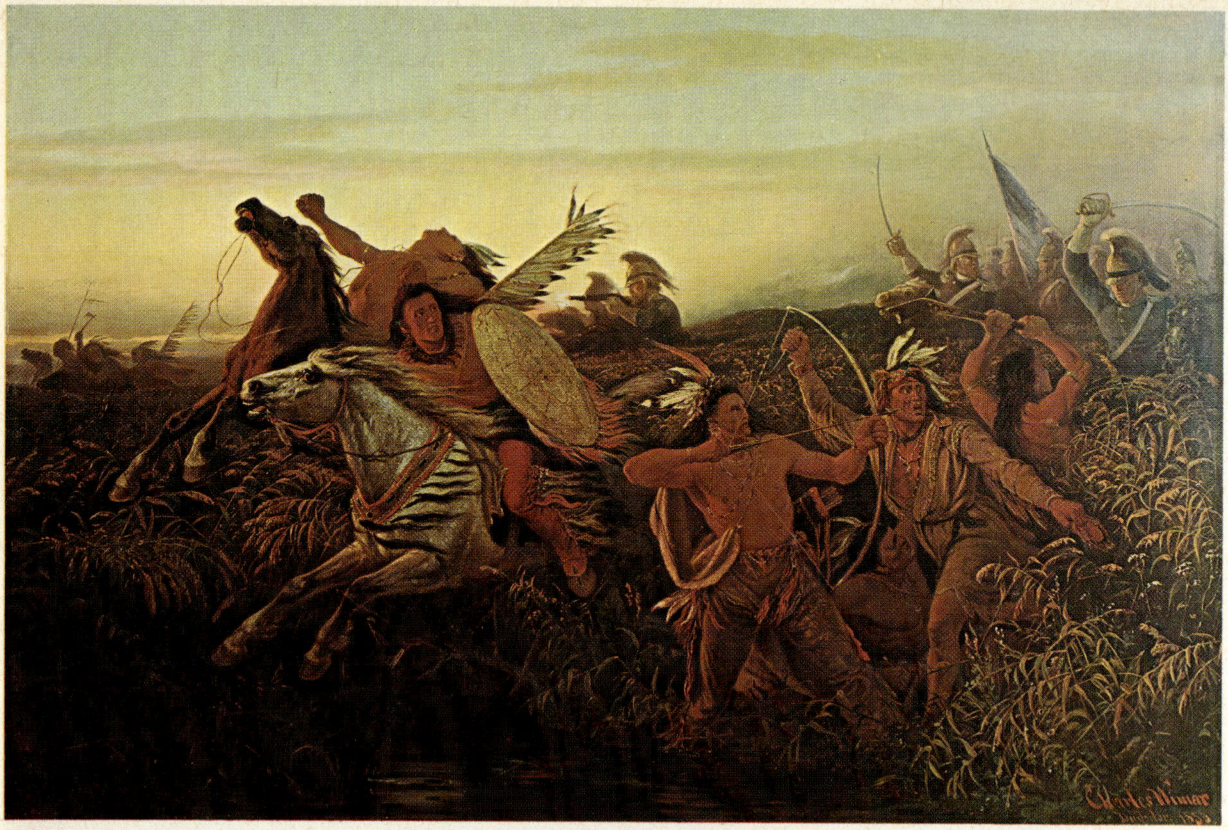
Charles Wimar

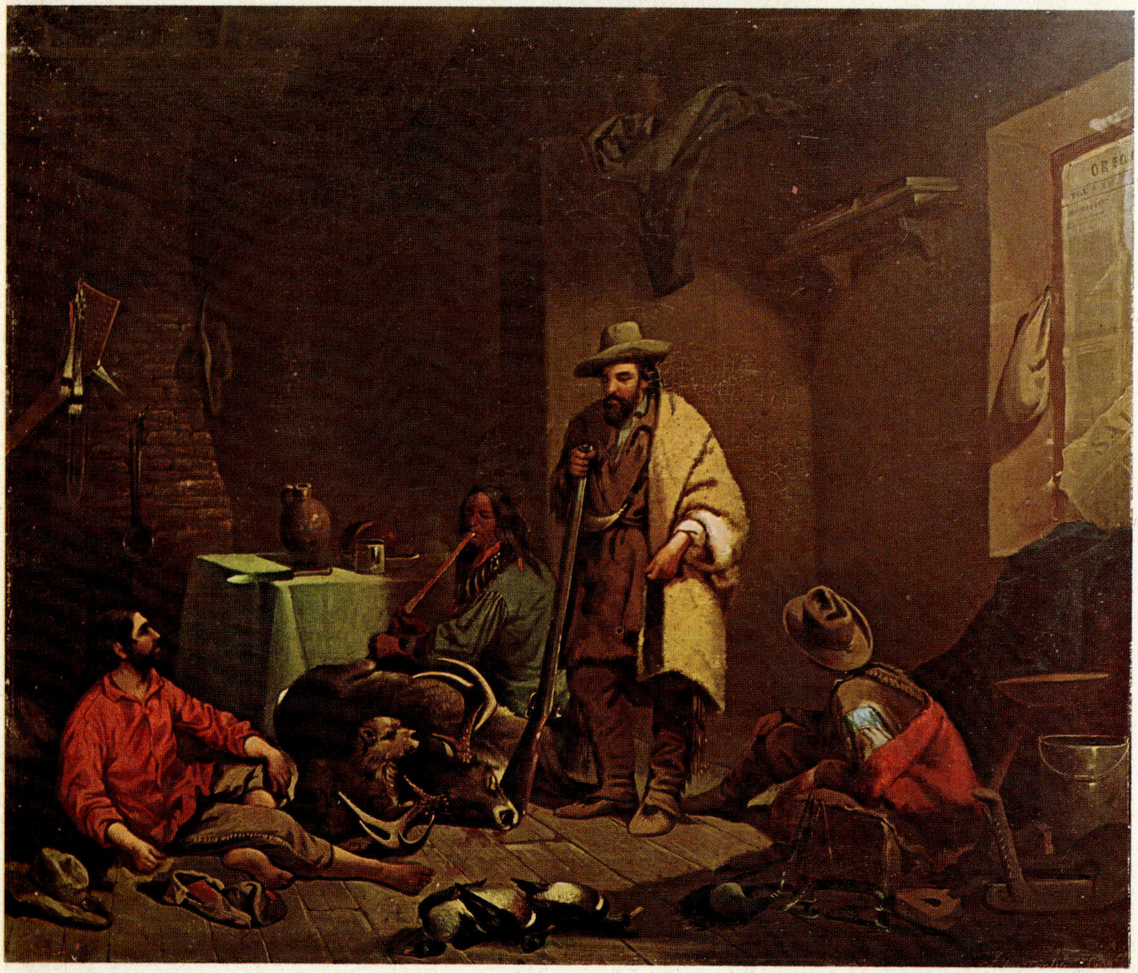

Left
CHARLES WIMAR
Indians pursued by American dragoons
Signed and dated *Dusseldorf* 1853, 33in by 46in
New York $50,000 (£20,833). 23.V.74
From the collection of the Noonday Club, St Louis

Right
CHARLES C. NAHL
Vaqueros roping a steer
Signed and dated 1866, 42in by 51in
Los Angeles $60,000 (£25,000). 4.III.74

Left
JOHN MIX STANLEY
'Hunters and traders'
Signed and dated 1862, 25¼in by 30¼in
New York $30,000 (£12,500). 23.V.74

Right
FRANK TENNEY JOHNSON, NA
Camp of the Blackfeet
Signed and dated 1938, 36¼in by 46¼in
Los Angeles $55,000 (£22,917). 4.III.74
From the collection of Mr and Mrs Ted Dalzell

EASTMAN JOHNSON, NA, after **EMANUEL LEUTZE**
Washington crossing the Delaware
With signature *E. Leutze,* painted in 1851,
40½in by 67⅞in
New York $260,000 (£108,333). 25.x.73
From the collection of Ambassador and
Mrs J. William Middendorf II. The original by
Leutze is in the Metropolitan Museum of Art,
New York

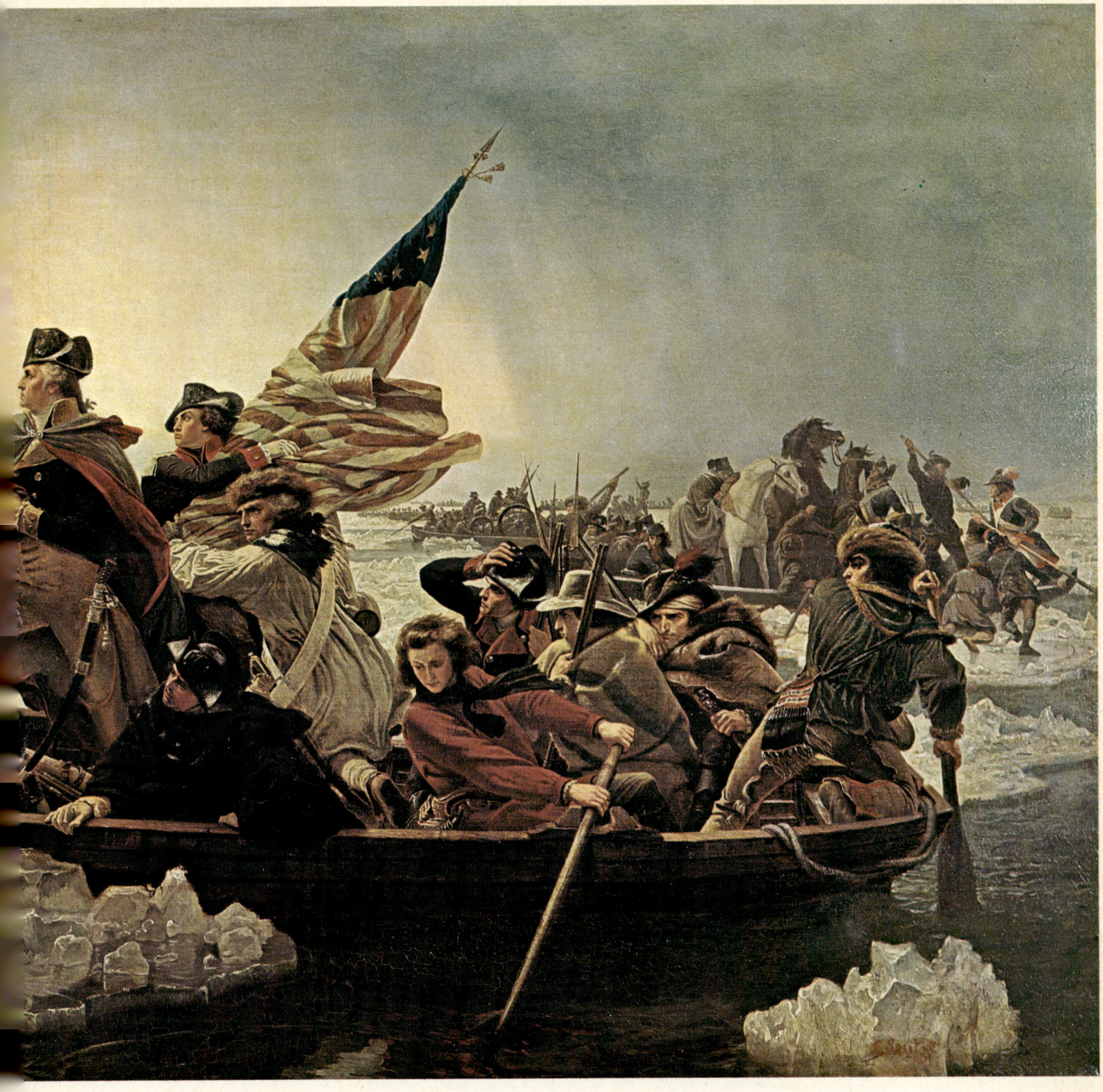

Above
ANDREW MELROSE
New York Harbor and the Battery
Signed, painted *circa* 1887, 22in by 36in
New York $37,500 (£15,625). 25.x.73

Below
GEORGE INNESS, NA
Landscape with figures
Signed and dated 1866, 12¼in by 18¼in
New York $35,000 (£14,580). 25.x.73

Opposite page Above
CHILDE HASSAM
The water garden
Signed and dated 1909, also signed with monogram and dated 1909 on the reverse, 24in by 36in
New York $140,000 (£58,300). 23.v.74
From the collection of the late Thérèse Lownes Noble

Below
MARTIN JOHNSON HEADE
Orchid and hummingbird
Signed, painted *circa* 1864, 15in by 20in
New York $27,000 (£11,250). 23.v.74

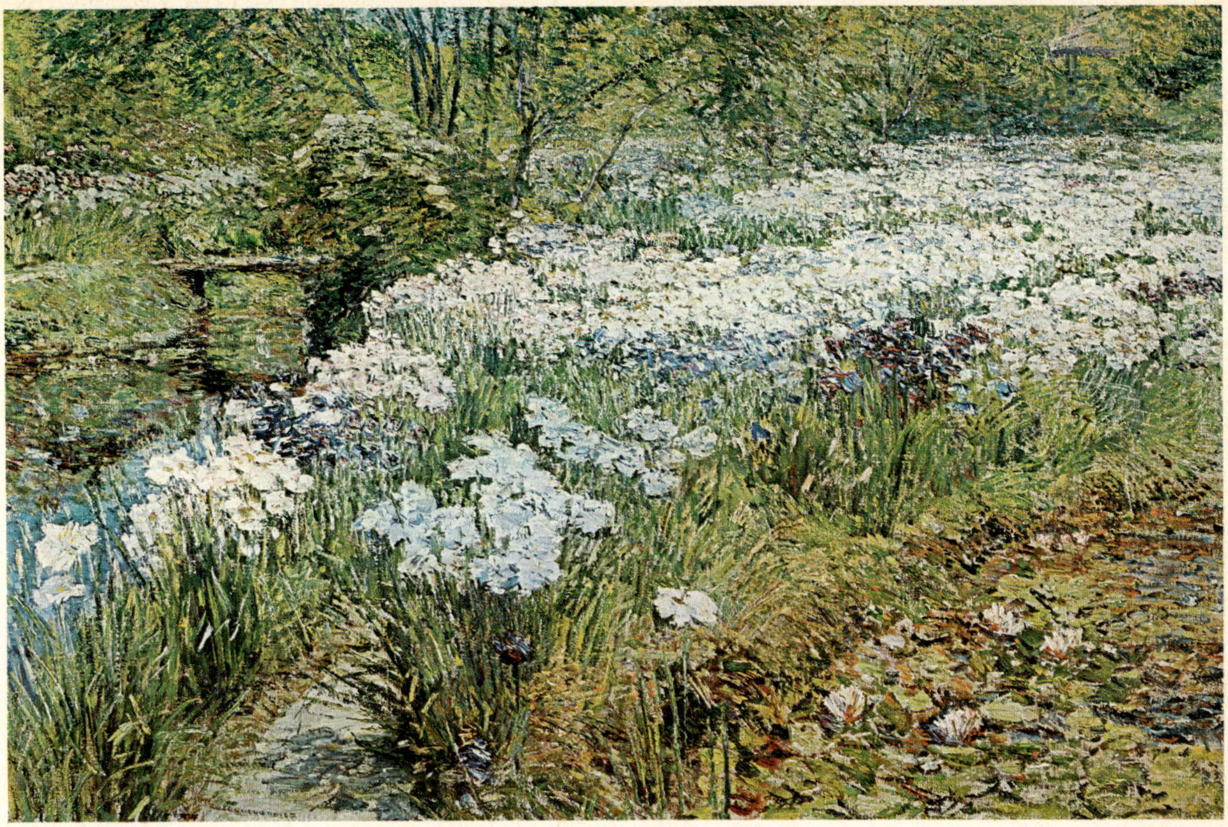

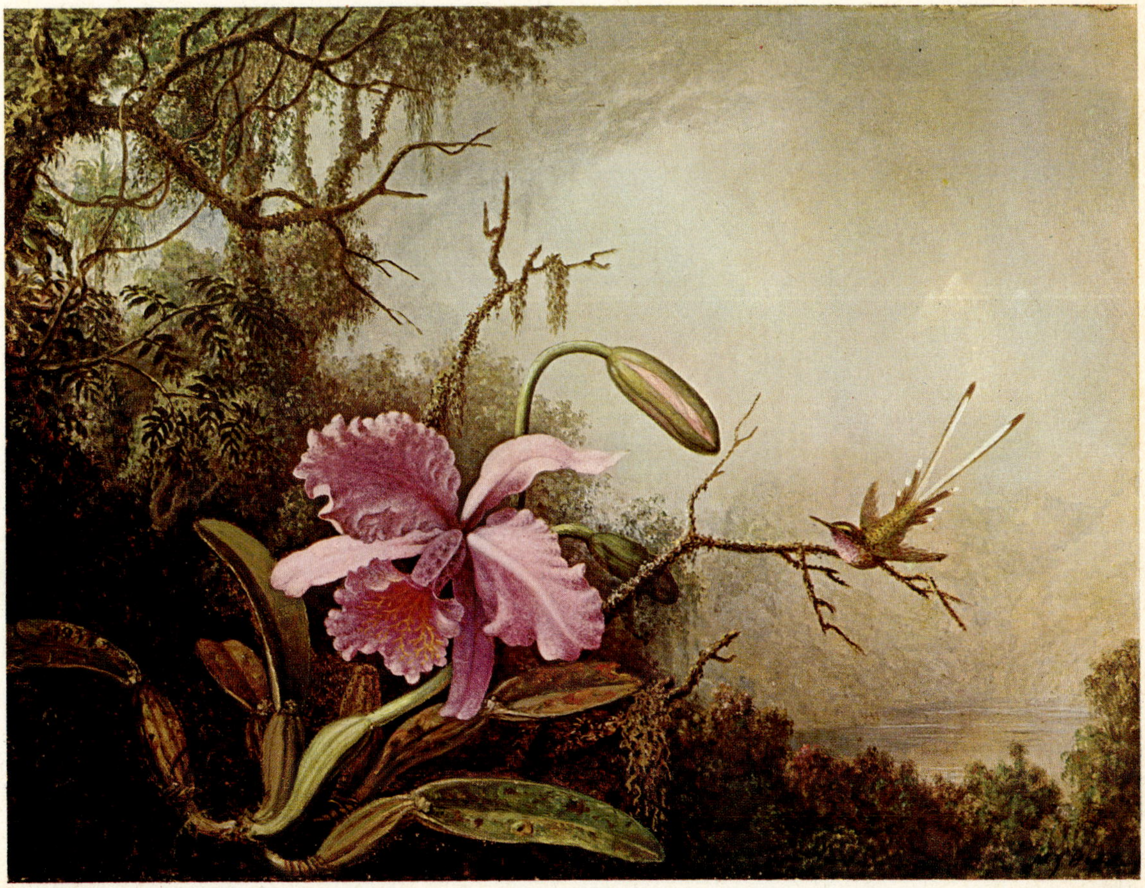

WINSLOW HOMER, NA
Fruit vendor at Nassau
Watercolour and pencil, signed and dated *Nassau July 14th*, 1885, 12½in by 9in
New York $65,000 (£27,083). 17.X.73
From the collection of the late Edwin C. Vogel

MAURICE B. PRENDERGAST
'*Splash of sunshine and rain*' (*Church of St Mark – Venice*)
Watercolour, signed and dated 1899, also signed and titled on an exhibition label affixed to the reverse, and signed, titled and dated 1904 on another label affixed to the reverse, 19¼in by 14½in
New York $67,500 (£28,125). 13.XII.73

EDWARD HICKS
The Peaceable Kingdom
16¾in by 20in
New York $65,000 (£27,083). 14.XI.73
From the Edith Gregor Halpert Folk Art Collection

Prints

JOHN JAMES AUDUBON
Night heron or Qua bird (plate CCXXXVI)
Hand-coloured engraving and aquatint by R. Havell after the drawing by Audubon, published in London, 1835
New York $3,100 (£1,292). 30.V.74
From the collection of Louise C. Morgan

176 PRINTS

ALBRECHT DÜRER
The sea monster
Engraving, *circa* 1498, 249mm by 289mm
New York $14,000 (£5,800). 14.v.74

ALBRECHT ALTDORFER
Landscape with a watermill
Etching, *circa* 1520, 177mm by 235mm
New York $82,500 (£34,375). 14.V.74
This work is one of the earliest pure landscapes in the history of western graphic art

HENDRIK GOLTZIUS
The three statues: *The Farnese Hercules*; *Emperor Commodius as Hercules*; and *The Apollo Belvedere* (illustrated)
Engravings, a set of three plates, second state with letters, each 418mm by 302mm
London £1,150 ($2,760). 11.VII.74

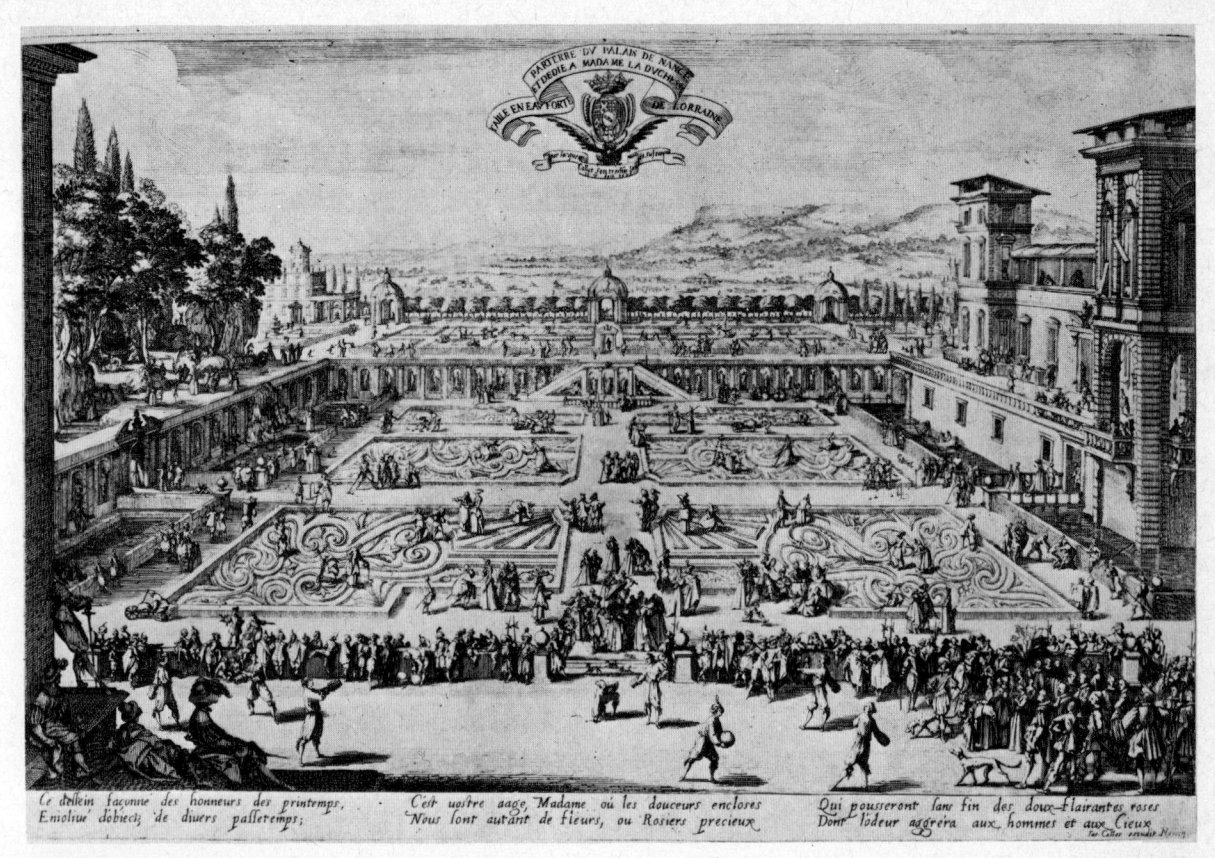

JACQUES CALLOT
Le parterre de Nancy
Etching, first state of two, 259mm by 387mm
London £1,400 ($3,360). 11.XII.73
From the collection of the late Dr Felix Somary

JACQUES CALLOT
Les Gobbi
Etchings, two of a set of twenty-one plates, the first state before numbers, each *circa* 65mm by 86mm
London £950 ($2,280). 28.III.74
From the collection of the late Dr Felix Somary

REMBRANDT HARMENSZ. VAN RIJN
'The Three Crosses' – *Christ crucified between the two thieves*
Drypoint and burin, fourth state of five, 385mm by 449mm
New York $90,000 (£37,500). 14.V.74

REMBRANDT HARMENSZ. VAN RIJN
The great Jewish bride
Etching, fifth (final) state, 221mm by 168mm
London £7,000 ($16,800). 11.XII.73
Formerly in the collection of Louis Galichon

REMBRANDT HARMENSZ. VAN RIJN
Abraham's sacrifice
Etching and drypoint, only state, 158mm by 134mm
London £2,800 ($6,720). 11.VII.74

GIOVANNI BENEDETTO CASTIGLIONE
Noah guiding animals into the ark
Etching, first state of two, 137mm by 97mm
London £650 ($1,560). 11.XII.73

GIOVANNI BATTISTA TIEPOLO
The young man leaning on an urn, from *Vari Capricci*
Etching, 141mm by 182mm
London £1,100 ($2,640). 28.III.74
From the collection of the late W. A. McDonald

WILLIAM BLAKE
The man sweeping the interpreter's parlour
Engraving on pewter, second state, 81mm by 164mm
London £2,100 ($5,040).
11.XII.73
Impression No 5, recorded by Keynes. Formerly in the collections of Dr Greville Macdonald and Ruthven Todd

WILLIAM BLAKE
The illustrations to Dante
Engravings, a set of seven plates, printed on India paper laid on wove paper, one of 100 sets pulled in 1892, each 272mm by 352mm
London £3,700 ($8,880). 11.VII.74

Above: GEORGE RICHMOND, RA
The Fatal Bellman
Line engraving, only state, 68mm by 47mm
London £520 ($1,248). 30.IV.74
From the collection of the late Kerrison Preston

Right: WILLIAM HOLMAN HUNT, RA
Afterglow in Egypt
Etching, proof before completion of the plate.
Inscribed and with artist's initials, size of sheet 225mm by 148mm.
London £410 ($984). 8.I.74
From the collection of Mrs Elizabeth Burt

SAMUEL PALMER
Above: Harvest under a crescent moon
Wood-engraving on Japan-type paper, from the 1932 edition of fifty, this impression numbered 9, 28mm by 79mm
London £620 ($1,488). 8.I.74
From the collection of the late Hon Robert Gathorne-Hardy

Left: The sleeping shepherd, early morning
Etching, on chine appliqué, fourth state, 95mm by 75mm
London £170 ($408). 2.VII.74

Left: HENRI DE TOULOUSE-LAUTREC
La loge au mascaron doré
Lithograph printed in colours, first state of two, 1893, numbered 69 from the edition of 100, 370mm by 290mm
New York $8,500 (£3,542). 8.XI.73

Below left: JAMES A. MCNEILL WHISTLER
Maude standing
Etching and drypoint, tenth state of twelve, printed in sepia, 227mm by 153mm
New York $6,800 (£2,833). 15.V.74
From the collection of George W. Vanderbilt
Formerly in the collection of Edward G. Kennedy

Below right: JACQUES VILLON
Danseuse espagnole, 1899
Aquatint, printed in colours, on Arches, signed in pencil, numbered 18/25, 507mm by 357mm
London £2,400 ($5,760). 20.XI.73

MAURICE PRENDERGAST
The breezy common
Coloured monotype, 1895–1905, signed and titled on the plate, 177mm by 229mm
New York $4,700 (£1,958). 14.II.74

MARY CASSATT
Gathering fruit
Drypoint and aquatint printed in colours, *circa* 1895, early impression of the final state, signed in pencil, 428mm by 300mm
New York $16,000 (£6,666). 15.V.74

EDWARD HOPPER
Night on the El train
Etching, 1920, signed in pencil, 188mm by 202mm
New York $5,400 (£2,250). 8.XI.73

188 PRINTS

HENRI DE TOULOUSE-LAUTREC
La châtelaine ou le tocsin
Lithographic poster printed in blue, first state before letters, 574mm by 452mm
London £800 ($1,920). 16.VII.74

HENRI DE TOULOUSE-LAUTREC
Invitation à une tasse de lait, 1900
Lithograph, only state, signed in pencil, inscribed *à Stern*, 267mm by 200mm
London £2,100 ($5,040). 20.XI.73

HENRI DE TOULOUSE-LAUTREC
Couverture de l'estampe originale, 1893
Lithograph printed in colours, signed in pencil and numbered 66, 565mm by 655mm
London £2,700 ($6,480). 16.VII.74

Photography as Art

By Graham Ovenden

Those of us who have long been acquainted with the warm seductive imagery of the Victorian camera, can only wonder at the comparative neglect of over a half century of this marvellous art. This neglect is even more difficult to understand when one considers the enthusiasm shown by the public and – albeit to a lesser extent – by the practitioners of the established fine art fraternity.

As photography covers two related yet 'opposite' poles of human interest, on the one hand the scientific both chemical and physical, and on the other, the artistic use of this mechanism which creates the visually emotive and beautiful, this crossing of the frontiers of science into art make it a particular child of the nineteenth century.

There are qualities inherent to the photographic image that transcend certain efforts in pictorial realism as practiced by the less precise handwork of the Victorian narrative painter. But even so, it is dangerous to confuse the photographic print with actuality. Its image is no less a transposition of the seen thing than the painted representation. The camera picture is the chemical reaction of the graph of light, and because of its tonal perfection one often forgets that it is the two-dimensional interpretation of a three-dimensional world, and not reality itself. If we also include the dimension of time, surely there is a paradox here. The 'common' quality of greatness in a work of art, ie: timelessness, seems hardly appropriate to the photographic image which is very much the product of a moment. And yet, in the hands of a great artist this instant of time can be expanded to encompass a multitude of emotions that will enrich our perception of the human experience. Simply, the chemical image of light can possess the psychological profundity of great art.

Another important virtue of the photographic medium is the technical ease with which the chemical image is produced, thus placing it within the scope of virtually all who attempt it, and this in turn must give a greater freedom of expression to those less academically trained than the 'fine' artist, but who are equally sensitive visually. Yet although there may be a degree of ease in making an image, this does not guarantee that any person placing a camera before a subject will create a masterpiece or even an aesthetically pleasing picture. Great photography is as rare as great painting, though the incidence of the naive genius is likely to be higher in the camera than the paint brush.

Main Street, Gorbals, looking North
From 'Old Glasgow', an album of forty carbon prints by Thomas Annan, published for the 'City of Glasgow Improvement Trust', the photographs of old closes, streets, etc., taken between 1868 and 1877 and including studies of the High Street, closes off the High Street, and off the Saltmarket
London £7,500 ($18,000). 21.VI.74

    Certainly one of the most visually exciting qualities encountered in the Victorian album is not necessarily that of great portraiture, but of social documentation, and it is doubly precious because of its rare existence in our modern equivalents. The innovation of the photographic medium seems to have inspired many inquisitive minds to immortalise their existence onto the light-sensitive paper. This type of self-expression at its least, collectively, creates an important visual document of our forefathers, and at its height can extend into the realms of great art, such as the work of Julia Margaret Cameron and Lewis Carroll.
    Even we, in this age of sated appetites for the visual media, can still marvel at the action of light on a silver salt, creating a miniature of our visual expanse. How much more remarkable must this have seemed to a society hitherto unacquainted with the precise magic of the camera image.
    Although the middle and upper classes are well documented in the Victorian album, the poorer members of society fare less well, this is particularly frustrating as the quality of the material that does survive from the festering slums of the great nineteenth-century industrial cities is extraordinarily high, both pictorially and in terms of human values. Perhaps the technical difficulties, particularly in the first two decades of photography, are the main reason for the scarcity of the purely social document. On the evidence of the work of the Newcastle amateurs, Hetling and Spence, and the searching journalism of Smith and Thomson, much has been lost by the inactivity of the nineteenth-century cameraman.

65, High Street, Glasgow
A plate from 'Old Closes and Streets, a Series of Photo-gravures 1868-1899' the illustrations taken from photographs by and the volume published by T. & R. Annan & Sons, 230 Sauchiehall Street, Glasgow, for 'The City of Glasgow Improvement Trust'
London £1,100 ($2,640). 21.VI.74

Yet if the Victorians wished to remain unobservant of their own social plight, in the realm of the grand tour and expeditionary feats of endurance nothing was overlooked. With the isolated exceptions, such as MacPherson, however, in the totality of the nineteenth-century achievement in photography and art, it is just these feats of endurance that now seem the most trivial and irrelevant.

Perhaps in this we see one of the limitations of the photographic medium. Topographical subjects seldom contain even a grain of genius, and even when the imagery is powerful, such as in the work of Maville, Atget or Sawyer, it is as much the social conscience and mystery which create atmosphere as the environments themselves.

To the Victorian amateur of intense dedication, however, the limitations of situation seem to matter little. While Frith and Bedford were battling with the sands of the Sahara, and Fenton and Robertson with even more unpleasant surroundings in the Crimea, less than a decade later passionate, yet monumentally silent, images were created by Mrs Cameron in her glazed hen-house, and masterpieces in miniature by Lewis Carroll in sunlit gardens.

It is relevant to notice the high degree of intellectual attainment of the Victorian photographic amateurs. Possibly it was their greater freedom and scope that allowed them

H. PEACOCK (?)
Tea time at Millhall, Sussex
Albumen print, *circa* 1865

experimentation (unlike those forced to live totally by commercial enterprise and open to the whims of a fickle public) and that enabled them to achieve a standard of such excellence. Indeed, it was an amateur, Mrs Cameron, who took the art to a pinnacle of achievement. In virtually all portraiture there are few images of the quality of Mrs Cameron's; her work is unique, certainly within the first half century of photography. Though her indulgence can be excessive and her sentiment perhaps at times overly feminine, in her great images of the Victorian intelligentsia we possess a document of the highest order. Even the romantic *richesse* of Hill and Adamson, or the elegance of Nadar, fall short of the genius of her vision. Her work, as Fry so rightly asserts, has the quality of great portraiture, this is manifest not only in her portrayal of the famous, but also in her images of children, from which emanates a riveting sense of presence. Possibly only Lewis Carroll achieved an equal profundity, but by very different means.

I mention Mrs Cameron in particular because her art, which is at the summit of pictorialism, seems to display a very relevant facet of the nineteenth century: that of the Romantic intellectual; it also acts as a contrast to the grinding poverty of the lower orders of society so magnificently rendered by Annan and Hetling. Photography in the hands of a person sensitive to his environment and predicament is open to the broadest style and interpretation; the critic who sees the photograph only as a means of recording is naive, not to say moronic.

Photography, like painting, evolves lineally, and it is particularly instructive to follow the evolution from Hill and Hetling to Annan, Thomson and Riss, to Martin, Hine and

A lady and a gentleman
Albumen print from the Coghill Family Album, *circa* 1862

JULIA MARGARET CAMERON
Portrait of Annie Cameron
A plate from the presentation album dedicated by Julia Margaret Cameron to her 'best beloved sister Mia' and containing fifty-eight photographs by Mrs Cameron and sixty-one others by various photographers
London £40,000 ($96,000). 21.VI.74

A study of a young girl
Attributed to Oscar Gustav
Rejlander, *circa* 1860, 180mm
by 154mm
London £600 ($1,440). 21.VI.74

Walker Evans in the direction of social observation, or to the school of portraiture as represented by Cameron, Nadar or Sanders.

In particular, taking the spectrum of photographic achievement during the last fourteen decades, its intimate humanity is revealed, and this must be one of the most precious qualities possessed by mankind.

It seems a little unjust that Roger Fry's prophetic utterances in that brief masterpiece, *Famous Men and Fair Women* should have been realised in spirit if not in practice – that one day the National Portrait Gallery would be suitably deprived of its purchasing grant, thereby necessitating the acquisition of photographic images rather than the costly painted representations – I wonder if he ever foresaw the competitive enthusiasm among museums and collectors now apparent in the auction rooms. It is regrettable that due to the general poverty of our National Museums, the institutions now dedicated to the building of a great national collection may find the task beyond their means.

A group including Tennyson and his sons in a garden
Anonymous, a plate from the presentation album dedicated by Julia Margaret Cameron to her sister Mia and containing fifty-eight photographs by Mrs Cameron and sixty-one by other photographers, 161mm by 138mm (see also p194)
London £40,000 ($96,000). 21.VI.74

Manuscripts and Printed Books

198 ORIENTAL MANUSCRIPTS AND MINIATURES
202 WESTERN MANUSCRIPTS
208 AUTOGRAPH MANUSCRIPTS, LETTERS, AND PROOFS
212 PRINTED BOOKS

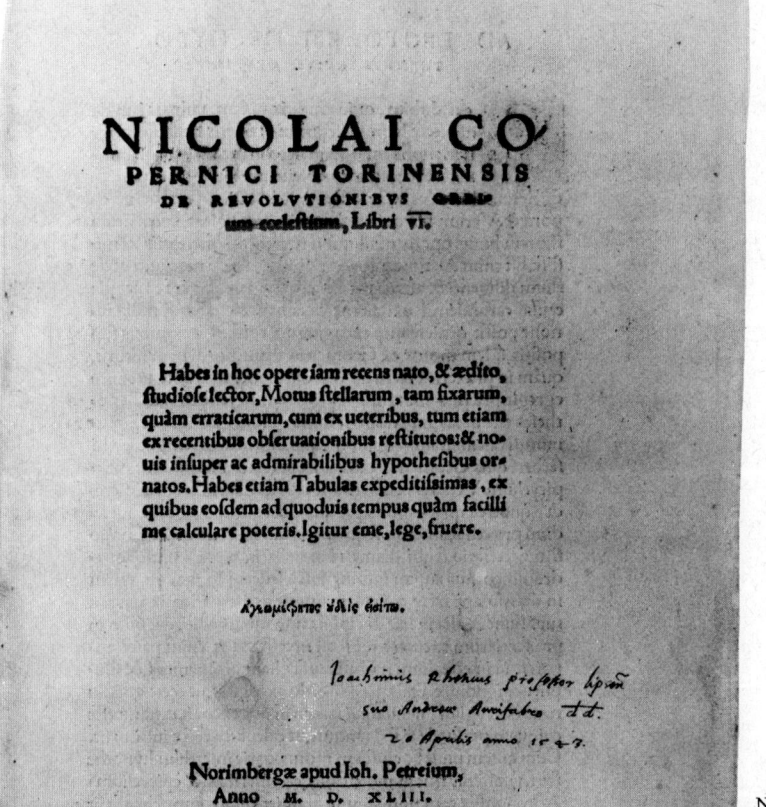

NIKOLAUS KOPPERNIK, called COPERNICUS
De Revolutionibus Orbium Coelestium
Presentation copy of the first edition, inscribed by Joachim Rheticus, who supervised the printing, to his pupil Andreas Goldschmidt, Nürnberg, 1543
London £44,000 ($105,600). 11.VI.74
From the celebrated collection of books on early scientific subjects formed by Harrison D. Horblit Esq

198 ORIENTAL MANUSCRIPTS AND MINIATURES

The hermitage of Vasishtha visited by Vishvamitra
Indian miniature from a series of illustrations to the *Rāmāyana*, [Kulu, *circa* 1690-1700]
London £2,600 ($6,240). 11.XII.73

COL JAMES SKINNER, CB
Persian manuscript for a rule-book of military exercises for Indian musket cavalry, with 33 coloured illustrations and 14 miniatures, Hansi, January 1824
London £1,600 ($3,840). 23.IV.74

Portrait of a bearded shepherd with goat and sheep
A Persian miniature by Riza-i'Abbasi, inscribed and signed by the artist, [Isfahan], 7th day of Ramazan 1041 [28th March 1632]
London £4,200 ($10,080).
23.IV.74
From the collection of Mrs Constance Sitwell

Opposite page
A disconsolate lady on a terrace with her companion
Indian miniature [Guler, circa 1760]
London £850 ($2,040).
11.XII.73

ORIENTAL MANUSCRIPTS AND MINIATURES 201

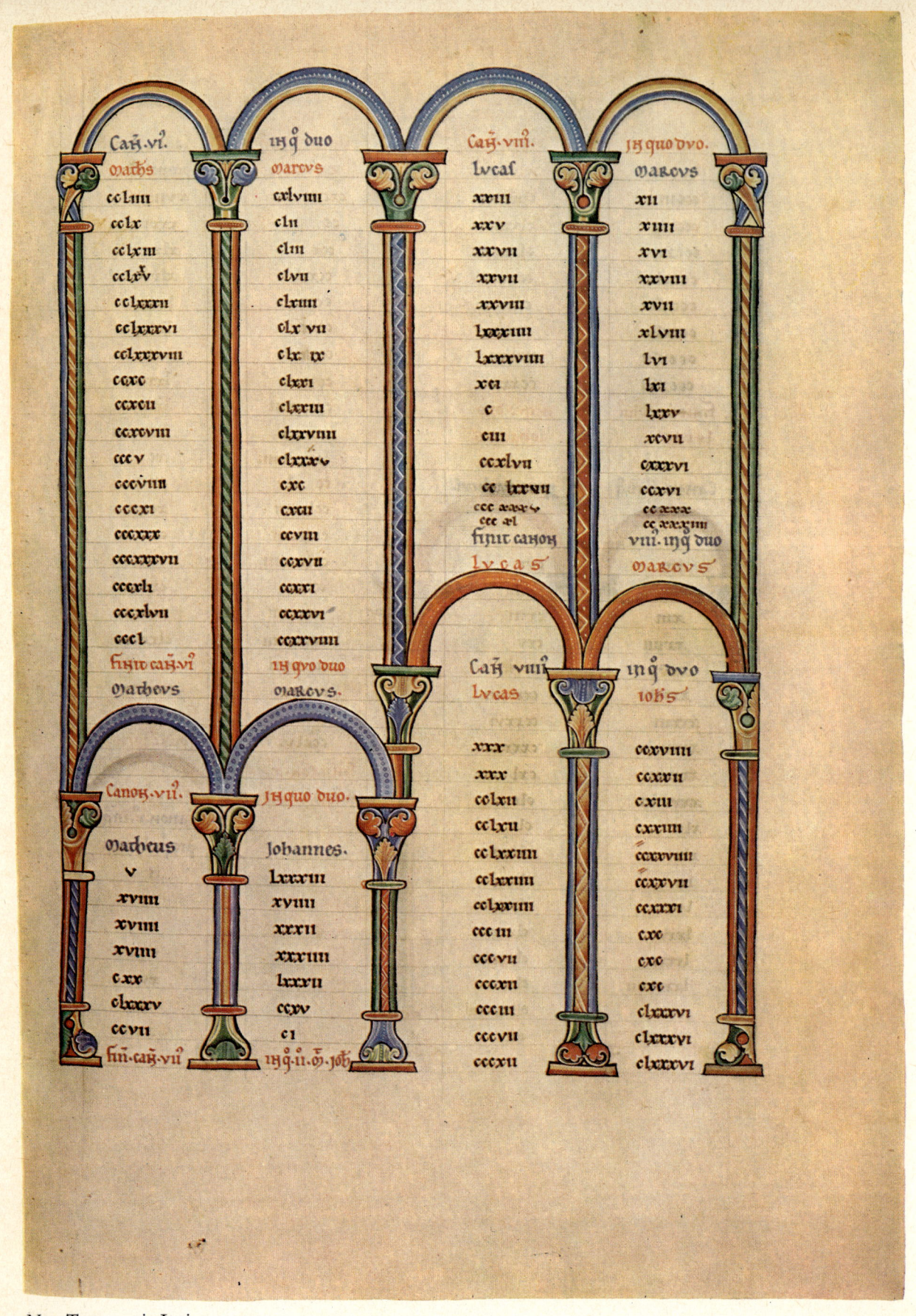

New Testament in Latin
Manuscript on vellum, with 12 pages of decorated Canon Tables and 36 large illuminated initials, [France (Auxerre?), third quarter of the twelfth century]
London £20,000 ($48,000).4.vi.74 One of the Hornby Manuscripts from the collection of the late Major J. R. Abbey

Minor Prophets in Latin, with gloss
Manuscript on vellum with decorated initials, [North-Eastern France, Anchin, third quarter of the twelfth century]
London £42,000 ($100,800). 4.VI.74.
One of the Hornby Manuscripts from the collection of the late Major J. R. Abbey

204 WESTERN MANUSCRIPTS

LIVY
Historia Romana, Decades I-III in the French translation of Pierre Bersuire
Manuscript on vellum, 3 vol., illustrated with 30 miniatures, including 3 quadripartite miniatures as illustrated,
[Central France?, second quarter of the fifteenth century]
London £75,000 ($180,000). 28.XI.73
From the collection of the late Sir Thomas Phillipps Bt (1792-1872)

Hours of the Virgin, use of Reims
Manuscript on vellum written for Jacques and Jeanne Cauchon, illustrated with 24 roundels depicting occupations of the months and signs of the zodiac and 19 large miniatures,
[Reims, *circa* 1430]
London £34,000 ($81,600). 4.VI.74
One of the Hornby Manuscripts from the collection of the late Major J. R. Abbey

206 WESTERN MANUSCRIPTS

CRISTOFORO BUONDELMONTI
Liber Insularum Archipelagi
Manuscript on vellum, illustrated with 79 illuminated maps, [France, *circa* 1525]
London £26,000 ($62,400). 28.XI.73
From the collection of the late Sir Thomas Phillipps Bt (1792-1872)

Herbal
Manuscript on vellum illustrated with coloured pen drawings of about 375 plants, [Northern Italy, second half of the fifteenth century]
London £9,500 ($22,800). 10.XII.73

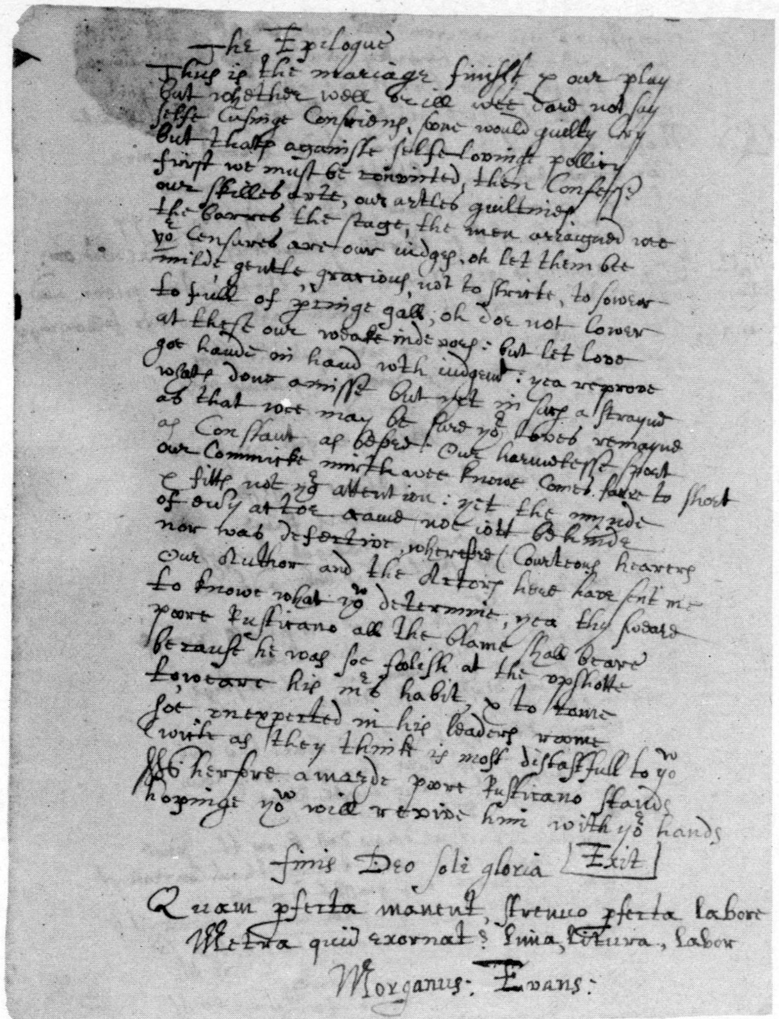

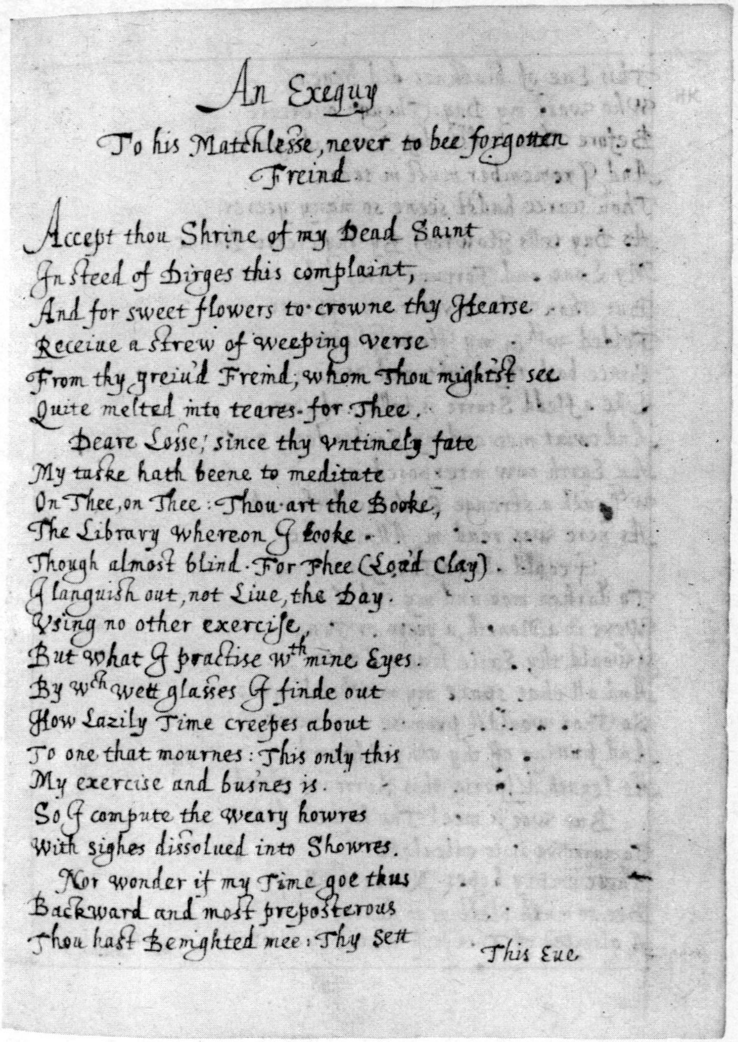

An Exequy

To his Matchlesse, never to bee forgotten Freind.

Accept thou Shrine of my dead Saint
Instead of Dirges this complaint,
And for sweet flowers to crowne thy Hearse
Receive a strew of weeping verse
From thy griev'd Freind, whom thou might'st see
Quite melted into teares for Thee.
Deare Losse; since thy vntimely fate
My taske hath beene to meditate
On Thee, on Thee: Thou art the Booke,
The Library whereon I looke
Though almost blind. For Thee (lov'd Clay)
I languish out, not Liue, the Day,
Vsing no other exercise,
But what I practise wth mine Eyes.
By wch wett glasses I finde out
How lazily Time creepes about
To one that mournes: This only this
My exercise and busines is.
So I compute the weary howres
With sighes dissolued into Showres.
Nor wonder if my Time goe thus
Backward and most preposterous
Thou hast Benighted mee: Thy Sett
_____ This Eve

Poetical Commonplace Book
Manuscript largely in the hand of Thomas Manne, containing 24 poems by Henry King, and others by Richard Corbett, Thomas Carew, Ben Johnson, etc., [circa 1625-44]
London £5,800 ($13,920). 26.vi.74
From the collection of the late Sir Thomas Phillipps Bt (1792-1872)

THOMAS HEYWOOD
Manuscript of a hitherto unknown tragicomedy freely adapted from Richard Johnson's novel *The Most Pleasant History of Tom a Lincolne*, transcribed by three hands, the principal one being Morgan Evans, [circa 1611-15]
London £45,000 ($108,000). 20.xi.73
From the collection of the Most Hon the Marquess of Lothian

ABRAHAM LINCOLN
Autograph letter to Brigadier General A. E. Burnside,
Executive Mansion, 26 Dec. 1861
New York $9,500 (£3,958). 28.11.74

THOMAS JEFFERSON
Autograph letter to Benjamin Rush discussing veterinary medicine, his correspondence with Mr Adams and the navy. Monticello, 6 March 1813
New York $4,100 (£1,708). 28.11.74
From the collection of the late J. William Middendorf Jr

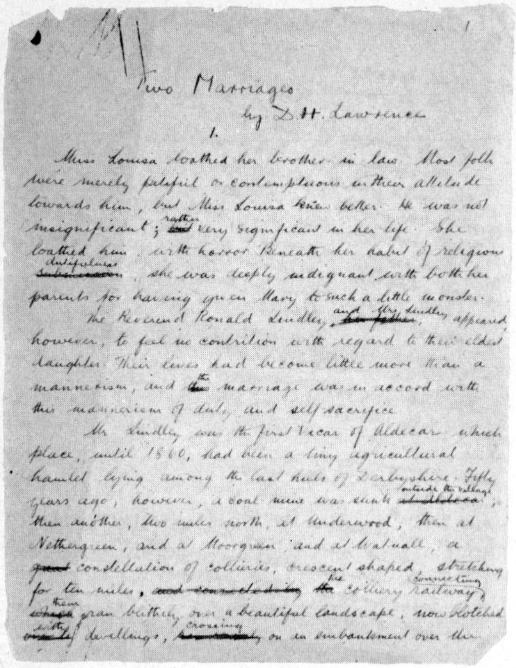

D. H. LAWRENCE
Two Marriages
Autograph manuscript of the story first published in *The Prussian Officer* as *The Daughters of the Vicar*
Los Angeles $7,000 (£2,916). 17.II.74

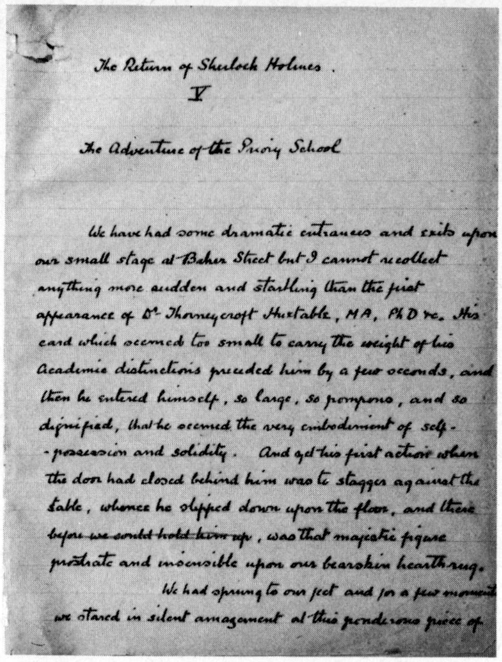

SIR ARTHUR CONAN DOYLE
The Adventure of the Priory School
Autograph manuscript of part V of *The Return of Sherlock Holmes*
New York $15,000 (£6,250). 28.II.74

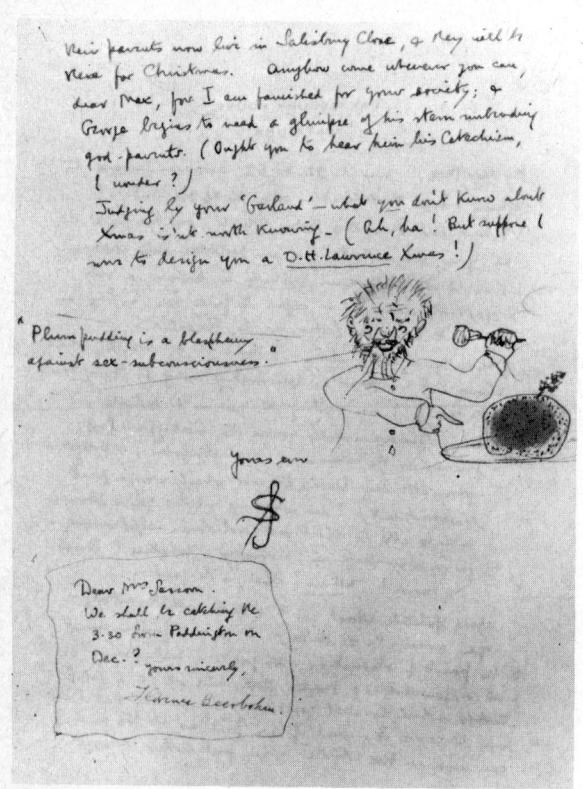

SIEGFRIED SASSOON
A series of 17 unpublished autograph letters to Max Beerbohm, 1937-42
London £1,600 ($3,840). 16.VII.74

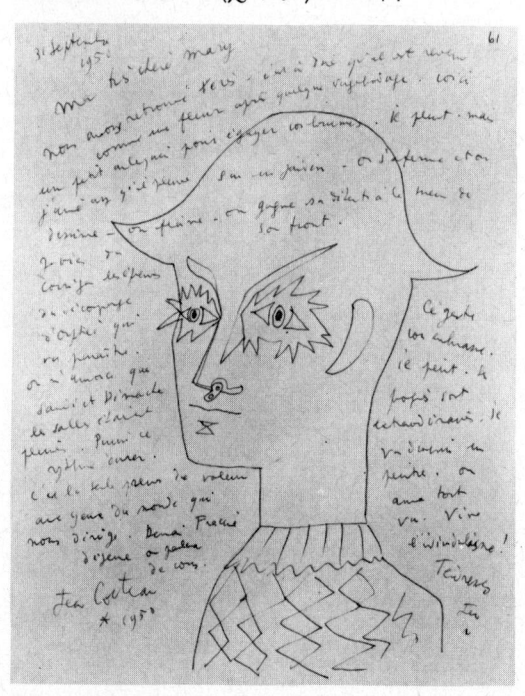

JEAN COCTEAU
A series of 205 autograph letters, 8 cards, and one telegram to his English translator Mary Hoeck, including 9 drawings and several poems, 1948-63
London £3,400 ($8,160). 16.VII.74

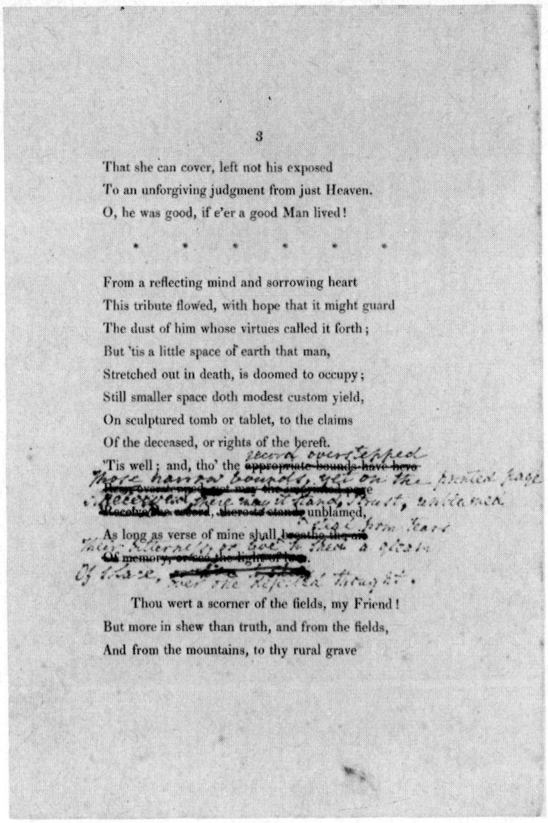

AUTOGRAPH PROOFS 211

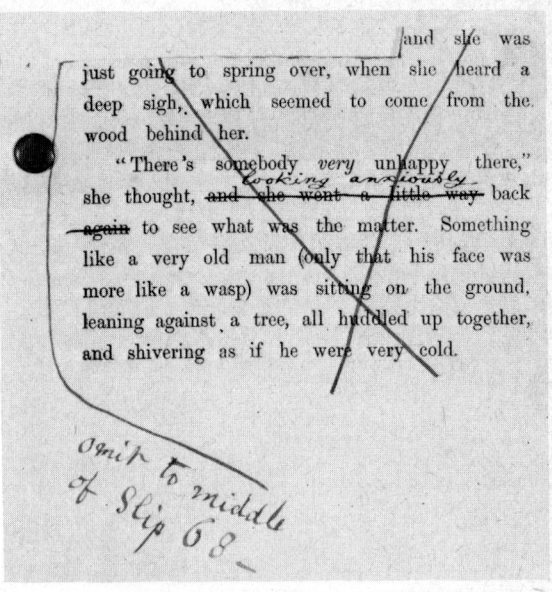

C. L. DODGSON ('Lewis Carroll')
Galley proofs for a suppressed portion of *Through the Looking Glass,* with autograph revisions by the author London £1,700 ($4,080). 3.VI.74
Left
WILLIAM WORDSWORTH [*Elegy on Charles Lamb*]
4 leaves, with revisions by the author in the hand of his wife Mary. [Privately printed, 1836]
London £2,600 ($6,240). 17.VI.74

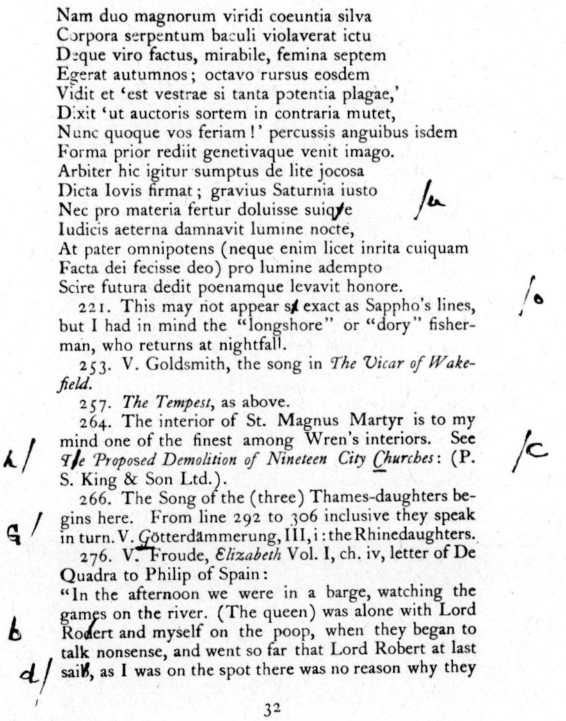

T. S. ELIOT
The Waste Land
Proof copy of the first English edition with autograph corrections by the author, Hogarth Press, 1923
London £600 ($1,440). 29.IV.74
From the collection of Mrs Ian Parsons

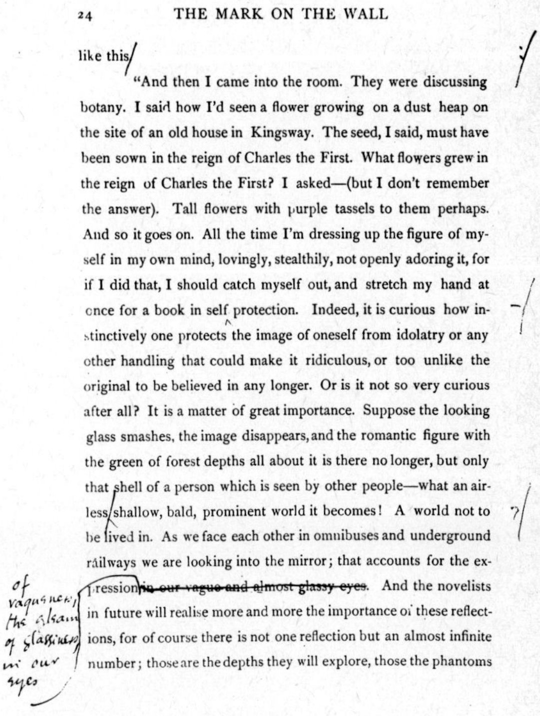

VIRGINIA and LEONARD WOOLF *Two Stories*
First edition, with autograph revisions by Virginia Woolf to her story *The Mark on the Wall,* Hogarth Press, 1917
London £750 ($1,800). 29.IV.74
From the collection of Mrs Ian Parsons

The Most Sacred Bible
A complete copy of the first edition of this translation, 1539
London £13,000 ($31,200). 26.XI.73

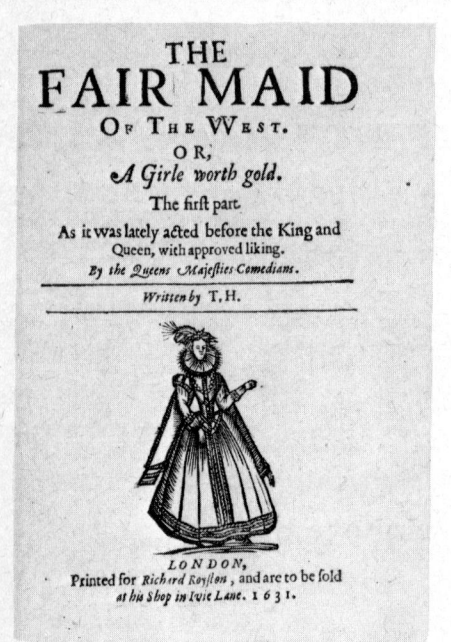

MICHAEL DRAYTON
Endimion and Phoebe
First edition, [1595], one of three known copies
London £19,500 ($46,800). 27.XI.73

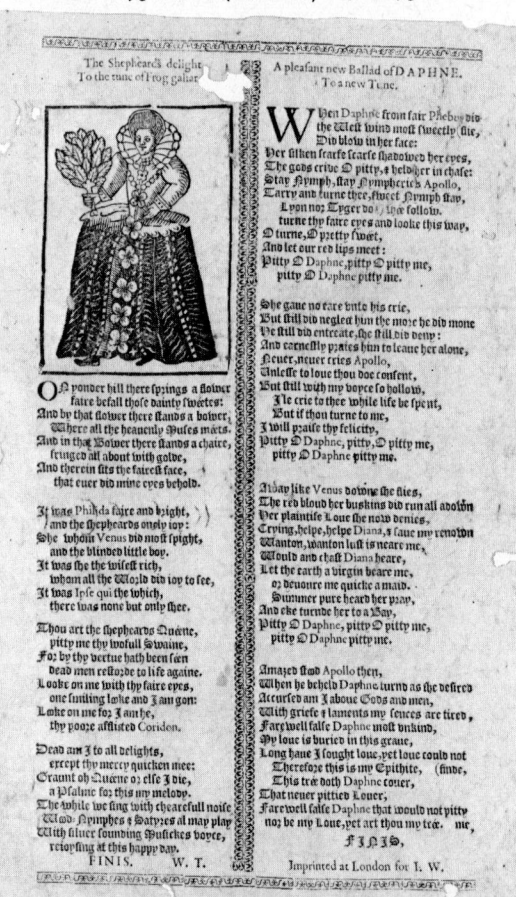

T[HOMAS] H[EYWOOD]
The Fair Maid of the West
First edition, 1631
London £4,000 ($9,600). 24.VI.74

Right
[NICHOLAS BRETON] *The Shepheards Delight*
[THOMAS DELONEY] *A Pleasant New Ballad of Daphne*
The only known copy of this broadside, [1624]
London £2,600 ($6,240). 26.XI.73
Early English printed books from the collection of the late Sir Thomas Phillipps Bt (1792–1872)

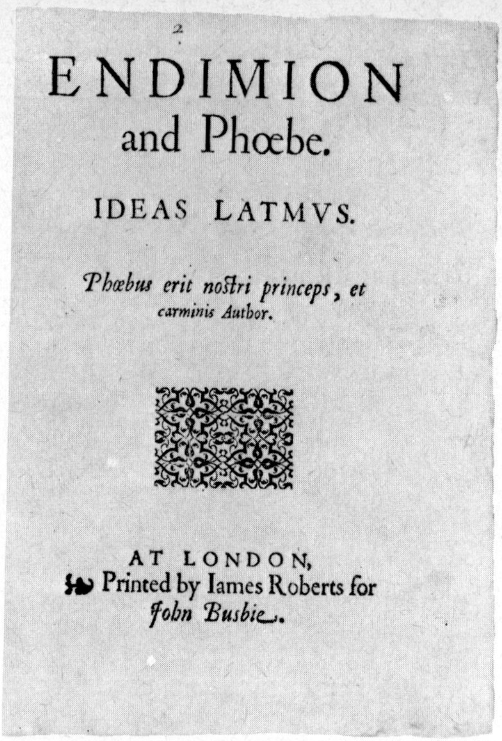

PRINTED BOOKS 213

PETER BIENEWITZ APIANUS
Astronomicum Caesareum
A fine copy of the first issue, containing 36 full-page woodcut astronomical figures with volvelles, coloured silk threads, and seed pearl markers, Ingolstadt, at the author's press, 1540
London £17,000 ($40,800). 10.VI.74
From the celebrated collection of books on early scientific subjects formed by Harrison D. Horblit Esq

SIR THOMAS MORE
Workes
First collected edition, bound in 2 vol., 1557
London £6,600 ($15,840). 25.VI.74
From the collection of the late Sir Thomas Phillipps Bt (1792-1872)

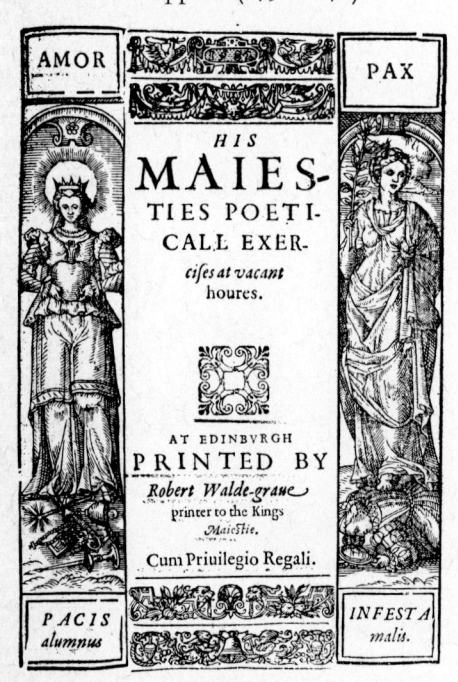

JAMES I, King of England
The Essayes of a Prentise in the Divine Art of Poesie, 1585; *Poeticall Exercises at Vacant Houres*, [1591]
First editions of the two works bound in one volume
London £6,500 ($15,600). 24.VI.74
From the collection of the late Sir Thomas Phillipps Bt (1792-1872)

SIR HUGH PLATT
The Floures of Philosophie with the Pleasures of Poetrie annexed unto them
The only known copy of the author's earliest work, 1581
London £7,500 ($18,000). 25.VI.74
From the collection of the late Sir Thomas Phillipps Bt (1792-1872)

JOHN MILTON
Paradise Lost
First edition, with the first title, 1667
London £8,800 ($21,120). 8.X.73
From the collection of George Goyder Esq

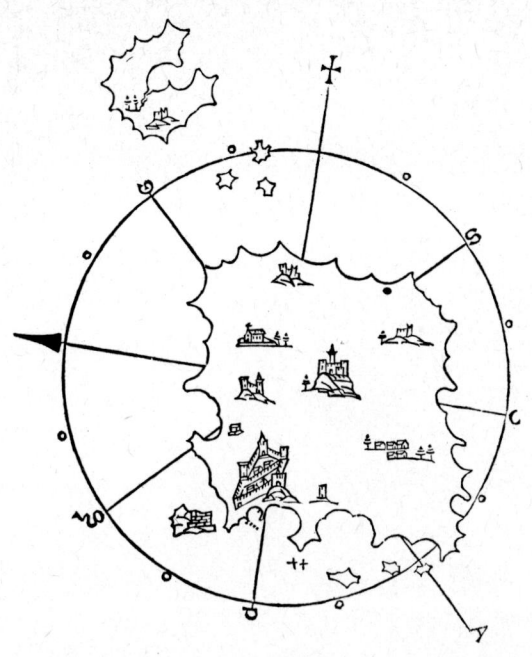

BARTOLOMMEO DALLI SONETTI
Isolario
First edition of the first book to contain printed nautical charts, with 49 woodcut maps,
[Venice, 1485?]
London £6,200 ($14,880). 10.VI.74
From the celebrated collection of books on early scientific subjects formed by Harrison D. Horblit Esq

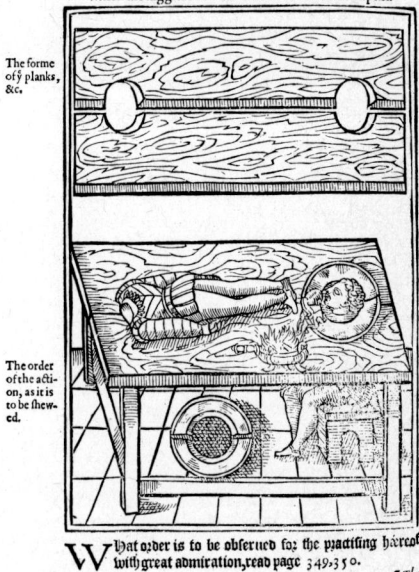

REGINALD SCOT
The Discouerie of Witchcraft, wherein the Lewde Dealing of Witches and Witchmongers is Notablie Detected
First edition, woodcut illustrations and diagrams, 1584
London £2,200 ($5,280). 18.III.74
From the collection of books on conjuring and magic formed by the late Roland Winder

Left
ST BRIDGET
[*Revelationes*]
The earliest extant Latin edition, illustrated with 14 full-page woodcuts and 13 large historiated initials,
[Lübeck], 1492
London Chancery Lane £11,000 ($26,400). 16.V.74
From the collection of Hr Sven Eriksson

Right
HARTMANN SCHEDEL
Liber Chronicarum
First edition of the 'Nuremberg Chronicles', illustrated with over 2,500 woodcuts, Nuremberg, 1493
London Chancery Lane £7,400 ($17,760). 16.V.74
From the collection of the late O. F. Grazebrook

216 PRINTED BOOKS

C.J. TEMMINCH AND FL. PREVOST
Les Pigeons
2 volumes, with 147 coloured plates, Paris, 1811-43
London £12,000 ($28,800). 26.11.74
From the collection of the Rt Hon the Earl of Cawdor

JOHN GOULD
A monograph of the Trochilidae or family of Humming-Birds
5 volumes with 360 hand-coloured plates, [1849]-61
New York $30,000 (£12,500). 9.IV.74

Bible, in German
2 vols. with numerous woodcut illustrations coloured by hand, Strasburg, 1485
London Chancery Lane £4,500 ($10,800). 16.V.74
From the collection of Mrs A. M. E. Lytle

Hortus Sanitatis. Ortus Sanitatis
Second Latin edition, with over 1000 woodcut illustrations coloured by hand, Strasburg, 1497
London £2,500 ($6,000). 8.X.73

GEOFFREY CHAUCER
Workes
First complete edition, with 15 woodcut illustrations, 1532
London £23,000 ($55,200). 26.XI.73
From the collection of the late Sir Thomas Phillipps Bt (1792-1872)

BARTHOLOMAEUS Anglicus
[*De Proprietatibus Rerum*]
First edition in English of this important medieval encyclopedia, printed by Wynkyn de Worde, [*circa* 1495]
London £5,500 ($13,200). 26.XI.73
From the collection of the late Sir Thomas Phillipps Bt (1792-1872)

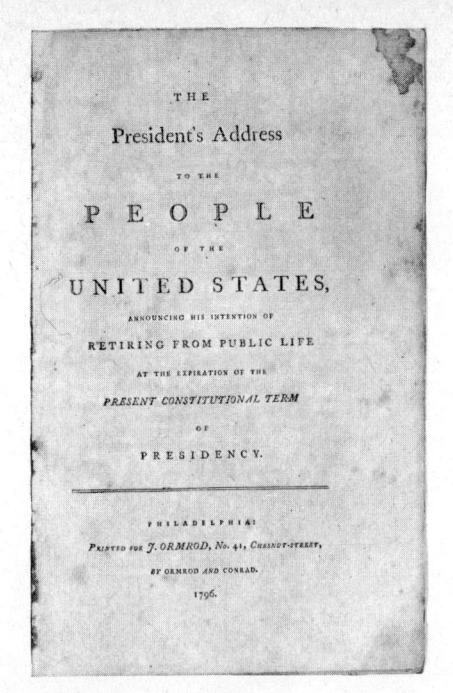

GEORGE WASHINGTON
The President's Address to the People of the United States announcing his intention of retiring from public life
First edition, Philadelphia, 1796
New York $12,000 (£5,000). 11.VI.74
From the collection of Harry J. Sonneborn

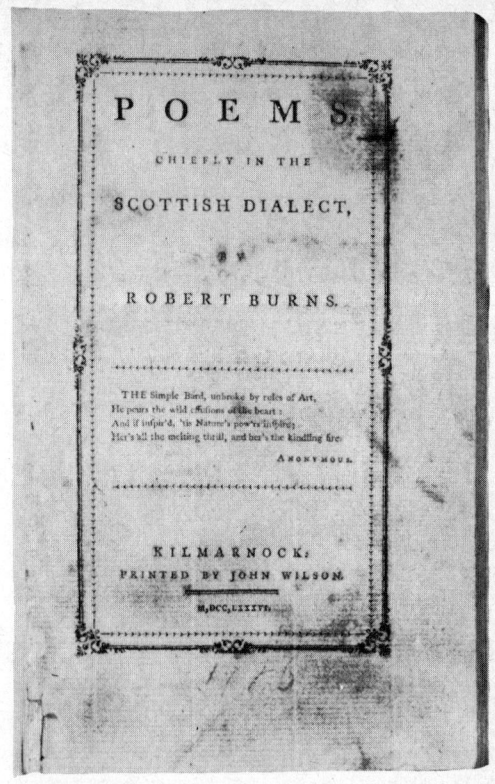

ROBERT BURNS
Poems, chiefly in the Scottish dialect
First edition, Kilmarnock, 1786, with the bookplate of James, Earl of Glencairn, one of Burn's earliest patrons
New York $10,000 (£4,166). 30.X.73

FREDRICH HINDRIK CHAPMAN
Architectura Navalis Mercatoria
First edition, with engraved pictorial title and 62 plates, Stockholm, 1768
London £3,600 ($8,640). 11.VI.74
From the celebrated collection of books on early scientific subjects formed by Harrison D. Horblit Esq

HOWARD E. JONES
Illustrations of the Nests and Eggs of Birds of Ohio
One of 35 copies with the plates coloured by hand, Circleville, [1879]-86
Los Angeles $19,000 (£7,916). 23.VI.74

J. H. CADDY
Scenery of the Windward and Leeward Islands
12 coloured aquatint views, 1837
New York $2,600 (£1,083). 18.XII.73

J. B. AUDEBERT and J. P. VIELLOT
Oiseaux Dorés ou à Reflets Metalliques
2 volumes with 190 plates printed in colours and gold, Paris, 1800-02
London £8,500 ($20,400). 26.II.74
From the collection of the Rt Hon the Earl of Cawdor

H. L. DUHAMEL DU MONCEAU
Traité des Arbres Fruitiers
6 volumes, with 422 plates printed in colour and finished by hand, Paris, [1807-35]
New York $27,500 (£11,458). 21.V.74
From the collection of Louise C. Morgan

JOHN J. AUDUBON and JOHN BACHMAN
The Viviparous Quadrupeds of North America
3 volumes, with 150 coloured lithographs, New York, 1845-48
New York $20,000 (£8,333). 30.X.73

JOHANNES BLAEU
Atlas Major, sive Cosmographia Blaviana
First complete edition, 11 volumes containing 597 engraved maps, plans, views, and plates of astronomical instruments, coloured throughout by hand, Amsterdam, 1662
London £25,000 ($60,000). 13.V.74

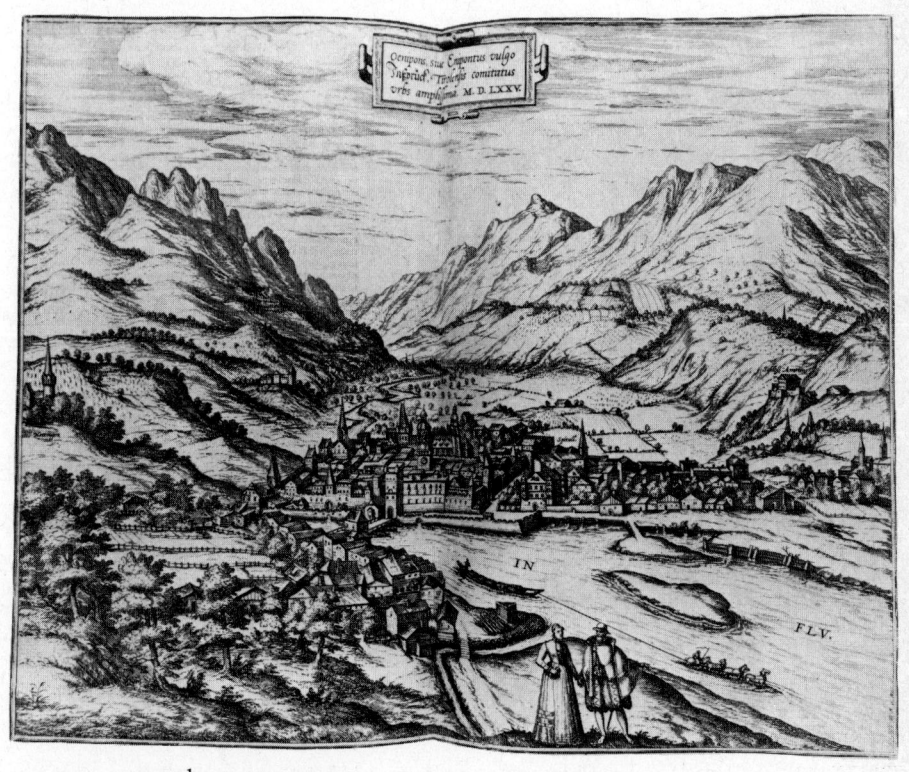

GEORG BRAUN and F. HOGENBERG
Civitates orbis terrarum
Vol. 1-4 (of 6) with 236 engraved views of towns, Cologne, 1581-82
London £9,500 ($22,800). 13.V.74

JOSIAH BOYDELL and JOHN WILLIAM EDY
Picturesque Scenery of Norway
2 volumes, with 80 coloured aquatint views, [1811]-20
New York $5,500 (£2,291). 9.IV.74

Specimens of Polyautography, consisting of Impressions taken from Original Drawings
The first artist's lithographs ever published, comprising 24 examples by Benjamin West, Thomas Stothard, Fuseli, and others, [1806-07]
London £3,500 ($8,400). 13.V.74

WILLIAM BLAKE *Illustrations of the Book of Job*
Proof impressions of the engraved title and 21 plates, 1825
London £2,800 ($6,720) 18.II.74

GUILLAUME APOLLINAIRE *L'Enchanteur Pourrissant*
24 woodcut illustrations, 7 initials and printer's device by André Derain, Paris, 1909
London £3,700 ($8,880). 2.IV.74

GORDON BOTTOMLEY
Frescoes from Buried Temples
Text printed from 35 intaglio plates, with 34 illustrations printed from blocks, woodcuts, or plates by James Guthrie, 1928
London £2,000 ($4,800). 19.II.74

226 PRINTED BOOKS

BLAISE CENDRARS
La Prose du Transsibérien et de la Petite Jehanne de France
The first four sheets for the 'livre simultané' illustrated with a large design by Sonia Delaunay,
normally joined to form an illustrated poem about 6 feet long, Paris, 1913
London £1,500 ($3,660). 2.IV.74

Works of Art

228 MEDIEVAL WORKS OF ART
230 GOTHIC WOOD CARVINGS
232 BAROQUE WOOD CARVINGS
234 RENAISSANCE WORKS OF ART
242 NINETEENTH-CENTURY WORKS OF ART
244 ICONS AND RUSSIAN WORKS OF ART
261 OBJECTS OF VERTU
266 MINIATURES

A Flemish enamelled gold and baroque pearl pendant in the form of a ship, Antwerp (?), second half of the sixteenth century, height 5½in
London £19,000 ($45,500). 10.VI.74
From the collection of the late Arturo Lopez-Willshaw

An English Nottingham alabaster of the Nativity, early fifteenth century, height 1ft 4¼in
London £5,500 ($13,200). 23.V.74

A Limoges enamel plaque showing St Valeria presenting her decapitated head to St Martial, thirteenth century, width 5in
London £2,000 ($4,800). 20.XII.73

A Rhenish Gothic ivory diptych carved with the Glorification of the Virgin and the Crucifixion, second half of the fourteenth century, each panel 2¾in by 4¾in
London £3,800 ($9,120). 20.XII.73
From the collection of Mrs E. Joseph

A North Italian Gothic Crucifix figure, *circa* 1250, height 8ft 2in
London £7,500 ($18,000). 1.VII.74
From the collection M Jean Charles de Geyndt

230 GOTHIC WOOD CARVINGS

A German lindenwood figure of St John, probably Franconian, late fifteenth century, height 3ft 4¾in
New York $8,500 (£3,541). 1.XI.73

An Eastern French polychrome wood group of St George and the dragon, sixteenth century, height 3ft 6½in
London £4,600 ($11,040). 23.V.74

A polychrome oak figure of St Michael, probably South French or Spanish, fifteenth century, height 5ft 10in
London £4,800 ($11,520). 1.VII.74
From the collection of the late Mr and Mrs Eric Bullivant

GOTHIC WOOD CARVINGS 231

A French group of St Martin and the beggar, sixteenth century, height 3ft 2in
London £3,400 ($8,160). 26.X.73

A South German limewood relief of the Presentation in the Temple, probably Swabian, *circa* 1490, height 3ft 6½in
London £6,500 ($15,600). 26.X.73

An Austrian polychrome wood figure of the Immaculata, from the workshops of Meinrad Guggenbichler (1649-1723), *circa* 1710, height 1ft 9in
London £4,800 ($11,520). 23.v.74
From the collection of Dr William M. Milliken

Right A South German giltwood *bozzetto* of the Baptism from the circle of Adam Ferdinand Dietz (1730-1777), *circa* 1770, height 8in
London £1,800 ($4,320). 23.V.74
From the collection of Dr William M. Milliken

Below A pair of Würzburg limewood figures of angels attributed to Johann Wolfgang van der Auwera (died 1756), *circa* 1740, height 1ft 1½in
London £5,000 ($12,000). 23.V.74
From the collection of Dr William M. Milliken

A German gold tazza, the bowl set with four rows of contemporary gold coins and the handles with classical coins, dated 1619, width 9½in
London £17,000 ($40,800). 10.VI.74
From the collection of the late Arturo Lopez-Willshaw

A Milanese rock crystal bowl by the Saracchi family of Milan, the head and neck of the dragon spout and the heads of the dolphin handles set with enamelled gold cartouches and a table-cut ruby in high gold collet, the remaining mounts of gold enamelled with panels of interlacing scrollwork separated by simulated rubies in translucent red enamel against white and green cartouches, second half of the sixteenth century, height 7⅛in, width 12½in
London £16,000 ($38,400). 10.VI.74
From the collection of the late Arturo Lopez-Willshaw

A Spanish enamelled gold and jewelled girdle of twenty-eight links, fashioned in the form of the Fire-steel of the Order of the Golden Fleece, last quarter of the sixteenth century, length 1ft 11½in
London £3,500 ($8,400). 10.VI.74

A Spanish enamelled gold pendant in the form of a standing female figure, last quarter of the sixteenth century, height 3⅛in
London £11,000 ($26,400). 10.VI.74
From the collection of the late Arturo Lopez-Willshaw

From left to right
A French (Fontainebleau School) carved boxwood hand mirror, third quarter of the sixteenth century height 8½in £4,000 ($9,600)

A French enamelled gold dagger and sheath with original case, probably Paris work for the Turkish market or perhaps made in the Constantinople palace workshops by a French craftsman, first half of the eighteenth century, length 1ft 3½in £4,400 ($10,560)

A German enamelled gold book cover, the binding enclosing a contemporary devotional work, dated 1667/8, 4¾in by 2½in £3,100 ($7,440)

The objects illustrated on this page were sold in London on 10th June 1974, from the collection of the late Arturo Lopez-Willshaw

238 RENAISSANCE BRONZES

Above left An Italo-Flemish bronze dog, first half of the seventeenth century, 6¼in London £2,900 ($6,960). 20.XII.73

Above right A Florentine bronze horse, late sixteenth century, 7in Florence L4,000,000 (£2,640; $6,318). 8.IV.74

Left A Venetian bronze figure of a triton, *circa* 1600, 5½in London £1,400 ($3,360). 20.XII.73

Below left One of a pair of bronze tritons, from the workshops of Niccoló Roccatagliata, late sixteenth/early seventeenth century, height 6½in New York $14,500 (£6,042). 2.III.74

Below right A Paduan bronze satyr from the workshops of Riccio, sixteenth century, height 8½in London £2,600 ($6,240). 1.VIII.74

RENAISSANCE BRONZES

A bronze figure of the Medici Aphrodite, Florentine, first half of the seventeenth century, height 1ft 10¼in
New York $7,500 (£3,125). 2.III.74

A bronze group of the Rape of the Sabine Women, from the workshops of Giovanni da Bologna, early seventeenth century, height 1ft 11¼in
New York $14,000 (£5,800). 1.XI.73
From the collection of the late Ruth Palitz

A North German amber cabinet, the doors opening to reveal a further door set with a mirror flanked by small drawers opening onto a chamber backed with mirror panels and *verre eglomisé* paintings of the Continents and of a fountain, second half of the seventeenth century, 3ft 6in by 2ft 11in
London £17,500 ($42,000). 20.XII.73
Formerly in the Kitson Collection and at Hever Castle

RENAISSANCE WORKS OF ART 241

A stained glass panel, Nuremberg, dated 1616, 1ft 3⅞in by 1ft 2⅞in New York $1,100 (£458). 1.XI.73

Below left A Nuremberg iron casket, second half of the sixteenth century, 11¾in by 7in London £8,500 ($20,040). 23.V.74

Below right A Norwegian gilt-copper-mounted drinking horn, fifteenth century, length 10in New York $3,000 (£1,250). 1.XI.73

A stained glass panel with an achievement of the arms of Jane Seymour, Queen of England, height 1ft 7in London £580 ($1,392). 1.VII.74

A German boxwood medallion in the manner of Christoph Weiditz, second quarter of the sixteenth century, diameter 2⅜in London £3,100 ($7,440). 20.XII.73 From the collection of W. Greenshields Esq

A pearwood and boxwood ship model, the *H.M.S. Marlborough*, English, early eighteenth century, height 2ft 11in, length 3ft
New York $20,000 (£8,333).
30.V.74
From the collection of Louise C. Morgan

A gold and silver damascened steel dish, the underside signed with the initials P intersecting Z for Placido Zuloaga of Madrid, third quarter of the nineteenth century, width 1ft 4in
London £1,150 ($2,760). 30.V.74

A bronze figure of a basset hound by Barye, stamped and numbered 12, French, mid-nineteenth century, height 6¼in
London £750 ($1,800). 28.XI.73

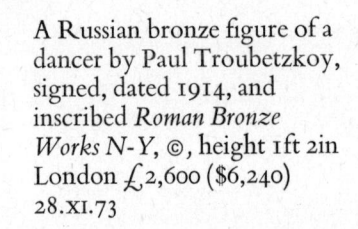

A Russian bronze figure of a dancer by Paul Troubetzkoy, signed, dated 1914, and inscribed *Roman Bronze Works N-Y*, ©, height 1ft 2in
London £2,600 ($6,240) 28.XI.73

A French bronze figure of the Turkish horse by Barye, signed, mid-nineteenth century, height 11¼in
London £3,100 ($7,440). 28.XI.73

A bronze group of a gazelle with a Cupid by Carl Paul Jennewein, signed, height 2ft 3in
New York $3,100 (£1,866). 27.X.73
Formerly in the collection of the Cranbrook Academy of Art, Bloomfield Hills, Michigan

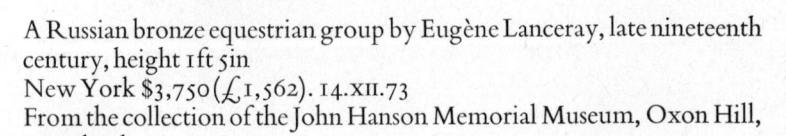

A Russian bronze equestrian group by Eugène Lanceray, late nineteenth century, height 1ft 5in
New York $3,750 (£1,562). 14.XII.73
From the collection of the John Hanson Memorial Museum, Oxon Hill, Maryland

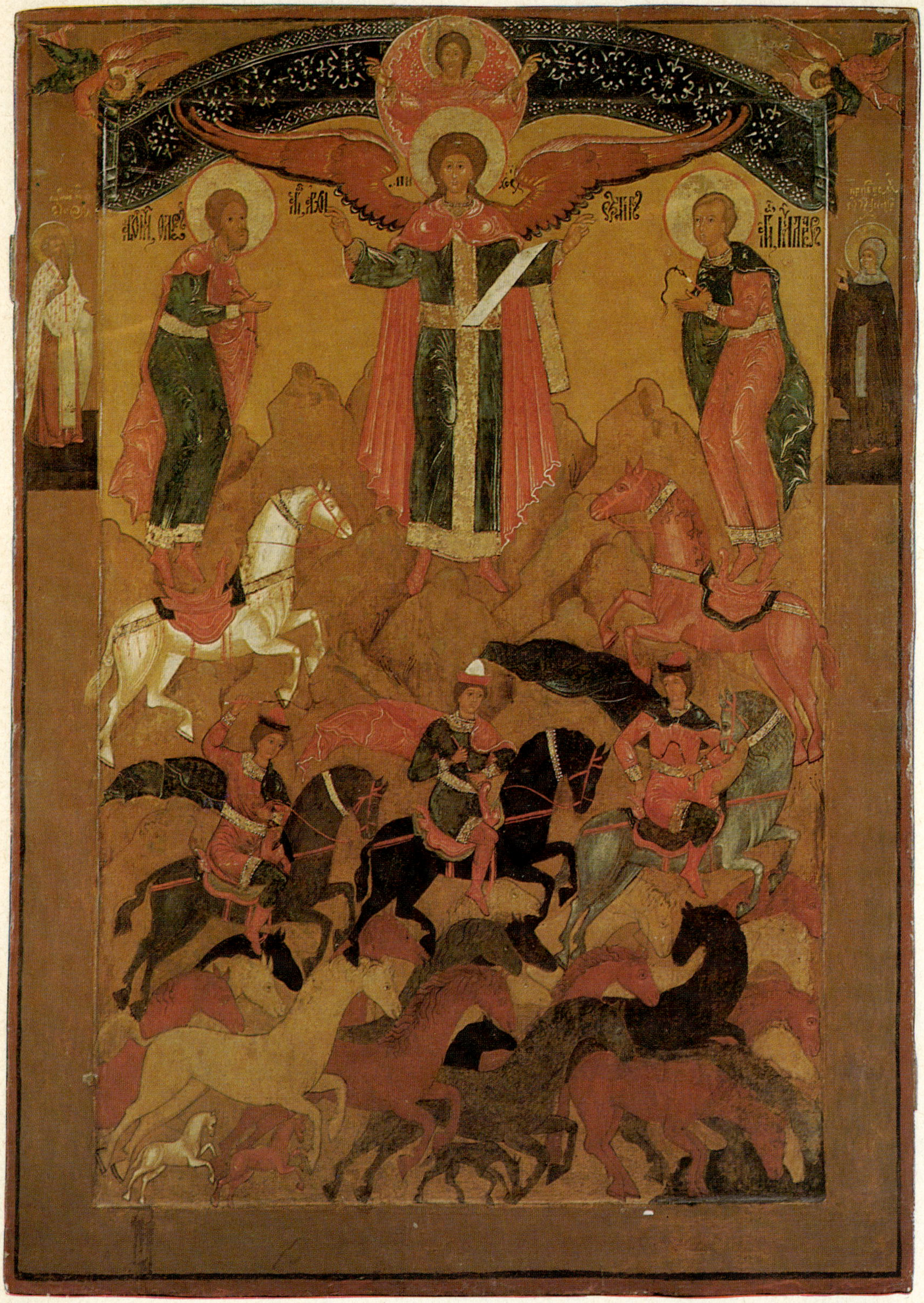

Above A Russian icon of the raising of Lazarus. North Russian, late sixteenth century, 28½in by 23in
London £6,000 ($14,400). 3.XII.73

Opposite page A Russian icon of St Flor and St Lavr. Central Russian, sixteenth century with extensive nineteenth-century restorations, 41in by 29in
London £7,200 ($17,280). 1.IV.74

246 ICONS

Left A Russian iconastas icon of the apostle Peter. Central Russian, *circa* 1500, 41½in by 20¼in
London £4,800 ($11,520). 1.IV.74
Probably from the same iconastas as the St Basil of Cesarae icon sold in these rooms on 30th October 1972 for £3,000 ($7,500)

Right A Russian icon of the Deisis. Central Russian, sixteenth century, 50½in by 35½in
London £10,000 ($24,000). 3.XII.73
Previously sold by Sotheby Parke Bernet New York on 30th November 1972 for $16,500 (£6,600)

A Russian icon of the Crucifixion. North Russian, sixteenth century, 33½in by 28½in
London £5,600 ($13,440). 1.IV.74

A Russian icon of Pokrov. Moscow School, *circa* 1700, 44in by 35in
London £3,600 ($8,640). 1.IV.74

A late nineteenth-century Russian icon of the Vernicle with later silver-gilt riza, workmaster's initials NG Moscow *circa* 1900, 12¼in by 10½in
New York $7,250 (£3,021). 18.V.74

A Russian icon of St Sophia, the Holy Wisdom. Novgorod School, late fifteenth/early sixteenth century, 14½in by 11in New York $14,000 (£5,833). 18.V.74

A Russian icon triptych with silver-gilt and shaded enamel decoration. The mounts by Vasili Agafanov, Moscow School, *circa* 1900, 12⅞in by 16⅛in New York $15,000 (£6,250). 13.XII.73

Right A pair of Russian wings of a triptych. Late seventeenth/early eighteenth century, 19in by 11¼in
New York $4,800 (£2,000). 18.V.74

248 'TYPICALLY RUSSIAN' ENAMEL

Left Fig 20 A gilded-silver and shaded enamel *kovsh* by Maria Semenova, Moscow, *circa* 1900 height 3½in
New York $4,500 (£1,875). 17.v.74

Centre left Fig 1 A gilded-silver, enamel and jewelled *charka* by Pavel Ovchinnikov, Moscow, 1877, height 1½in
New York $1,100 (£458). 17.v.74

Centre Fig 13 A gilded-silver and enamel sherbet dish by Anton Kuzmitchev, Moscow, *circa* 1900, height 6½in
New York $3,500 (£1,458). 17.v.74

Right Fig 2 A pair of gilded-silver and enamel candlesticks by Pavel Ovchinnikov, Moscow, 1884, height 4in
New York $3,500 (£1,458). 17.v.74

Fig 5 A gilded-silver and enamel punch bowl set by Ivan Chlebnikov, Moscow, 1884, diameter of tray 13⅛in
New York $21,000 (£8,746). 17.v.74

Fig 10 A gilded-silver and enamel tea set by Ivan Saltykov, Moscow, 1894, height of teapot 4½in
New York $12,000 (£5,000). 17.v.74

'Typically Russian' Enamel

By Robert C. Woolley

When Peter the Great opened his famous 'Window to the West' by creating on what had been only a swamp, the city of St Petersburg, the craftsmen of Russia were forced to adopt the more advanced Western precepts and influences of artistic endeavour. However, a major section of the Russian crafts community, mainly based in Moscow, resisted this forced Westernisation and continued to work in the Old Russian or Pan-Slavic styles.

The Pan-Slavic movement, as it is called, was given its greatest encouragement during the reign of Czar Nicholas I (1825-1855). Nicholas, a militarist czar basically interested in the glorification of 'all the Russias', felt that Russian artistic expression, particularly in the decorative arts, should reflect the heritage and the stylistic motifs of ancient Russia rather than blindly assimilate whatever style was fashionable in the West as dictated by its primary exponent in Russia, the international society of St Petersburg. Drawing upon strong near-Eastern and Byzantine influences, objects created by the craftsmen of the Pan-Slavic movement do not readily appeal to Western taste and are always dubbed 'typically Russian'. The colours, the decorative designs, and the shapes of many of the objects are exotic and brilliant, related more closely in feeling to the wildly colourful St Basil's Cathedral on Red Square in Moscow than to the Winter Palace in Leningrad.

Perhaps the greatest and most popular expression of the Pan-Slavic movement is the silver and enamel work produced in Moscow from the 1870s to the Revolution in 1917.

Pavel Ovchinnikov, one of the best and most original of the artisans working in this tradition, founded his firm in Moscow in 1851. His production was of such good quality that his firm received an 'Imperial Warrant' in 1872 and Ovchinnikov became one of the Court silversmiths.

Works by Ovchinnikov cover the whole range of enamelling: *cloisonné* or filigree enamel (where the enamel colours are painted into and surrounded by *cloisons,* or filigree wire 'cages', applied on a flat gilded-silver surface), *champlevé* enamel (where the design is cut out of the surface of the piece being decorated and the enamel colours applied in the interstices and then polished flush with the overall surface after firing), *pliqué-à-jour* enamel (where the filigree cagework of the object to be decorated is lined with a thin sheet of silver foil to which translucent enamel colours are applied; after firing the silver sheet is removed with acid leaving a fragile and beautiful 'stained glass window' effect). Ovchinnikov is credited with having revived the *cloisonné* enamel technique which had its Russian origins during the late sixteenth and seventeenth centuries. The *champlevé* enamel technique developed later, but the *pliqué-à-jour* enamel process may have been original to the firm of Ovchinnikov, although all the different enamelling styles were also used by Ovchinnikov's rivals.

Most designs for the enamel objects made during this period were based on Old Russian forms. The *charka,* or single handled drinking cup made by Ovchinnikov in 1877 (Fig 1), finds its antecedents in the drinking vessels of Medieval Russia. This example is decorated with multicoloured *cloisonné* enamel on a stippled silver-gilt ground and set with semi-precious stones. The pair of chamber candlesticks, made by Ovchinnikov in 1884 (Fig 2), have unusual feet fashioned in the form of chickens, the stylistic basis of which comes from Russian mythology. The decorative details of the candlesticks can be found in the exuberant architectural forms of seventeenth-century Moscow. The liqueur set made by Ovchinnikov after 1896 (Fig 3) shows a strong Byzantine influence in the exotic enamel colours of the stylised leaves and flowers.

The *kovsh,* or single-handled ladle, made by Ovchinnikov after 1896 (Fig 4), is probably the most typically Russian of the objects made during this period. Ladles of similar zoomorphic form date from pre-Christian times in Russia and the use of *kovshi* for ceremonial purposes originated during the seventeenth century. This *kovsh* was obviously made to commemorate a wedding ceremony. The front is decorated with the Russian Imperial Eagle and the sides with two nuptial scenes.

The quality of Ovchinnikov's art is generally high. Although most of his earlier work (the production in the 1870s and 1880s) is executed in solid, opaque and translucent enamel colours, the later pieces (those made from *circa* 1890 to the Revolution) are more desirable to today's collectors. These later pieces such as the wedding *kovsh* (Fig 4), are enamelled all over and the enamel colours are actually shaded within the *cloisons* rather than being solid colours. Obviously, enamelling of this type is more elaborate and harder to execute than the more ordinary enamel work of the objects illustrated in figures 1, 2, and 3.

The objects created by Ovchinnikov and his contemporaries were intended for Russian consumption as they suited the wealthy bourgeois Moscow taste of the period with its interest in traditional Russian motifs blended with sumptuousness. Pavel Ovchinnikov was the first silversmith in Russia to set up a school to train craftsmen in the technical and aesthetic sides of the manufacture of enamel work. At its peak, the school had up to 130 students for five to six years' training periods.

One of the most successful contemporaries of Ovchinnikov was Ivan Chlebnikov who worked in Moscow from 1869 to 1918. The punch bowl set, made by Chlebnikov in 1884 (Fig 5), is very similar in execution to the work of Ovchinnikov and is in purely Russian taste. The Easter egg made by Chlebnikov, *circa* 1900 (Fig 6), is executed in shaded all over enamel of good quality and has more subtle colouring than the punch bowl set. Although certainly Russian in flavour, the egg has an aesthetic quality which appeals to the non-Russian eye. The cigarette case, made by Chlebnikov in 1889 (Fig 7), is executed in fine silver filigree work and *pliqué-à-jour* enamel, which give the case a brilliant multi-coloured transparency when light passes through it.

One of the few firms which worked primarily in Pan-Slavic taste, yet was situated in St Petersburg rather than Moscow, was the firm of G. P. Gratchev. Gratchev's establishment was founded in 1866 and continued manufacturing until 1917.

Probably on account of the cosmopolitan atmosphere of St Petersburg, the work of Gratchev is not quite as typically Russian as the work of his Moscow contemporaries. The cigarette case by Gratchev, *circa* 1900 (Fig 8), is Pan-Slavic in design, but the enamel colours are muted and subtle, not quite as exotic as they would have been in Moscow. The same is true of

'TYPICALLY RUSSIAN' ENAMEL 251

Fig 6 A gilded-silver and enamel Easter egg by Ivan Chlebnikov, Moscow, *circa* 1900, height 3in
New York $4,200 (£1,680). 13.XII.73

Fig 9 A gilded-silver and enamel bottle by G. P. Gratchev, St Petersburg, *circa* 1900, height 6¾in
New York $2,100 (£840). 30.XI.72

Fig 11 A gilded-silver and enamel egg by Ivan Saltykov, Moscow, *circa* 1900, height 3½in
New York $4,000 (£1,600). 13.XII.73

Fig 7 A gilded-silver and *pliqué-à-jour* enamel cigarette case by Ivan Chlebnikov, Moscow, 1889, length 4⅛in
New York $2,000 (£800). 30.XI.72

Fig 8 A gilded-silver and enamel cigarette case by G. P. Gratchev, St Petersburg, *circa* 1900, length 3⅝in
New York $450 (£180). 1.V.73

the covered flask by Gratchev, *circa* 1900 (Fig 9), whose colours are basically tones of blue with a few translucent red enamel highlights. Perhaps this flask is the best example of Gratchev's compromise between working in St Petersburg and creating objects for the Muscovite taste.

Ivan Saltykov was one of the most prolific silversmiths and enamellers of the period. He worked only from 1884 to 1897, but his output must have been extensive as many examples of his work are extant today. Generally his production was intended for a less affluent clientele and is, subsequently of only average quality. The tea set made by Saltykov in 1894 (Fig 10), is executed in standard, shaded *cloisonné* enamel on a stippled, gilded-silver ground. Fortunately the tea set is still complete and in its original fitted oak box. The Easter egg by Saltykov, *circa* 1900 (Fig 11), is of high quality. It is enamelled all over with a cream coloured ground; and the flowers, foliage and birds are painted with subtle gradations of colour. The egg opens in the middle and contains two enamelled egg stands which screw into the top and the bottom to form two egg cups.

Although most objects created in Pan-Slavic taste were sold in Russia, the firm of Anton Kuzmitchev (working in Moscow from 1886 to 1897) retailed a number of objects through the New York firm of Tiffany & Co. Figure 12 is one such object. This gilded-silver bowl is decorated both in *cloisonné* and *pliqué-à-jour* enamel and is marked on the base, 'Made for Tiffany & Co.'. The goblet made by Kuzmitchev, *circa* 1900 (Fig 13) is executed in *champlevé* and *pliqué-à-jour* enamel and bears the coats-of-arms of Moscow, Kiev and St Petersburg. This type of sherbet goblet was not exclusively made by Kuzmitchev, as similar examples are known by both Ovchinnikov and Feodor Rückert.

Fig 3 A gilded-silver and enamel liqueur set by Pavel Ovchinnikov, Moscow, *circa* 1900, height of flask 9¾in
New York $4,900 (£1,960).
30.XI.72

'TYPICALLY RUSSIAN' ENAMEL 253

Left Fig 12 A gilded-silver and enamel tazza by Anton Kuzmitchev, Moscow, *circa* 1900, made for Tiffany & Co., height 3¾in
New York $3,000 (£1,400).
13.XII.73

Right Fig 16 A gilded-silver and enamel *kovsh* by Fabergé, Moscow, *circa* 1900, length 3¼in
New York $2,200 (£880).
27.IV.72

Fig 14 A gilded-silver and enamel casket by Feodor Rückert, Moscow, *circa* 1900, length 7in
New York $4,500 (£1,800).
28.X.70

Fig 4 A gilded-silver and enamel *kovsh* by Pavel Ovchinnikov, Moscow, *circa* 1900, length 13in
New York $10,000 (£4,000).
27.IV.72

'TYPICALLY RUSSIAN' ENAMEL

Feodor I. Rückert, a Moscow German, was one of the very best craftsmen of the time. Although he had his own factory, much of his production was retailed by Fabergé both in Moscow and in St Petersburg. Many pieces signed by Rückert, in fact, also bear the marks of the firm Fabergé so that Rückert's work is now generally considered by connoisseurs of Russian enamel to be comparable to that of the esteemed Fabergé.

The House of Fabergé was, of course, the forerunner in the development of Russian objects which appealed to more international, cosmopolitan Western taste. However, this did not stop Fabergé from taking commercial advantage of the traditional taste of the Russian bourgeoisie by selling objects made in the Pan-Slavic manner.

Rückert drew great inspiration from Russian enamel work of the sixteenth and seventeenth centuries, using typically Russian colour combinations. He particularly used silver-gilt husk marks and beads raised on the ends of silver-gilt pins, often in combination with semi-precious cabochons. The casket made by Rückert, *circa* 1900 (Fig 15), also bears an enamel view of the Kremlin, but the enamel decoration of the body more closely resembles the style of Rückert's contemporaries than his own unique style. The small Fabergé *kovsh* (Fig 16) with the interesting animal-formed handle was made in Moscow, undoubtedly by Rückert although the *kovsh* bears only Fabergé hallmarks. The style of enamelling is very similar to that of the Rückert casket illustrated on figure 14. The mammoth *kovsh* with its ladle, by Rückert (Fig 17) – which appeared in last season's Art at Auction – is a marvellous expression of Rückert's talent. The bearded man on the front comes from Russian mythology; the colours and shape of the *kovsh* are extraordinarily flamboyant and exotic.

Left Fig 22 A gilded-silver and enamel bowl by Vassili Agafanov, Moscow, *circa* 1900, length 6in
New York $2,600 (£1,040). 1.v.73

Below Fig 21 A gilded-silver and enamel tea set by Maria Semenova, Moscow, *circa* 1900, height of teapot 4 in
New York $9,500 (£3,800). 13.XII.73

'TYPICALLY RUSSIAN' ENAMEL 255

Fig 15 A gilded-silver and enamel casket by Feodor Rückert, Moscow, *circa* 1900, length 4in
New York $4,000 (£1,600). 1.v.73

Fig 19 A gilded-silver and enamel casket by Gustav Klingert, Moscow, 1896, length 5¼in
New York $2,300 (£920). 1.v.73

Above Fig 23 A gilded-silver and enamel presentation goblet by Vassili Agafanov, Moscow, *circa* 1900, height 16in
New York $11,000 (£4,400). 27.IV.72

Right Fig 18 A gilded-silver and *pliqué-à-jour* enamel *kovsh* by Gustav Klingert, Moscow, *circa* 1880, length 7½in
New York $2,300 (£920). 27.IV.72

The *pliqué-à-jour* enamel *kovsh* (Fig 18), was made by Gustav Klingert, a Moscow silversmith working from 1865 to 1916. His work is more restrained than Rückert's and followed the more ordinary, accepted patterns of taste of the period. The casket made by Klingert in 1896 (Fig 19), is of good quality yet decorated in red, white and blue only and executed in solid colour tones.

The women of Russia were ably represented during this period by Maria Semenova, the daughter of Vassili Semenov, one of the best makers of Russian niello work. She headed her own factory from 1896 to 1904 and employed nearly one hundred craftsmen. Her work is greatly admired today, probably because her designs have a certain feminine subtlety of colour which is generally missing in the more garish work of her contemporaries. The *kovsh* (Fig 20) and the tea set (Fig 21) by Maria Semenova are executed in pastel colours of charming refinement.

The *Art Nouveau* movement of Western Europe often influenced Russian craftsmen and was assimilated and translated into purely Russian expression. The two-handled bowl (Fig 22) by Vassili Agafanov, working *circa* 1900, is a Russian version of the *Art Nouveau* style. Agafanov's hallmark of often mistaken for that of the Fabergé workmaster Victor Aarne. However, as Aarne worked only in St Petersburg, most pieces of Russian enamel marked in Cyrillic with the initials B.A. are probably by Agafanov. The presentation goblet (Fig 23) by Agafanov was given by the Dowager Empress Maria Feodorovna to an Englishman as a 'souvenir' of her visit to England in 1907. Such a gift for such a seemingly minor event gives one an idea of the vast production of Russian enamel pieces which must have been necessary to satisfy the demands of Russian society at the time. The 'purely Russian' character of the enamels and their technical virtuosity appealed to many people in pre-Revolutionary Russia, an appeal which continues to the present day.

Fig 17 A gilded-silver and shaded enamel *kovsh* and ladle by Feodor Rückert, Moscow, *circa* 1900, height of bowl 11¼in
New York $21,000 (£8,400). 30.XI.72

RUSSIAN WORKS OF ART 257

A Russian *cloisonné* enamel Easter egg by
Feodor Rückert, 3½in
London £5,200 ($12,480). 13.V.74

A Russian imperial presentation *cloisonné* enamel tea service, teapot 6¾in
London £8,000 ($19,200). 18.II.74
Presented by His Imperial Majesty Czar Nicholas II to Munshi Mohd. Abdul Karim, C.I.E., Indian Secretary to
H.M. Queen Victoria, Empress of India, at Balmoral Castle, October 3rd, 1896

258 RUSSIAN WORKS OF ART

From left to right
Above A Fabergé carved hardstone figure of an officer of the Imperial Horse Guards. Workmaster Henrik Wigström, St Petersburg, *circa* 1900, height 7½in $25,000 (£10,410)
A Fabergé gold-mounted rock crystal, red enamel and bloodstone imperial seal, St Petersburg, *circa* 1900, height 3in $12,000 (£5,000)
A Russian gold, enamel and bloodstone military seal by Samuel Arnd, St Petersburg, late nineteenth century, height 3⅞in $8,000 (£3,333)
A Fabergé carved hardstone figure of a captain of the 4th Harkovsky Lancers regiment. Workmaster Henrik Wigström, St Petersburg, 1914-1915, height 5¼in $23,000 (£9,583)
Below A Fabergé jewelled, gold and enamel-mounted nephrite card case. Workmaster Henrik Wigström, St Petersburg, *circa* 1900, 3½in by 2⅜in $7,500 (£3,125)
A Fabergé gold and translucent blue enamel cup. Workmaster Alfred Thielemann, St Petersburg, *circa* 1900, height 2¼in $8,500 (£3,541)
The objects illustrated on this page were sold in New York on 17th May 1974

RUSSIAN WORKS OF ART

From left to right
Above A two-colour gold and white translucent enamel lighter, Moscow, *circa* 1900, height 3⅛in $5,000 (£2,083)
A gold-mounted, gilded-silver, white enamel and jewelled double frame. Workmaster Karl Gustav Armfelt, St Petersburg, *circa* 1900, height 3¼in $16,000 (£6,666)
A gold, enamel and diamond cane handle. Workmaster Michael Perchin, St Petersburg, 1900, height 3⅜in $11,500 (£4,792)
Centre A two-colour gold and diamond snuff box. Workmaster Michael Perchin, St Petersburg, *circa* 1900, height 13/16in $10,500 (£4,375)
A translucent pink enamel imperial presentation egg, St Petersburg, *circa* 1890, height 1½in $12,000 (£5,000)
Below A gold, translucent enamel and jewelled cigarette case. Workmaster's initials in Cyrillic C.B., St Petersburg, *circa* 1900, length 3⅜in $10,000 (£4,167)
A gold-mounted and translucent white enamel stamp moistener. Workmaster Henrik Wigström, St Petersburg, *circa* 1900, height 1¾in $4,000 (£1,666)
A jewelled two-colour gold and translucent enamel *carnet-de-bal*. Workmaster Henrik Wigström, St Petersburg, *circa* 1900, length 2⅞in $5,000 (£2,083)
The Fabergé objects illustrated on this page were sold in New York on 17th May 1974

1. Russian silver and *cloisonné* enamel casket, maker's initials F.M., 4¼in £2,100 ($5,040) 18.II.74. **2.** One of a pair of Russian malachite urns, Alexander I period, 12in £5,200 ($12,480) 13.V.74. **3.** A Russian silver and enamel *kovsh* by Ovtchinnikov, 9in £5,800 ($13,920) 13.V.74. **4.** A Russian parcel-gilt *kovsh*, 1751, 11in £3,200 ($7,680) 25.X.73. **5.** A Fabergé gold and diamond commemorative snuff box, Moscow, c. 1910, 1½in $9,000 (£3,750) 17.V.74. **6.** A Fabergé silver-gilt, shaded enamel and *pliqué-à-jour* spoon, workmaster Feodor Rückert, St Petersburg, c. 1895, 8½in $1,900 (£791) 19.VI.74. **7.** A Fabergé silver-gilt and enamel glue pot, workmaster Anders Johan Nevalainen, 2⅞in £800 ($1,920) 13.V.74. **8.** A Fabergé gold and enamel heart-shaped *bonbonnière*, workmaster Henrik Wigström, 1¾in £2,700 ($6,600) 13.V.74. **9.** A Fabergé silver and enamel photograph frame, workmaster Anders Johan Nevalainen, 3¼in £1,200 ($2,888) 13.V.74. **10.** A Fabergé gold and enamel miniature frame, workmaster Michael Perchin, 4¼in £1,900 ($4,560) 13.V.74. **11.** A Fabergé agate figure of a gorilla, St Petersburg, c. 1900, 4in $12,000 (£5,000) 17.V.74. **12.** A Fabergé photograph frame, 6in £4,200 ($10,080) 18.II.74. **13.** A Fabergé gold-mounted, nephrite, diamond and white enamel frame, with portrait miniature of Czar Nicholas II, workmaster Henrik Wigström, St Petersburg, c. 1910, 4⅞in $20,000 (£8,333). 17.V.74. **14.** A Fabergé parcel-gilt silver and enamel miniature helmet, workmaster Michael Perchin, St Petersburg, c. 1890, 5⅜in $3,800 (£1,583). 17.V.74

OBJECTS OF VERTU 261

A historic Frederick the Great presentation snuff box by Jordan and Daniel Baudesson, Berlin, *circa* 1760, 3¾in
London £86,000 ($206,400). 10.VI.74
From the collection of Her Majesty Queen Frederika, the Queen Mother of the Hellenes
This box was presented by Frederick the Great, King of Prussia, to one of the Dukes of Brunswick, most probably Ferdinand-Albrecht, Duke of Brunswick-Wolfenbüttel, who was a prominent General on the Prussian side in the Seven Years War, during which he commanded the English and Hanoverian troops and was victorious over the French at the Battle of Minden

A Louis XV gold and enamel *tabatière* by Jean Moynat, Paris, 1749, Fermier Général Antoine Leschandel, 3in
London £26,000 ($62,400). 10.VI.74
Formerly in the collection of Rene Fribourg
Jean Moynat was received Master in Paris on 5th October 1745 and worked until his death in 1761

A gold and jewelled royal presentation snuff box, the lid centred with an enamel miniature of King Gustav III of Sweden, *circa* 1775, 3in
London £5,500 ($13,200). 10.VI.74
Formerly in the collection of the Earl of Cromartie
This box was presented to John Mackenzie, Lord MacLeod (1727-1789), by King Gustav III of Sweden

A Louis XV three-colour gold oval snuff box by Jean Ducrollay, Paris, 1762, Fermier Général Jean-Jacques Prévost, 2⅝in
London £5,200 ($12,480). 10.VI.74
Jean Ducrollay was received Master in Paris on 26th July 1734

An early Louis XV gold snuff box by Noël Hardivillier, the lid chased in the manner of Juste-Aurèle Meissonnier, Paris, 1733, Fermier Général Hubert Louvet, 2⅝in
London £6,000 ($14,400). 10.VI.74
Formerly in the collection of Count Thure Bonde
Noël Hardivillier was received Master in Paris on 4th June 1729

A Louis XV gold and enamel snuff box by Jean-Joseph Barrière, the cover centred by a *grisaille* miniature, the lip engraved *Constant à Paris*, Paris, 1765, 2½in
New York $26,000 (£10,833). 31.X.73

A four-colour gold and enamel snuff box, the cover centred by an oval *grisaille* enamel plaque bearing the Paris date letter for 1771, maker's mark illegible, the lip stamped with St Petersburg assay marks, 3in
New York $14,000 (£5,833). 31.X.73

A Louis XV two-colour gold and enamel snuff box by Charles le Bastier, Paris, 1764, Fermier Général Jean-Jacques Prévost, 3¼in
London £3,100 ($7,440). 10.XII.73
Charles le Bastier was received Master in Paris on 20th December 1754

An Empire gold and enamel *tabatière* by Gabriel Raoul Morel, decorated *en plein* with scenes after Teniers, Paris, early nineteenth century, 3¼in
London £4,200 ($10,080). 10.XII.73

A gold and mother-of-pearl snuff box, probably Dresden, unmarked, *circa* 1750, 3in
New York $14,000 (£5,800). 31.X.73

A Swiss gold and enamel snuff box in the form of a lion, *circa* 1820, 3⅛in
New York $6,600 (£2,750). 31.X.73
From the Connolly Collection, Boston
Formerly in the collection of King Farouk

A George III gold and enamel *nécessaire* attributed to James Cox, in the form of an upright cabinet on stand, the front opening to reveal five graduated drawers, the back with a glass painting of a gallant and a lady, the interiors of the doors inset with mirrors; the hinged pagoda top revealing a compartment for writing implements and the exterior decorated with small shaped vignettes of flowers in blue *basse-taille* enamel, *circa* 1760, 8⅝in London £6,000 ($14,400). 10.XII.73

MINIATURES

Left
A miniature of a nobleman by Nicholas Dixon, 2¾in
London £1,350 ($3,240).
26.XI.73

Right
A miniature of a nobleman by D. Gibson, 2¾in
London £1,350 ($3,240).
26.XI.73

A miniature of a lady by Samuel Cooper, signed with monogram and dated 1659, 3in
London £8,800 ($21,120).
29.IV.74

Left
A miniature of a young lady by D. Gibson, 2⅝in
London £3,100 ($7,440).
24.VI.74
From the collection of the Misses Fannie and Ida Edelson

Right
A miniature of a lady by Mathew Snelling, 2½in
London £1,550 ($3,720).
26.XI.73

Left
A miniature of Miss Hay by John Smart, signed and dated 1773 in full, 2in
London £3,000 ($5,760). 25.III.74
From the collection of Mrs W. A. Hay

Right
A miniature of Miss Elizabeth Hay by John Smart, signed and dated 1778, 1⅝in
London £3,400 ($8,160). 25.III.74
From the collection of Mrs W. A. Hay

Below left
A miniature of Peter Johnston Esq by John Smart, signed and dated 1803, 3½in
London £3,300 ($7,920). 26.XI.73
From the collection of Lady Nicholas Gordon Lennox

Below right
A miniature of Samuel Pepys Cockerell by Richard Cosway, signed and dated 1793 in full on the reverse, 3in
London £1,300 ($3,120). 26.XI.73
From the collection of Mrs Hilda Pemberton

Left
A miniature of Mrs George Aubry by John Smart, signed and dated 1787 I, 2⅝in
London £3,800 ($9,120). 24.VI.74
From the collection of the Rt Hon Lady Kilmarnock

268 MINIATURES

A miniature of Captain John Prince by Simon Jacques Rochard, signed and dated March 1817, 3in
London £1,050 ($2,520). 26.XI.73
From the collection of Mrs H. M. Burton

A miniature of Sir Richard Fanshawe, Bart by Samuel Cooper, 2in
London £1,650 ($3,960). 17.XII.73
From the collection of Major R. G. Fanshawe

A miniature of Mrs John Prince née Ainslie by Jean Baptiste Augustin, signed and dated *Paris* 1815, 3in
London £1,550 ($3,720). 26.XI.73
From the collection of Mrs H. M. Burton

Right A miniature of Robert Devereux, KG, 2nd Earl of Essex by Isaac Oliver, 2in
London £2,500 ($6,000). 26.XI.73
Now in the National Portrait Gallery, London

Arms and Armour

An English tilting helm formerly hung over the tomb of the 8th Lord De La Warr in Broadwater Parish Church. The skull with six raised ribs at the back, the front protected by a reinforcing plate extending down the comb and reaching to the visor pivot, over this, the visor of a single plate with narrow slit sight, above which is an applied reinforcing plate with scalloped edge; on the right side of the visor a triangular opening protected by a heavy outward turned flange. The skull is carried down at the back and attached to it is an extension plate with hole for bolting to the backplate, the visor is secured to the chin defence with a hinged latch locked in place by a spring-loaded bolt, around the neck rivet holes originally securing the lining. Late fifteenth century.
London £22,000 ($52,800). 12.II.74
This helm has been in Broadwater Parish Church for several centuries. It was stolen about 1850, but was recovered shortly afterwards.
Now in Her Majesty's Tower of London

A pair of German flintlock holster pistols, signed on the locks *Schmeiser à Eisenach*, the barrels in two stages with moulded girdle between, the fore parts etched with false damascus twist, the breeches chiselled with a trophy, the whole against a gold fish-roe ground, the locks with flat face chiselled against a gold ground, signed and dated 1728, the steels chiselled in high relief with a grotesque mask, the stocks of root walnut carved with scrollwork, the steel furniture chiselled against a gold ground, the pommel caps and the side plates with four medallion heads, silver escutcheons with a monogram of the letter F in gold surmounted by a princely crown. Length 20in
London £25,000 ($60,000). 19.III.74
From the collection of the late William Goodwin Renwick. Presumably commissioned by Johann Wilhelm, Duke of Sachsen-Eisenach (1698–1729) for presentation to the nobleman whose initial F is set in mirror monogram on the thumb-plate. The portrait on the pommel cap is probably that of Johann Georg, those chiselled on other mounts perhaps represent his predecessors as Dukes of Sachsen-Eisenach, Johann Georg I (1668–1686) and Johann Georg II (1686–1698)

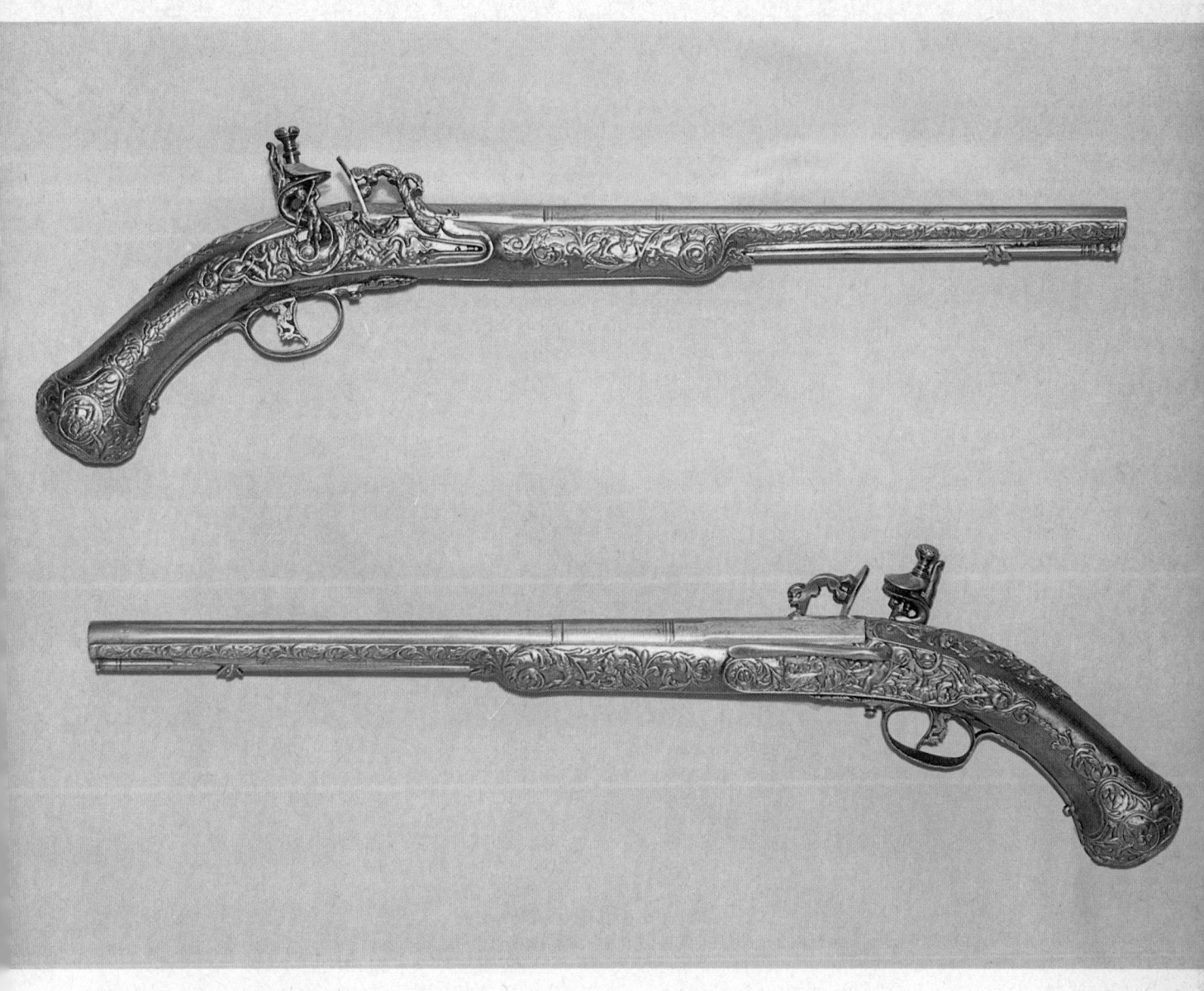

A pair of Brescian snaphaunce pistols, stocked entirely in steel, attributed to Stefano Scioli, the barrels in three stages, octagonal at the breech with two moulded girdles, the locks chiselled in exceptionally high relief, the plates with infant tritons riding a sea serpent and with Leda and the swan, the cocks with an infant triton spearing a dolphin with a trident, the arm of the steel with a dolphin and a winged harpy, the iron stocks wrought in one piece with simulated pommels, the fore-stocks with scrolling foliage and a triton in combat with a dragon, the side-plates with a similar subject, the top of each butt with a man rising from a flower struggling with a serpent, the trigger guards and butt caps chiselled with Roman profile heads, the pommels with oval cartouches enclosing busts of a man in full bottomed wig and armour and of a woman in contemporary dress, belt hooks and steel ramrods. *Circa* 1700. Length 21in
London £18,500 ($44,400). 12.XI.73
From the collection of the late William Goodwin Renwick

Left A late sixteenth-century Polish close helmet, the visor wrought with a grotesque human mask with moustaches. Possibly made for a pageant.
London £1,150 ($2,760). 18.VI.74
From Her Majesty's Tower of London

Right An 1814 pattern officer's helmet of the Royal Horse Guards, the badge with crowned GR cypher, the front with an oval plaque inscribed *Royal Horse Guards, Blue*, circa 1814.
London £1,000 ($2,400). 17.XII.73
From the collection of Mrs H. M. Sullivan

Left A late sixteenth-century German black and white three-quarter armour.
London £1,600 ($3,840). 18.VI.74
From Her Majesty's Tower of London

Right A composite mainly South German field armour, mostly Augsburg, probably by Anton Peffenhauser, third quarter of the sixteenth century.
London £5,000 ($12,000). 12.II.74
This armour is composed of elements from four suits: helmet and shoulder guard, Italian, mid-sixteenth century; breastplate, tassets, gorget, arms, gauntlets and legs from an Augsburg armour, third quarter of the sixteenth century; backplate, third quarter of the sixteenth century

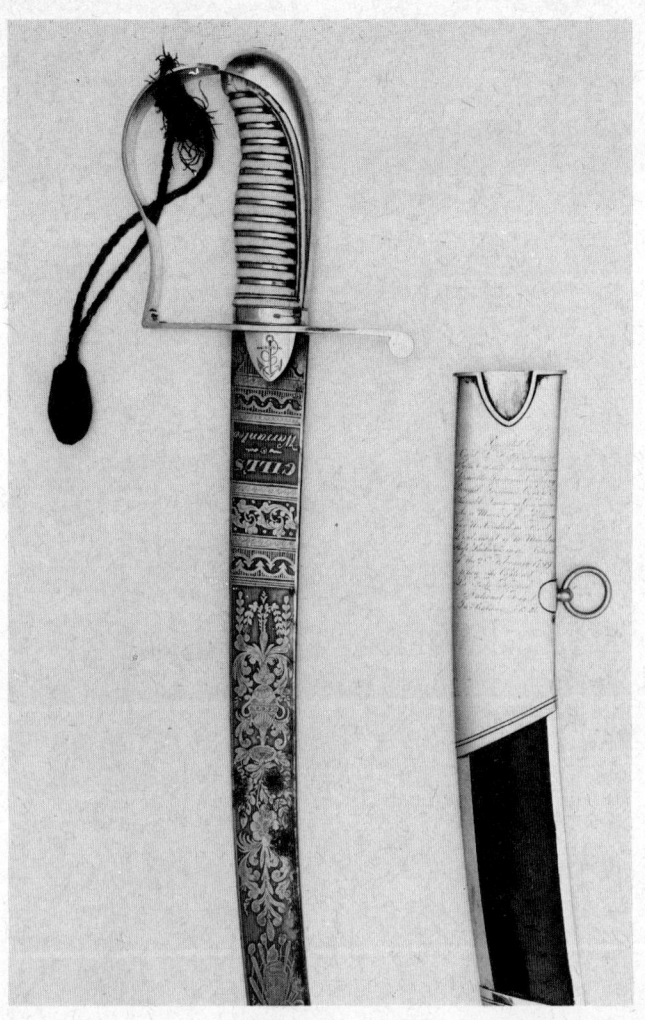

Left A gold-mounted naval officer's presentation fighting sword, the blade etched with eastern trophies and inscribed *Gill's Warranted*, the hilt with ivory grip, the gold-mounted leather scabbard inscribed *Presented to Cptn L.F. Hardyman By the Calcutta Insurance Office, Calcutta Insurance Company, Bengal Insurance Company & Amicable Insurance Company As a Mark of their Esteem for His Conduct as First Lieutenant of His Majesty's Ship La Sybille in the Action of the 28th February 1799 when she Captured La Forte French National Frigate In Belasore Roads. Circa* 1800. 36½in
London £1,600 ($3,840). 16.IV.74 From the collection of Brigadier T. St. G. Caulfield

Centre A gold and enamel hilted naval presentation small-sword, the blade inscribed on the forte *IWM à Solingen*, the hilt of chased gold, the underside of the guard inscribed *PRESENTED to CAPTN LUCIUS FERDINAND HARDYMAN by the Insurance Office of Madras for his Gallant Conduct in the Capture of the FRENCH FRIGATE LA FORTE on the Night of the 28th February 1799*, London Hallmark 1799–1800, maker's mark of John Ray and James Montague. 41½in
London £9,000 ($21,600). 16.IV.74 From the collection of Brigadier T. St. G. Caulfield
Lucius Ferdinand Hardyman (1771–1834) was First Lieutenant of the Sybille when she engaged the French Frigate La Forte on the night of the 28th February 1799. He succeeded to the command when Captain Edward Cooke was mortally wounded and successfully concluded the action. He became Rear-Admiral in 1830

Right A Field-Marshal's baton, presented to Hermann Goering by the Italian aircraft manufacturer Gianni Caproni, the baton of ivory surmounted by the National Socialist Symbol in oxidised silver on a malachite hemisphere and *semé* with T-shaped ornaments of malachite, and with two silver friezes cast and chased with figures and scenes illustrative of the Rise of the N.S.D.A.P. between 1914 and 1939, signed by the artist Emilio Monti. Length 19½in
London £2,400 ($5,760). 8.X.73

An English flintlock fowling piece by Andrew Dolep, the barrel in three stages, the lock signed *Dolep,* walnut full-length stock profusely inlaid with scrolling silver wire, steel furniture. *Circa* 1690. Length 54in
London £13,500 ($32,400). 8.x.73
Andrew Dolep, first recorded in 1681 working for Sir Philip Howard, was appointed gunmaker to Lord Dartmouth, Master General of the Ordnance and was admitted to the London Gunmaker's Company. He enjoyed royal patronage during the reign of Queen Anne and died in 1713

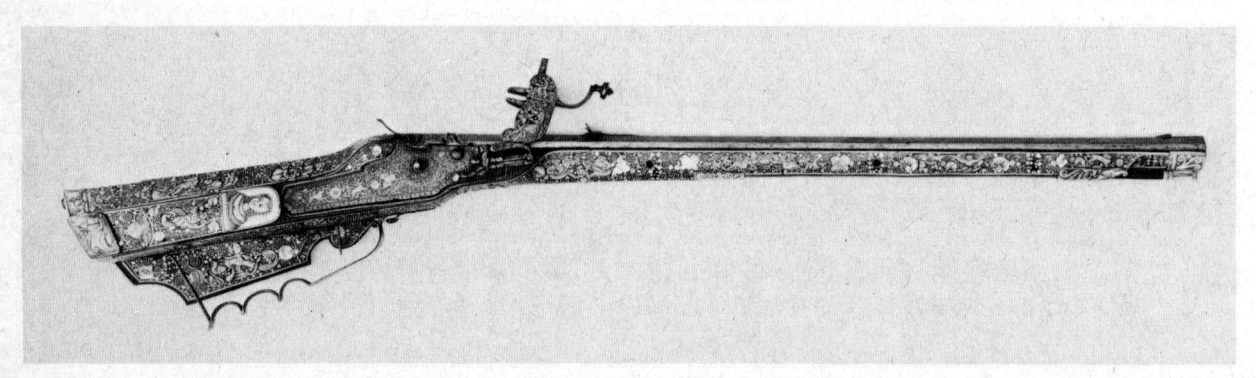

A Silesian wheel-lock sporting rifle, the octagonal barrel rifled with seven grooves, signed on the top flat *Georg Grosser,* numbered I on the tang, full-length walnut stock, profusely inlaid with stag-horn and engraved mother-of-pearl, the trigger guard damascened in silver with gilt borders, original ramrod. Mid-seventeenth century.
Length 39½in London £12,000 ($28,800). 12.xi.73. From the collection of the late William Goodwin Renwick

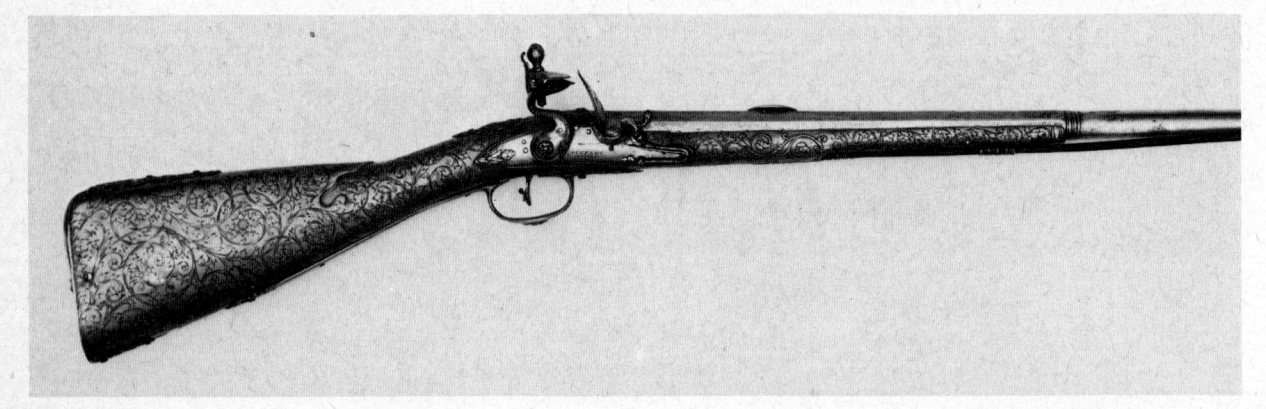

A Brescian flintlock fowling piece by Stefano Scioli, the barrel of Spanish form, stamped over the breech with a crowned leaf(?), the lock with rounded plate signed *Stefano Scioli,* three-quarter stock entirely of brass finely engraved, brass furniture, wood ramrod. Early eighteenth century. Length 55in
London £5,600 ($13,440). 19.iii.74. From the collection of the late William Goodwin Renwick

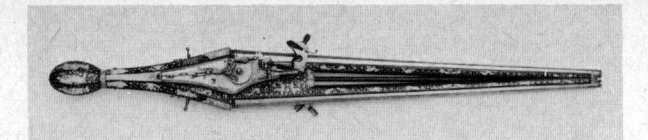

A Northern French wheel-lock double-barrelled holster pistol, barrelsmith's mark, *P.M.* over a star, probably from Sedan, the locks each stamped with the mark *G.L.* and two stars. Early seventeenth century. Length 30½in London £14,500 ($34,800). 19.III.74

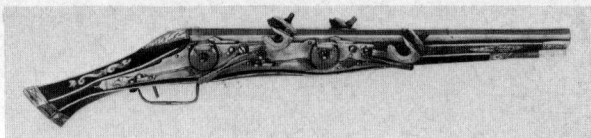

A South German wheel-lock pistol, firing three superimposed shots in succession from a single octagonal barrel, with left and right-hand locks, the right-hand plate bearing two locks firing the first and third charges, the left-hand lock firing the second charge, the three locks fired in succession by a single trigger, walnut full stock inlaid with stag-horn, the barrel stamped *H.K.* with an orb. Third quarter of the sixteenth century. Length 26in London £26,000 ($62,400). 12.XI.73

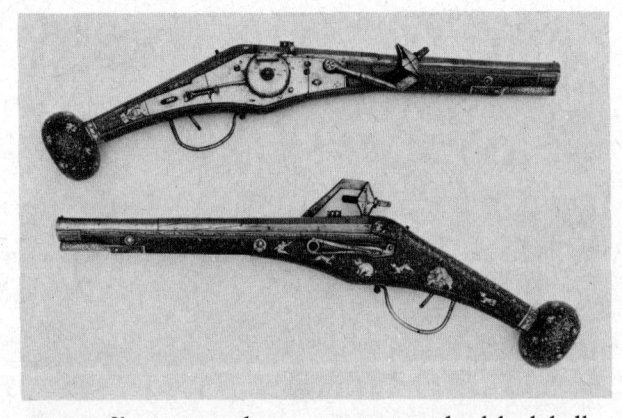

A pair of late sixteenth-century Saxon wheel-lock ball butted holster pistols, barrelsmith's mark an antler within a shield and the initials *H.B.*, the stocks in the manner of Klaus Hirt of Wasungen. Length 22in London £21,000 ($50,400). 19.III.74.

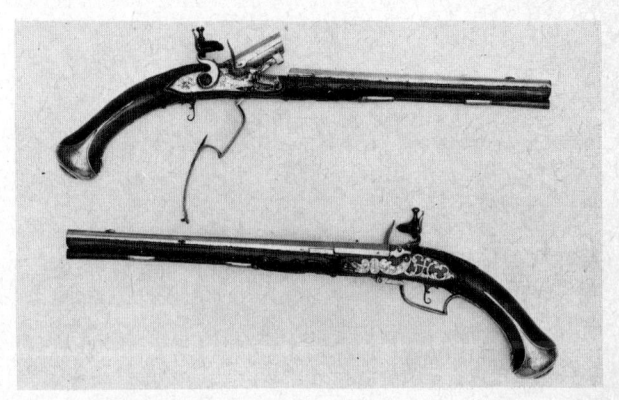

A pair of German flintlock breech-loading holster pistols, the locks signed *Schirmer*, the side-plates engraved with the arms of Augustus II, King of Poland and Elector of Saxony (1670-1733). *Circa* 1725-30. Length 22in London £7,800 ($18,720). 12.XI.73

The six pistols illustrated above were part of the collection of the late William Goodwin Renwick

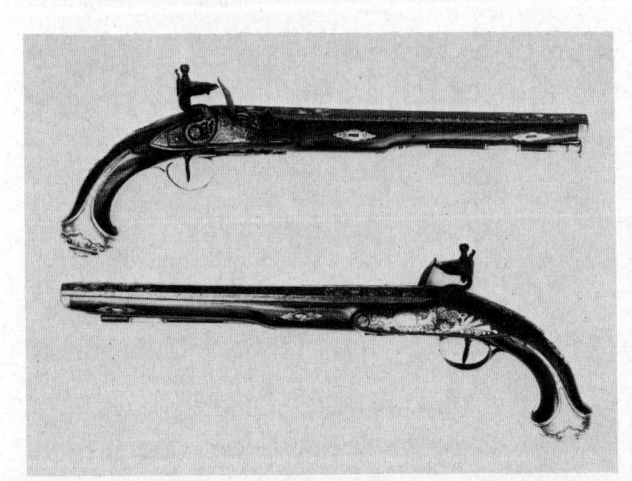

A pair of Indian flintlock holster pistols of English form, inscribed *Lucknow Arsenal,* and *A Col. Claude Martin, circa* 1780. Length 17in
London £4,200 ($10,080). 16.IV.74
From the collection of Brigadier T. St. G. Caulfield. Claude Martin, a deserter from the French Army in India joined the British and was Superintendent of Artillery to the Nawab of Oudh. He established the manufacture of fine firearms at Lucknow Arsenal

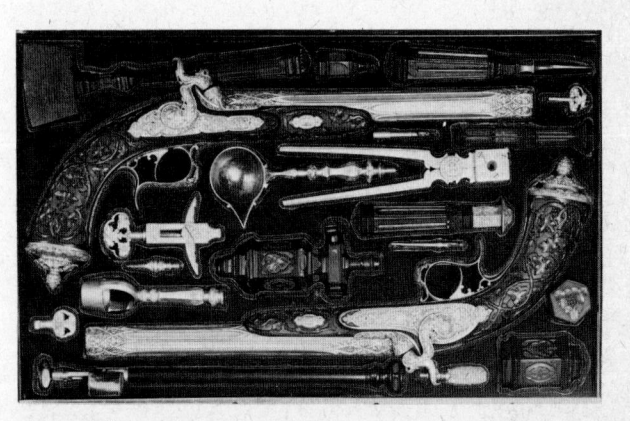

A pair of French presentation percussion cap target pistols, possibly by Moutier Le Page, carved ebony stocks, in original ebony case centred with the crowned initials *K.H. Circa* 1860. Length 16in
Los Angeles $18,000 (£7,500). 16.IX.73
This pair of pistols is thought to have been presented after the Treaty of Paris by Napoleon III to the Russian Grand Duke Konstantine Nicholaivich

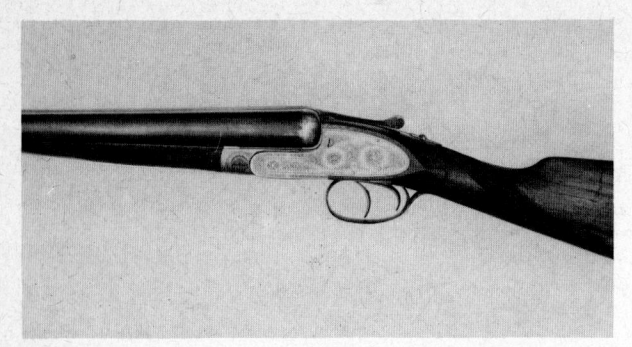

One of a pair of 12-bore double-barrelled sidelock ejector sporting guns by J. Purdey & Sons, inscribed *Made of Sir Joseph Whitworth's Fluid Pressed Steel*, the frames engraved with tight floral scrollwork and flower heads, well-figured walnut stocks, serial nos. 22709/22710. Length 44¾in
London £4,700 ($11,280). 16.IV.74

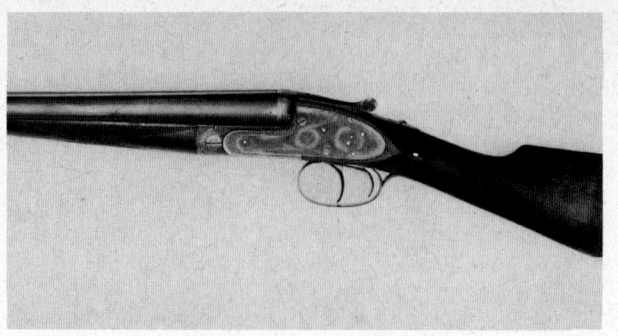

One of a pair of 16-bore sidelock ejector sporting guns by J. Purdey & Sons, serial nos. 25399/25400, walnut butts, the oval gold escutcheons initialled *HS 1 & 2* respectively. Length 44⅜in
London £6,000 ($14,400). 16.IV.74

A 10 gauge double-barrelled shotgun, 22¼-inch barrel stamped *J. Stevens and Co., Chicopee, Falls. Mass.*, serial no. 927
Los Angeles $10,000 (£4,160). 17.IX.73
From the collection of the late Gerald G. Fox
This is the gun used by Wyatt Earp to kill Curly Bill and by U.S. Marshall Heck Thomas to kill Bill Doolin

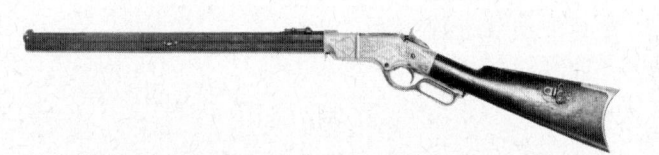

A .44 rim-fire lever-action repeating rifle, stamped *Henrys Patent, Oct. 16. 1860, Manufactured by the New Haven Arms Co. New Haven. Ct.*, serial no. 8298. Length 43½in
Los Angeles $7,000 (£2,900). 18.XI.73
From the collection of the late William Goodwin Renwick

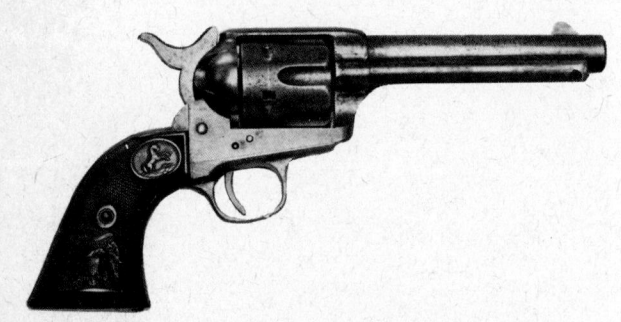

A .45 Colt S A revolver, the barrel reduced to five inches and stamped *Colts Pt. F.A. Mfg. Co., Hartford. Ct., U.S.A.* serial no. 69562
Los Angeles $20,000 (£8,333). 18.IX.73
From the collection of the late Gerald G. Fox
This is the hand gun that Marshal Wyatt Earp carried in his pursuit of the outlaw Curly Bill

A 9mm Persian Luger semi-automatic pistol with 8-inch barrel, the receiver struck with the arms of Persia and with adjustable rear sight to 800 yards, Persian serial no., original chequered walnut grips, the frame with detachable butt locking lug, associated magazine. Length 12½in
London £350 ($840). 12.II.74

Silver and Metalwork

The Petzolt Cup. A German silver-gilt standing cup and cover, the waisted circular body finely embossed and chased in low relief with six scenes depicting stages in the mining of silver. Underneath the foot is a lengthy Latin inscription recording the posthumous presentation of the cup in 1626 by Veit Georg Holtzschuher to Andreas Imhoff, together with a shield of the Holtzschuher Arms, maker's mark of Hans Petzolt, Nuremberg, *circa* 1625, height 18½in
London £40,000 ($96,000).25.x.73
From the collection of His Grace the Duke of Hamilton and Brandon

278 SILVER

One of a pair of Dutch salts, signed by Michiel de Bruyn van Berendrecht of Utrecht, 1650, height 8¼in
Los Angeles $20,000 (£8,333). 21.x.73

Above right One of a pair of Dutch tazze emblematic of summer and winter. Signed by Adam van Vianen of Utrecht, 1627, height 6¾in
London £30,000 ($72,000). 25.x.73
From the collection of His Grace the Duke of Hamilton and Brandon

A Dutch tazza. Maker's mark of Adam van Vianen of Utrecht, 1628, height 4¼in
London £24,000 ($57,600). 25.x.73
From the collection of His Grace the Duke of Hamilton and Brandon

A German parcel-gilt tankard. Maker's mark of Melchior Gelb, Augsburg, *circa* 1620, height 9½in
London £10,000 ($24,000). 9.v.74
From the collection of the late Dr Felix Somary

SILVER 279

An early George III silver-gilt casket in contemporary German style. Maker's mark of William Cripps, London, 1760, width 5¾in
London £1,050 ($3,520). 20.VI.74

A German silver-gilt standing cup and cover. Maker's mark of Veit Moringer, Nuremberg, *circa* 1560. The jewels added in the late eighteenth/early nineteenth century for William Beckford, height 14in
London £24,000 ($57,600). 25.X.73
From the collection of His Grace the Duke of Hamilton and Brandon

A Dutch beaker. Maker's mark ? a pillar, Enkhuizen, 1656, height 8¼in
London £3,200 ($7,680). 9.V.74
From the collection of Mrs W. R. Tomkinson

A Louis XVI soup tureen, cover and stand. Maker's mark of Henry Auguste, Paris, 1787, length of tureen 17¼in, length of stand 21in
New York $38,000 (£15,833). 18.VI.74

A pair of Italian silver-gilt small candlesticks. Maker's mark of Luigi Valadier, Rome, *circa* 1770, height 6½in
New York $20,000 (£8,333). 18.VI.74
Formerly in the collection of J. P. Morgan, Esq

Below A Dutch oval punch bowl. Maker's mark of Gregorius van der Toorn, The Hague, 1768, width 24¾in
London £12,000 ($28,800). 25.X.73
From the collection of Mrs D. Gavronsky

282 SILVER

Left An American porringer. Maker's mark of Paul Revere, Boston, *circa* 1780, diameter 5⅜in
New York $13,000 (£5,416). 17.XI.73

Below One of a pair of American sauce boats. Maker's mark of Zachariah Brigden, Boston, *circa* 1760, length 6¼in
New York $8,750 (£3,645). 17.XI.73

An American sugar dish and teapot. The teapot unmarked, but both pieces recorded in Revere's daybook. Paul Revere, Boston, 1791, heights 7⅛in and 6¾in
New York $30,000 (£12,500). 25.I.74
From the collection of Francis S. Parker Esq

A William III oval casket. Maker's mark of Pierre Harache, Senior, of London, *circa* 1700, width 5¾in
London £3,600 ($8,640). 28.II.74

A Charles II oval sugar or sweetmeat box. Maker's mark B.B., crescent below, London, 1676, width 7¼in
London £18,000 ($43,200). 28.II.74

A Charles II tankard. Maker's mark of Arthur Manwaring, London, 1677, height 8in
London £6,500 ($15,600). 20.VI.74

A William and Mary teapot. Maker's mark B.B., a crescent below, London, 1689, height 5in
London £4,200 ($10,080). 25.X.73

284 SILVER

One of a pair of George II sauce boats and stands (not illustrated). Maker's mark of Paul de Lamerie, London, 1733/39, length of boats 9⅜in, length of stands 9½in
New York $46,000 (£19,167). 4.VI.74

Left A George II cake basket. Maker's mark of Paul de Lamerie, London, 1740, length 14½in
New York $33,000 (£13,750). 4.VI.74
This basket was made for Charles Noel Somerset, 4th Duke of Beaufort who married Elizabeth, daughter of John Berkeley of Stoke Gifford, co. Gloucester, in 1740.

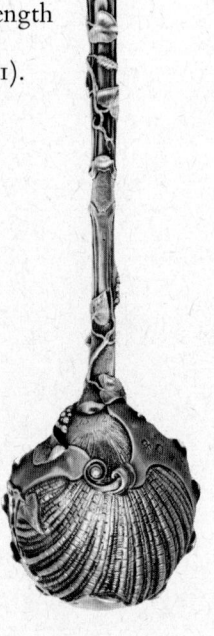

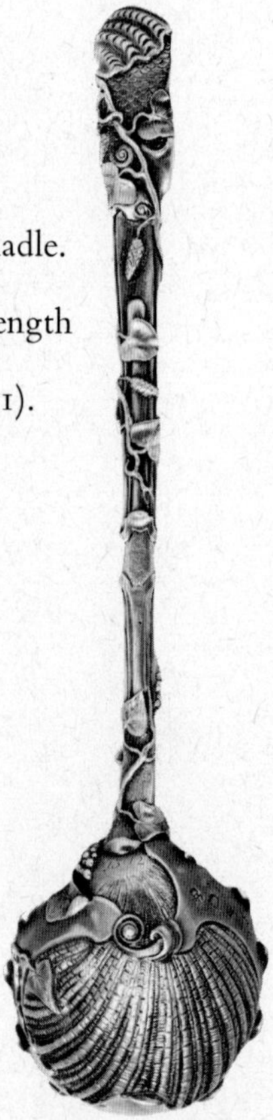

A George II rococo soup ladle. Maker's mark of Paul de Lamerie, London, 1738, length 14¾in
New York $9,100 (£3,791). 4.VI.74

A George II two-handled cup and cover. Maker's mark of Paul de Lamerie, London, 1739, height 13¾in
New York $37,000 (£15,417). 4.VI.74
Formerly in the collection of the Rt Hon Lord Tredegar

Above A pair of George III table candlesticks, formed as a sailor and girl in period dress. Maker's mark of Samuel Siervent, London, 1762, height 7¾in
London £1,700 ($4,080). 8.XI.73

Below right One of a pair of George III silver-gilt salvers on foot. Maker's mark of Benjamin Smith I of Rundell, Bridge & Rundell, London, 1807, diameter 12in
London £3,600 ($8,640). 20.VI.74
The Arms are those of Charles, 4th Duke of Richmond and Lennox, 1764-1819.

Below One of a pair of George II oblong tea caddies. Maker's mark of Peter Archambo, London, 1745, height 5in
London £850 ($2,040). 20. VI.74

A George II oval cake basket. Maker's mark of Thomas Farren, London, 1737, width 13in
London £5,500 ($13,200). 9.V.74

286 SILVER

A George III oval punch bowl. Maker's mark of D. Smith and R. Sharp, London, 1786, width 15in
London £2,500 ($6,000). 28.II.74
The Arms are those of Fitzgibbon, for John Fitzgibbon (1748-1802), created Viscount Fitzgibbon in 1793 and Earl of Clare in 1795.
From the collection of the Most Hon the Marquess of Waterford

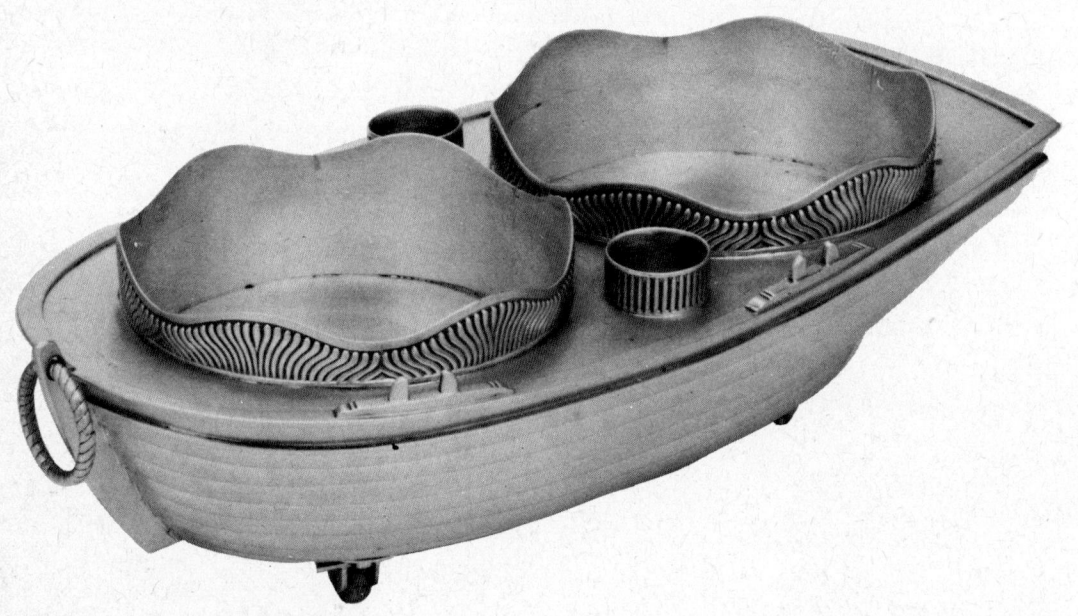

One of a pair of George III decanter wagons, formed as clinker-built pinnaces. Maker's mark of William Burwash, London, 1813, length 13in
London £3,200 ($7,680). 28.II.74

SILVER 287

A Victorian parcel-gilt table snuff box in the form of a military tent. Maker's mark of Joseph Angell III for Ridgway, Agent, 42 Leicester Square, London, 1850, length 8¼in
New York $2,800 (£1,167). 4.VI.74

A Victorian silver-gilt shaped oblong card case. Maker's mark of Nathaniel Mills & Sons, Birmingham, 1852, height 4in
London £165 ($396).
15.XI.73
From the collection of Mrs J. M. Douglas

Left One of a pair of Victorian pagodas. Maker's mark of Robert Hennell IV, London, 1864, height 21in
New York $16,000 (£6,666).
1.VI.74
From the collection of Louise C. Morgan

Right A Victorian model of the Bishop Rock lighthouse, Scilly Isles. Maker's mark of Edward Barnard & Sons, London, 1858, height 29½in
London £1,900 ($4,560). 21.II.74

288 SILVER

Left An Indian wine ewer with vase-shaped body. Maker's mark of P. Orr & Sons, Madras, *circa* 1870, height 14¾in
London £200 ($480). 21.III.74

Right A Victorian emu egg casket with silver-gilt mounts. Maker's mark of George Angell, London, 1871, height 8¾in
London £220 ($528). 6.XII.73

Below A William IV soup tureen with cover and stand, presented to Robert Stephenson on completion of the first Birmingham to London Railway, 1837. Maker's mark of G. R. Collis & Co., Birmingham, 1837, length 21in
Los Angeles $15,000 (£6,250). 21.X.73

SILVER 289

Left A William IV wine ewer. Maker's mark of John Bridge of Rundell, Bridge & Rundell, London, 1831, height 10¼in
London £520 ($1,248). 21.III.74

Right A George IV silver-gilt inkwell. Maker's mark of John Bridge of Rundell, Bridge & Rundell, London, 1823, height 3¼in
London £600 ($1,440). 21.II.74

Below A George III centrepiece. Maker's mark of Paul Storr of Rundell, Bridge & Rundell, London, 1817, height 24½in
London £3,200 ($7,680). 20.VI.74

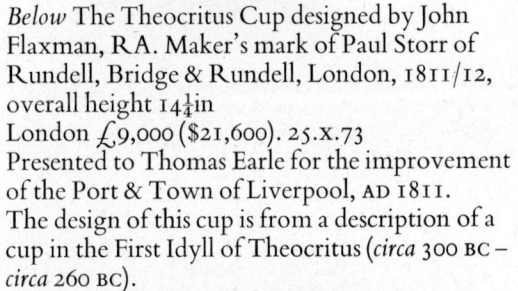

Below The Theocritus Cup designed by John Flaxman, RA. Maker's mark of Paul Storr of Rundell, Bridge & Rundell, London, 1811/12, overall height 14¼in
London £9,000 ($21,600). 25.X.73
Presented to Thomas Earle for the improvement of the Port & Town of Liverpool, AD 1811.
The design of this cup is from a description of a cup in the First Idyll of Theocritus (*circa* 300 BC – *circa* 260 BC).
From the collection of Sir Hardman Earle Bt

Above A pair of Victorian figure salts in romantic eighteenth-century costume. Maker's mark of Robert Garrard of R. & S. Garrard & Co., London, 1856, height 7in
London £1,000 ($2,400). 21.II.74

A Victorian electrogilt 'Please remember the grotto' inkstand. Maker's mark of Elkington, Mason & Co., London, 1851, width 9½in
London £170 ($408). 21.III.74
This cry was raised in the streets by small children, who collected old shells, etc., built a little 'grotto' and knelt beside it with their caps ready for pennies.

One of a pair of Victorian silver-gilt candelabra. Maker's mark of E. C. Barnard, London, 1876, the base of one also engraved *Habowski, Fecit, 1876*, height 43in
Los Angeles $17,000 (£7,084). 20.VI.74

A Paris porcelain circular chinoiserie plaque mounted in silver-gilt, the porcelain from the Clignancourt factory, *circa* 1780. The mounts maker's mark of Paul Storr of Rundell, Bridge & Rundell, London, 1815, diameter 22in
New York $15,000 (£6,250). 4.VI.74

292 SILVER

Right An early Victorian wine jug. Maker's mark of William Elliott, London, 1847, height 11¾in
London £360 ($864). 24.I.74

Above A William IV silver-gilt dessert stand of naturalistic inspiration. Maker's mark of Benjamin Preston for Kensington Lewis, London, 1834, height 6¼in
London £360 ($864). 21.II.74

Below A George IV silver-gilt shaped circular sideboard dish. Maker's mark of Edward Cornelius Farrell, London, 1823, diameter 27in
London £1,400 ($3,360). 20.VI.74

'Benvenuto Cellini' and the nineteenth-century Collector and Goldsmith

By John Culme

From a modern point of view one of the least sympathetic of nineteenth-century stylistic phenomena is the obsession with Cellini. By 1840, when the satirist Comte Horace de Viel-Castel claims to have been shown 'Joan of Arc's sword chased by Benvenuto Cellini', this mania had reached a point where ridicule was justified.[1] As little as twenty years earlier, however, this would have been impossible. While the extreme poles of seriousness and parody are easily distinguished, 'Cellini' objects force a reassessment of more critical distinctions between replication and mannerism, forgery and copy, sophistication and aesthetic double-dealing.

'I don't know what kind of thing this Tankard attributed (doubtless falsely) to Benvenuto Cellini will turn out to be, but one must remember, and I beg you to remember, that it is better to give a considerable sum for things of undoubted authenticity, than to buy at a lower price carvings that are uncertain, problematic and second rate', wrote William Beckford in 1818.[2] For the period, Beckford was an unusually discriminating collector. His doubts about this so-called Cellini tankard show him to be considerably in advance of others in the same field. By the close of the eighteenth-century, the goldsmiths of London were as accustomed to selling both old and new plate as were their successors of the mid-nineteenth century. In 1786, for instance, Sophie v. la Roche was told by a London goldsmith that 'Those antique, well-preserved pieces . . . often find a purchaser more readily than the modern.'[3]

When, in 1823, the contents of Beckford's Fonthill were offered for sale and the Abbey opened to the public, William Hazlitt observed that it looked like 'a cathedral turned into a toy shop', and that the only proof of taste which Beckford, the 'industrious *bijoutier*', had shown in his collection was 'his getting rid of it.'[4] George, Prince of Wales, no less criticised than Beckford for his flamboyant taste, was another early collector of old plate and plate in the 'antique' manner. His collection included a pair of dishes in seventeenth-century style made in 1810, one of which was centred by an original plaque of 1678.[5] He continued to buy

1 *Les Français peints par Eux-Mêmes*, Paris, 1840, vol I, p 128, Comte Horace de Viel-Castel, *Les Collectionneurs*
2 William Beckford, *Life at Fonthill 1807-1822*, London, 1957, letters translated and edited by Boyd Alexander, p 245
3 Sophie v. la Roche, *Sophie in London*, London, 1933, journal translated by Clare Williams, pp 171/2
'Antique' for the purposes of this article means 'old' rather than 'classical'
4 *London Magazine*, November, 1822. Centenary edition of W. Hazlitt's *Works*, London, 1934, vol 18, pp 173/4
5 E. Alfred Jones, *The Gold and Silver of Windsor Castle*, Letchworth, 1911, p 194, pl XCVIII

objects of this nature for the remainder of his life. As George IV, he purchased a silver-gilt mounted nautilus cup and cover from Rundell, Bridge & Rundell which had come from the Wanstead House sale in 1822. It is said that John Flaxman, then head of Rundell's design department, supposed the piece to be a work of Cellini's. Though sixteenth-century in origin, the cup has since been proved to bear the mark of the Nuremberg silversmith, Nicholas Schmidt.[6]

The tendency to esteem old works, even to produce faithful copies, naturally led to the making of new works in the old idiom. Rundell, Bridge & Rundell, with extensive interests in the manufacture and sale of jewellery as well as plate, were not alone in exploiting the 'antique'. A notable workshop of the period, brilliantly utilising old designs for new wares, was headed by the working silversmith, Edward C. Farrell. His early career remains a mystery, but from the time of entering his first mark in 1813,[7] when he was about thirty-eight, Farrell was being commissioned to copy and refurbish old works, tasks which clearly influenced his modern pieces.[8]

The years immediately following the peace of 1815 were important for the English collector of sixteenth- and seventeenth-century items, since German Renaissance objets d'art figured so greatly on the London market.[9] At this period Kensington Lewis, the retail silversmith most closely associated with Edward C. Farrell, was to figure prominently. Like other establishments, Lewis's stock was varied, but seems to have especially reflected the approved 'antique' taste. In 1816 he bought from the sale of the Duke of Norfolk a heavily chased seventeenth-century German tankard.[10] By 1826 he was sufficiently well known to receive a notice in the fashionable magazine, Ackerman's *Repository*: 'Mr. Lewis, silversmith of St James's Street, has in his possession twelve very curious silver ornaments, apparently for the table, by the celebrated Italian artist, Benvenuto Cellini . . .'[11] In order to supplement his stock with compatible modern objects, Lewis employed Farrell, and their association seems to have lasted from about 1816 until 1833/34. As the maker, Farrell received no contemporary acclaim for his work, while Lewis gained considerable publicity when one of his chief patrons, The Duke of York, died, and a 'GRAND CANDELABRUM' from Farrell's workshop, together with various corresponding items, were sold in 1827, less than ten years after they had been made.[12]

By the late 1830s Lewis's concern as a goldsmith had declined after a movement towards heavy naturalism.[13] He retired to devote his energies to prestigious property development.[14] In general, the retail establishments of London maintained their interest, if more broadly based, in the sale of 'antique' plate. Perhaps the most well known of these, a firm which continued the tradition until the Edwardian period, was Lambert & Rawlings of Coventry Street. While the Farrell/Lewis *oeuvre* had tended towards the fantastic, the Lambert &

---

6 Ibid p 4, pl II
7 Goldsmiths' Hall Library, makers' marks books, vol 4, fol 23, no 3
8 Sotheby's, lot 59, 20th June, 1974; a silver-gilt dish, maker's mark of Edward C. Farrell, London, 1822, the centre with a seventeenth-century Flemish plaque signed with the initials PG in monogram
9 Gerald Reitlinger, *The Economics of Taste*, London, 1963, p 67
10 Ibid p 625
11 Rudolph Ackerman's *Repository*, London, 1826, vol VII, pp 303/4
12 Christie's, 19th, 20th and 21st March, 1827. *The Times*, 23rd March, 1827, p 3b. *The Gentleman's Magazine*, March, 1827, p 266, and April, 1827, pp 358/9
13 Sotheby's Belgravia, lot 135, 21st February, 1974; a silver-gilt dessert stand, maker's mark of Benjamin Preston, London, 1834, stamped: 'K. LEWIS St. JAMES'S St.'
14 *The Survey of London*, London, 1960, vol XXIX part I, p 361

Detail

Fig 1 A silver-gilt cup and cover in late sixteenth-century style, chased with scenes from the lives of Solomon and David, 30½in high, marked on lip, base and cover with a pseudo-seventeenth-century town letter for Zürich, and a device in a shield intended to represent the maker's mark of Abraham Gessner (1552-1613) of Zürich, mid-European, *circa* 1870.
London £2,200 ($5,280). 30.V.74

Rawlings house style reflected the way in which old designs could be copied and adapted for domestic use. Nevertheless, they also drew inspiration from original works, as shown by a matching pair of tazze. One of these was Flemish and of about 1660, the other was made in London in 1829 by the workshop of Charles Fox who was subsequently described, but not by name, as one of Lambert & Rawlings's 'best artists'.[15] The firm's connection with Charles

15 H. R. Forster, *The Stowe Catalogue priced and annotated,* London, 1848, p 147, lots 779 and 780. The tazze appeared again at Sotheby's, lots 40 and 41, 20th April, 1972.

Fox and his descendants is well known, and Fox's designers show themselves to have been impressed by the styles of the seventeenth-century.

From the early 1840s the atmosphere both for craftsmanship and collecting changed. A new and more professional spirit was injected into the trade, largely through entrepreneurs such as Jean Valentin Morel. Having studiously recaptured the techniques of the *cinquecento*, these men were unashamed at 'possessing a portion of that spirit of commercial enterprise which has stimulated so much exertion in this modern field of competition . . .'[16] Continuing exhibitions encouraged this rivalry, and brought dignity and widespread recognition to their re-creations as modern works of art. This pride in modern pieces caused critics to begin to explode the myth which surrounded the name of Cellini;[17] by 1858, and the Art Treasures Exhibition at Manchester, Matthew Digby Wyatt was able to say of the Earl of Warwick's cup that it was 'in all respects worthy of Cellini; and if not by his hand, is certainly the production of an artist of equal merit.'[18]

Antonio Cortelazzo, a self-taught virtuoso metalworker, was elevated from his career as a Cellini imitator to a position where he was heralded as a new Benvenuto Cellini, by the English connoisseur, Sir Austen H. Layard, who commissioned original works from him.[19] Johann Karl Bossard of Lucerne, on the other hand, always made a virtue of his accomplished imitations,[20] unlike the unknown maker of a large silver-gilt cup of about 1870,[21] purporting to be a genuine work of the sixteenth-century (Fig 1) Zürich silversmith, Abraham Gessner.[22] This cup had evidently been made to deceive, and was the type of production which the United Kingdom Customs Act of 1842 unwittingly encouraged. Section six to the amendment of this Act specifically exempted from duty items of 'gold or silver plate being of foreign manufacture, and of an ornamental kind, and having been made or wrought previous to the year 1800 . . .', and as such did not need to be import-marked.[23]

The great art sales of the late nineteenth-century gave collectors the opportunity to become more discerning at the same time as the impetus given to manufacturers and retailers by the international exhibitions was exhausted. There was no longer any place for the nineteenth-century imitator of Cellini, since collectors and museums could more easily buy high quality sixteenth- or seventeenth-century pieces, and the middle classes could obtain mass-produced electrotypes, or objects which had entered into the vernacular, long-known in the trade as the 'Cellini' style.[24]

The gradual change of emphasis on Benvenuto Cellini is finally seen not as an aspect of the history of plate, or even of taste in certain objects. 'Cellini' becomes a measuring-rod of craftsmanship, a goal towards which metalworkers will be assumed to want to move.

16 *Descriptive Particulars of a collection of Silver, Silver Gilt and Enamel'd Plate . . . Manufactured and Designed by Joseph Angell*, London, 1851, p 3
17 Shirley Bury, *The lengthening shadow of Rundell's*, part 3, *The Connoisseur*, April, 1966, p 221a
18 *Art Treasures of the United Kingdom*, edited by J.B. Waring, London, 1858
19 J. Culme, *Antonio Cortelazzo and the Narishkine Tea Service, Art at Auction, 1971-72*, pp 422/3
20 Thieme & Becker, vol 4, p 399. Marc Rosenberg, *Der Goldschmiede Merkzeichen*, Frankfurt, 1890, p 511, no 2548
21 Sotheby's Belgravia, lot 148, 30th May, 1974
22 Marc Rosenberg, *Der Goldschmiede Merkzeichen*, Frankfurt, 1911, pp 940/1, no 5775
23 J. Paul de Castro, *The Law and Practice of Hall-Marking Gold and Silver Wares*, London, 1926, pp 312/3
24 *The Art Journal*, illustrated catalogue of the Great Exhibition, 1851, p 189, a 'CLARET-JUG after Cellini' shown by Martin, Baskett & Martin of Cheltenham. A similar jug is illustrated in *Yesterday's Shopping*, Newton Abbot, 1969, a facsimile of The Army & Navy Stores Catalogue of 1907, p 606, no 1080

Above left and right A pair of 'wriggled-work' marriage plates by Stephen Cox of Bristol, *circa* 1730, diameter 8¼in £420 ($1,008).
Above centre A late Stuart flat-lidded 'wriggled-work' tankard, maker's mark I.L. in a shield struck inside the base, *circa* 1680-90, height 6⅛in £850 ($2,040)

A broad-rimmed plate or paten by Lawrence Dyer, engraved with the arms of George Griffith, Bishop of St Asaph, Wales, from 1660-1666, *circa* 1660, diameter 9⅝in £400 ($960)

A Charles I or Cromwellian flagon, 'hallmarks' of the maker RB stamped on cover and an indistinct touch inside base, *circa* 1640-50, height 10½in £720 ($1,728)

A 'wriggled-work' plate, maker's mark on reverse L.A. a fleur-de-lis between within a heart, *circa* 1690, diameter 8½in £260 ($624)

The pieces shown on this page are from the collection of the late R. F. Michaelis, sold in London on 12th November 1973

Left
Two German pewter and wood tankards by Andreas Haas, Kulmbach, maker's mark only, *circa* 1700, heights 8¾in $2,100 (£875)

Below left
A pewter Adam and Eve charger, probably by François Briot, Montbéliard, or Caspar Enderlein, Nuremberg, apparently unmarked, *circa* 1600, diameter 18¾in $3,900 (£1,625)

Below right
A large pewter weavers' guild tankard, probably German, marks obscured by action of cover on handle, sixteenth century, height 17½in $2,000 (£834)

The objects illustrated on this page were in the collection of the Benjamin and Mary Siddons Measey Foundation sold in New York 3rd November 1973

Coins and Medals

Renaissance bronze portrait medal of Giovanni Pico della Mirandola (1463-94), by Niccoló Spinelli, called Fiorentino
Zürich SF65,000 (£9,286; $22,286). 27.V.74

A Greek tetradrachm of Lampsacos, *circa* 160 BC
Zürich SF24,000 (£3,429; $8,229). 27.V.74

A Roman silver medallion of the Emperor Constans (AD 337-350), struck at Trier
Zürich SF55,000 (£7,857; $18,857). 27.V.74

300 COINS AND MEDALS

Henry VII, sovereign,
London mint (1504-07)
£20,000 ($48,000)

Charles I, triple unite, 1644,
Oxford mint £9,000 ($21,000)

James I, rose ryal of thirty
shillings (1605-06)
£4,300 ($10,320)

George II, two-guineas, 1735
£4,700 ($11,280)

Alfred the Great, King of
Wessex, silver penny, *circa* AD
887-99 £1,400 ($3,360)

Victoria, pattern five-pounds
1839 £5,700 ($13,680)

From the collection of the late J. H. Barnes, sold in London on 26th June 1974

Coin Sales

By T. G. Eden

This season has seen several very fine collections of coins passing through the saleroom representing every field in numismatics, at a time when prices have risen dramatically over a relatively short period. Probably the season's most interesting sale was the collection of Continental coins and medals sold on 12th June, which had been uncovered quite by chance in the owner's woodshed. Among the coins were many important Italian pieces of the sixteenth and seventeenth centuries including a ducatone of Bologna, of which only three other examples are known. This realised the record price for an Italian coin of £22,000 ($52,800).

On June 26th, the late J. H. Barnes' collection of Roman and English gold coins was sold and a record price of £20,000 ($48,000) was established for an English gold coin, a sovereign of Henry VII. In fact, it was during Henry's reign that the 'Sovereign' was first introduced as a coin denomination and very few examples remain in private hands. Moreover the sale, as a whole, which totalled £471,556 set a record for any coin sale held in London.

It has been many years since a specialised sale of Renaissance medals has been held, but in May, Sotheby & Co. A.G. Zürich, sold a comprehensive collection which aroused wide interest. A very beautiful bronze portrait medal of Giovanni Pico della Mirandola by Niccoló Fiorentino, considered the only contemporary casting (circa 1500) in existence, fetched 65,000 SFR (£9,286; $22,286). Some fine ancient coins were also sold in Zürich and included a silver medallion of the Emperor Constans (A.D. 337-350). Roman medallions are all great rarities since they were only struck in small quantities for presentation purposes; consequently, all known examples are very well documented in reference books. This piece, however, came to light quite recently without any known provenance and clearly caused a great deal of comment, resulting in a record price of 55,000 SFR (£7,857; $18,857).

From this season's results, as shown by strong prices and higher attendance in the saleroom, it is obvious that numismatics are attracting more interest from both collectors and investors.

Roman aureus of Domitian (81-96AD) £6,400 ($15,360)

Roman aureus of Septimius Severus (193-211AD) £8,200 ($19,680)

Roman aureus of Tetricus I (270-273AD) £9,500 ($22,800)

Ancient British stater of Verica, King of the Atrebates tribe £2,600 ($6,240)

Gaulish stater of Criciru, King of the Suessiones tribe £1,150 ($2,760)

Ancient British stater of Tasciovanus, King of the Catuvellauni tribe £2,000 ($4,800)

From the collection of the late J. H. Barnes, sold in London, 26th June, 1974

COINS AND MEDALS

1. Italy, Bologna, Gregory XIII (1572–85), ducatone, year VIII £22,000 ($52,800)
2. Essen, Anna Salome (1646–88), thaler, 1660 £14,000 ($33,600)
3. Italy, Modena, Alfonso IV (1658–62), ducatone, 1659 £16,000 ($38,400)
4. Bronze portrait medal of Pietro-Maria Rossi, Count of San-Secondo, fifteenth century £700 ($1,580)
5. Silver portrait medal of Christian V of Denmark and Charlotte Amalia, 1675 £1,400 ($3,360)
From the collection of Continental coins and medals sold in London on 12th June 1974

COINS AND MEDALS

1. Anglo-Gallic, Edward the Black Prince (1355-75), Hardi d'or London £3,000 ($7,200). 15.V.74

2. Scotland, Mary (1542-1567), testoon London £1,700 ($4,080). 15.V.74

3. Anglo-Gallic, Henry VI (1422-1436), angelot London £3,400 ($8,160). 15.V.74

4. Denmark, Christian VI, ducat, 1730 from the wreck of the Danish frigate 'Wendela' (lost 1737) London £680 ($1,632). 8.XI.73

5. Egypt, Ptolemy IV (221-204BC), octodrachm New York $9,000 (£3,750). 13.III.74

6. Rhodes, tetradrachm, *circa* 360BC London £4,500 ($10,800). 15.V.74

7. U.S.A., Eagle, 1799, trial striking in copper London £1,800 ($4,320). 14.XII.73

304 ORDERS, MEDALS AND DECORATIONS

The Imperial Russian Order of St Alexander-Nevesky, awarded to Peter Alexeievich Moritz, Private Secretary to Empress Maria Alexandrovna and Privy Councillor to Czar Alexander II
London £5,500 ($13,200). 5.VII.74

A Victoria Cross group for the Great War (1914-18) awarded to Captain E. D. Bellew, 7th Canadian Infantry
London £6,000 ($14,400). 5.VII.74

Clocks, Watches and Scientific Instruments

A gilt-metal planetarium clock by Thouverez
signed *Thouverez à Paris Année 1797*,
height 530 mm
London £10,000 ($24,000). 24. VI. 74
From the collection of Major A. Heathcote

GEORGE GRAHAM No 272   A small ebony-veneered quarter-repeating bracket timepiece, the 4¾-inch dial signed *Graham London* and with pendulum aperture, mask and leaf lower spandrels and pendulum adjustment and strike/silent dials in the upper corners, the movement with latched dial and plates, ringed pillars, pull quarter repeat, chain fusees and lenticular pendulum bob, the similarly signed backplate numbered 272, height 10in
London £36,000 ($86,400). 18.III.74
On Thomas Tompion's death in 1713 George Graham, his partner and nephew by marriage, succeeded to his business and continued his series of numbers

THOMAS TOMPION No 131   A grande sonnerie walnut longcase clock, the three-train movement with a 10-inch dial signed *Tho Tompion Londini fecit,* contained in a burr-walnut case, both movement and case numbered 131, height 7ft 1 in. London £30,000 ($72,000). 28.VI.74
Thomas Tompion, 1639-1713, became a Brother in the Clockmakers' Company in 1671. In 1703 he was elected Master of the Clockmakers' Company, began numbering clocks between 1680 and 1685 and it is reasonable to place this example between 1685 and 1695.
Right   JOHN KNIBB   A month olivewood parquetry longcase clock, the 10-inch dial signed *John Knibb Oxon fecit,* contained in an olivewood and walnut case, height 6ft 7½in. London £22,500 ($54,000). 28.VI.74
John Knibb, 1650-1722, younger brother of Joseph to whom he was apprenticed in about 1664, took charge of the Oxford business when Joseph moved to London and became a Freeman in 1673

1. A mahogany 'lighthouse' clock by Simon Willard, Roxbury, Mass., *c*.1825, 29in $20,000 (£8,333) 26.I.74.
2. A George II mahogany wheel barometer attributed to John Bradburn and Justin Vulliamy, with hygrometer and thermometer, 4ft 2in £5,400 ($12,960) 28.VI.74.
3. A George III mahogany wheel barometer, signed *Whitehurst, Derby*, 3ft 6¾in £3,600 ($8,640) 28.VI.74.
4. A Federal mahogany shelf clock by Simon Willard, Grafton, Mass., *c*. 1795, the dial inscribed *Simon Willard, Grafton 40*, above an oval inscribed *For Samuel Fiske, Roxbury*, 34½in $16,000 (£6,666) 17.XI.73. **5.** An English gilt-metal carriage clock, the 4-inch dial signed *James McCabe. Royal Exchange London 3180*, probably *c*. 1860, 8½in £3,500 ($8,750) 8.IV.74. **6.** A gold and agate English *nécessaire*, the whole surmounted by a gilt metal verge watch No. 1324 by Robert Sellers of London, *c*. 1760, 5½in SF39,000 (£5,200; $12,480) 16.XI.73. **7.** An Art Deco lapis lazuli, jade and onyx desk clock set with diamonds by Black, Starr and Frost, New York, *c*. 1925, 7¾in $17,000 (£7,083) 29.V.74. **8.** An English brass and ormolu skeleton clock, the white enamel dial inscribed *Jeffreys & Gilbert*, late 19th century, 13½in £600 ($1,440) 19.XII.73. **9.** A walnut quarter-repeating bracket timepiece, the 6-inch dial signed *Joseph Knibb, London*, the backplate signed *Joseph Knibb Londini fecit*, 12in £11,000 ($26,400) 18.III.74. **10.** A veneered ebony quarter-repeating bracket clock, the 4½ inch dial signed *Thomas Tompion Londini Fecit*, the similarly signed backplate numbered 225, *c*. 1700, 9½in £27,000 ($64,800) 18.III.74. **11.** A silver-mounted ebony quarter-repeating bracket clock, the 4-inch dial signed *Wm. Webster Exchange Ally*, 9in £21,000 ($50,400) 18.III.74.

CLOCKS

From left to right

A walnut marquetry longcase clock, the 10-inch dial signed *John Wise Londini Fecit,* height 6ft 9½in London £4,800 ($11,520). 18.III.74

A Federal inlaid mahogany longcase clock by Simon Willard, Roxbury, Massachussetts, the dial inscribed with maker's name, *No. 1551* and *Warranted for Mr T. and J. Brown,* the interior of the door affixed with the label of Simon Willard and the original bill of sale dated November 4, 1799, height 7ft 2in   New York $10,000 (£4,166). 26.I.74

A mid-eighteenth-century Dutch automaton longcase clock, the dial signed *Jan Henkels Amsterdam,* height 8ft 1½in London £3,800 ($9,120). 15.X.73 From the collection of the Rt Hon Lord Hollenden

A mahogany month longcase regulator, the 12-inch circular silvered dial signed *John Moore and Sons, Clerkenwell, London,* also signed on a bracket at the right hand side of the movement supporting the winding arbor *THIS REGULATOR Made By John Moore and Sons, Clerkenwell, London Feby. 1835. No. 9921,* the plinth faced with an applied carved coat of arms of Heathcote impaling Perceval (for Sir William Heathcote, 5th Baronet), height 6ft 9in London £5,500 ($13,200). 20.V.74

A William and Mary marquetry month longcase clock, the 11-inch dial signed *Jeremie Gazuet Londini fecit,* height 6ft 8½in. London £3,600 ($8,640). 4.II.74

From left to right
Above
A gold-cased detached lever watch by Thomas Cummins No. 4-25, hallmarked 1824, diameter 55 mm
London £4,600 ($11,040). 18.III.74

A gold quarter striking keyless lever clockwatch, signed *Dent au Brassus No. 21962*, diameter 56 mm
Zürich SF19,000 (£2,530; $6,072). 16.XI.73

Centre
BREGUET NO. 124
A gold-cased perpetuelle or self winding watch, with quarter repeating and calendar, subsidiary dial for seconds, with apertures for the day of the week and for the phases and age of the moon, *circa* 1800, diameter 58 mm
London £7,800 ($18,720) 18.III.74.

SYLVAN MAIRET NO. 114
A slim gold cased cylinder watch, mid-nineteenth century, diameter 47 mm
London £1,100 ($2,640). 24.VI.74

Below
BREGUET NO. 4514. A brass cased chronometer deck watch, diameter 64 mm
London £4,200 ($10,080). 18.III.74.

A gold, enamel and pearl-set keyless lever watch, with minute repeating, perpetual calendar and chronograph, diameter 56 mm
Zürich SF54,000 (£7,200; $17,280). 16.XI.73
From the collection of Sam Bloomfield Esq

EDOUARD JUVET, FLEURIER, NO.41607
A Swiss gold and enamel watch for the Oriental market, *circa* 1820, length 58 mm
New York $6,250 (£2,604).
30.X.73

A gilt metal and crystal cased cruciform verge watch by Henry Gebart, *circa* 1620, length 65 mm
London £7,000 ($16,800).
24.VI.74

JAMES COX, LONDON
A gold and enamel watch with revolving paste-set bezel and with *scènes galantes*, *circa* 1770, diameter 50 mm
New York $12,000 (£5,000).
29.V.74

A gold and enamel watch and fob by George Prior of London, the case enamelled with a naval battle scene, the handle with a band of rubies and an emerald, the fob with small plaques of naval scenes, 1818
Los Angeles $7,500 (£3,125). 4.II.74
From the collection of George Maximoff Esq

Above right
A repoussé gold pair cased quarter repeating verge watch and chatelaine by Cabrier of London, *circa* 1730, length 190 mm
Zürich SF39,000 (£5,200; $12,480). 16.XI.73

312 SCIENTIFIC INSTRUMENTS

A gilt-metal box compendium by Le Sieur du Ferrier, signed and dated 1611, 95mm by 80mm
London £4,000 ($9,600). 24.VI.74

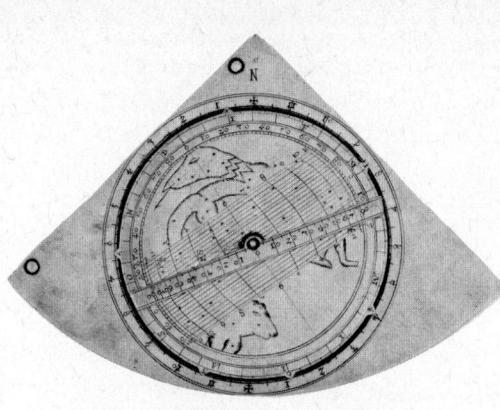

A brass quadrant by John Prujean, seventeenth century, radius 108 mm
London £1,200 ($2,880). 10.XII.73

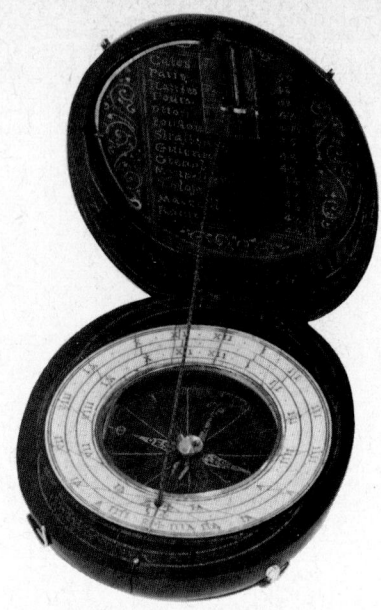

An oval lignum vitae pocket sundial, *circa* 1600, 74 mm by 60 mm
London £800 ($1,920). 24.VI.74

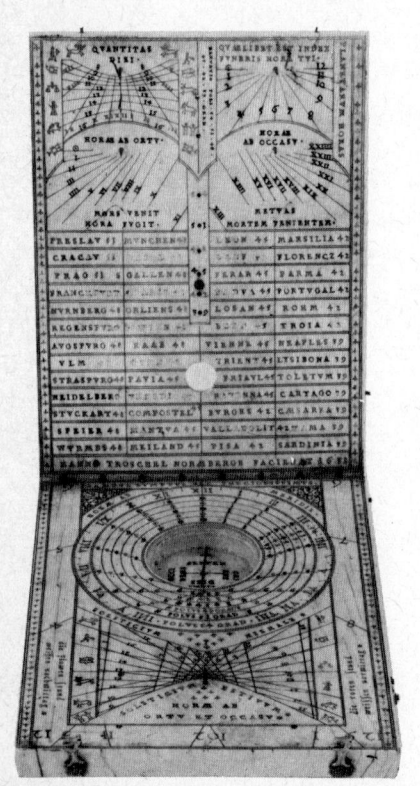

An ivory tablet dial by Hans Troschel of Nuremberg, 1631, 157 mm by 112 mm
London £3,800 ($9,120). 24.VI.74

A gilt metal nocturnal by Ioannes Valen dated 1577, diameter 102 mm
London £2,100 ($5,040). 15.X.73

Antiquities, Islamic, Tibetan, Nepalese and Primitive Works of Art

A Benin bronze head of an oba, the crown of the head with a hole for the receipt of an ivory tusk, Nigeria, height 13⅜in
London £28,000 ($67,200). 8.VII.74

A Benin bronze altar stand composed of a Queen Mother flanked by two rows of four female attendants standing on a rectangular, hollow platform and surrounding a rectangular opening, Nigeria, 14in by 10⅞in London £20,000 ($48,000). 8.VII.74

A Benin bronze figure of a flute player with finely cast features, Nigeria, height 25in
London £185,000 ($444,000). 8.VII.74
From the collection of the late R. Sturgis Ingersoll

316 AFRICAN ART

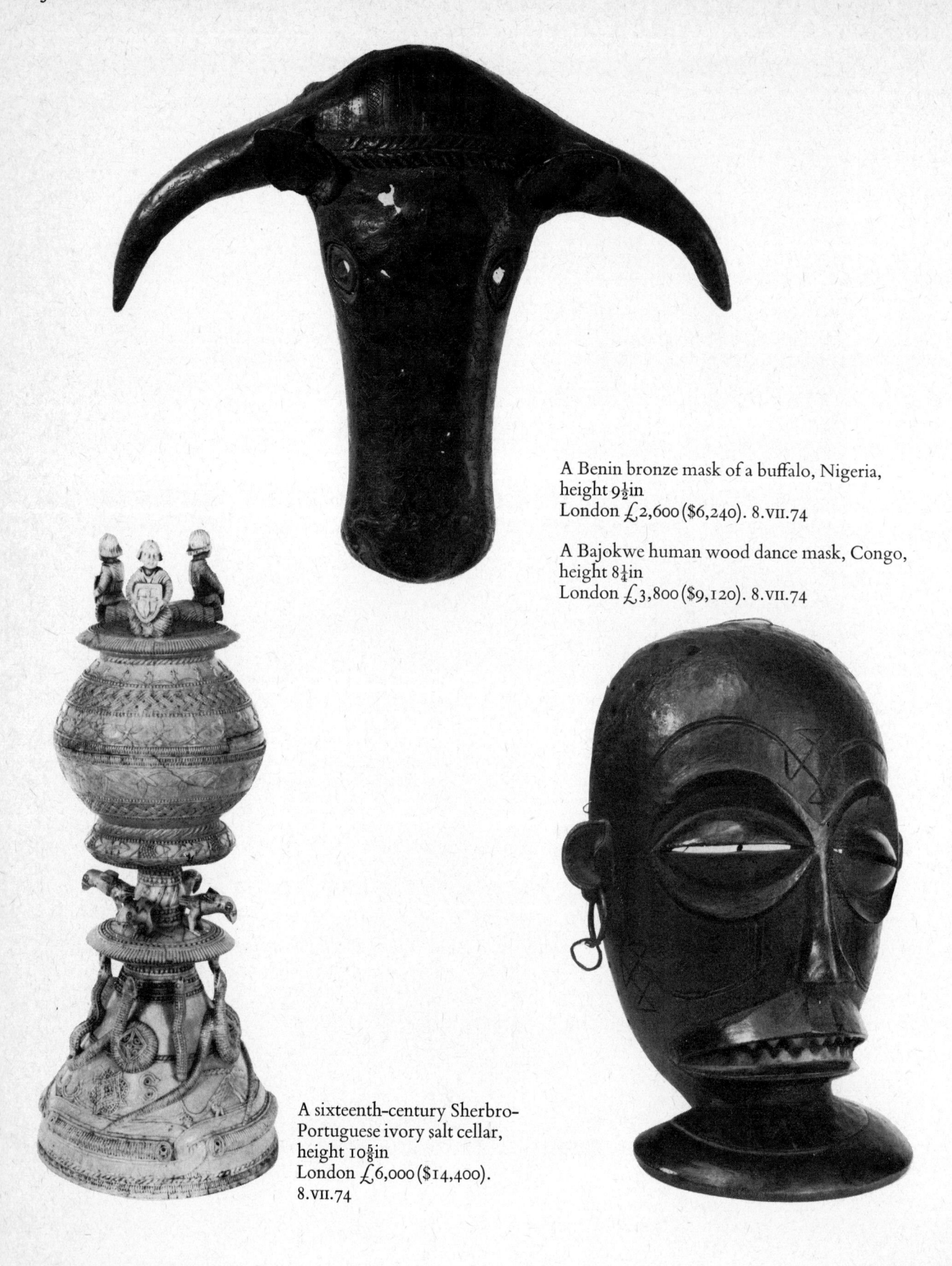

A Benin bronze mask of a buffalo, Nigeria,
height 9½in
London £2,600 ($6,240). 8.VII.74

A Bajokwe human wood dance mask, Congo,
height 8¼in
London £3,800 ($9,120). 8.VII.74

A sixteenth-century Sherbro-
Portuguese ivory salt cellar,
height 10⅝in
London £6,000 ($14,400).
8.VII.74

A Tlingit wood *potlach* ladle, length 23½in
London £6,500 ($15,600). 8.VII.74

A Central Mexican stone mask,
Teotihuacan III-IV, Classic, *circa* AD
250–750, height 5in
New York $10,000 (£4,167). 23.IV.74
Right
A Maori carved wood 'presents' box,
New Zealand, height 6in
London £7,200 ($17,280). 8.VII.74

Right
A Salish wood spindle
whorl, Southern Coast of
British Columbia, diameter
8⅝in
New York $36,000 (£15,000).
14.XI.73
Left
A Cree Indian chief's regalia,
height 61in
London £5,200 ($12,480).
8.VII.74

318 ISLAMIC WORKS OF ART

One of three late fifteenth-century Persian mosaic tile panels, Timurid, dated 885 H. (1480–1481), height 33¼in
New York $28,000 (£11,667). 7.XII.73
From the collection of the Hagop Kevorkian Fund

ISLAMIC WORKS OF ART 319

A late twelfth/early thirteenth-century Iranian pottery bowl, probably Rayy or Kashan, diameter 8 $\frac{1}{16}$ in
New York $54,000 (£22,500). 4.v.74
From the collection of Dr and Mrs Fred Olsen

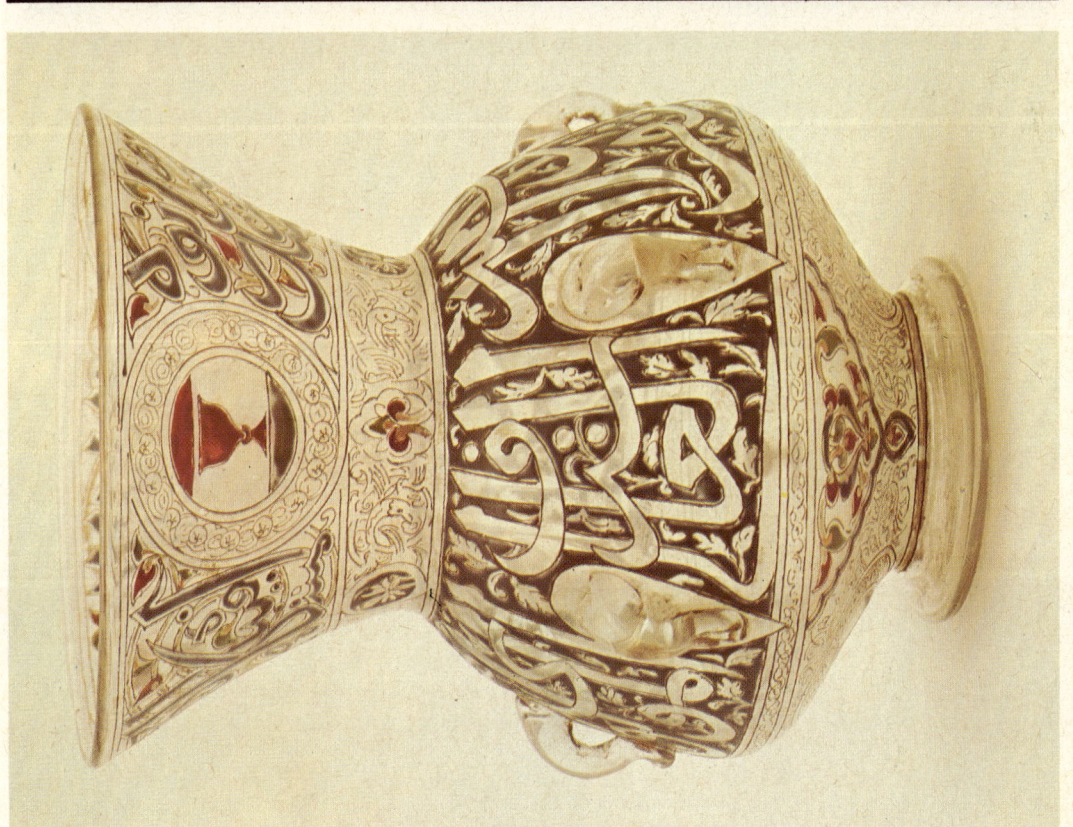

A fourteenth-century Mamluk enamelled glass lamp, Damascus or Aleppo, height 11 $\frac{5}{16}$ in
New York $38,000 (£15,833). 4.v.74
From the collection of the Hagop Kavorkian Fund

320 TIBETAN AND NEPALESE WORKS OF ART

Left
A Sino-Tibetan gilt bronze figure of Dhyanibuddha Amitayus, *circa* 1700, height 16 1/16 in
New York $6,750 (£2,813). 28.XI.73

Right
An early Nepalese bronze figure of Tara, tenth/twelfth century, height 8 5/16 in
New York $19,000 (£7,917). 28.XI.73

Below left
A fifteenth-century Nepalese Pata depicting the Mandala of a Tantric deity, 29¾in by 50in
London £5,200 ($12,480). 29.IV.74

Below right
A fifteenth-century Tibetan gilt-bronze figure of the Dhyanibodhisattva Maitreya, height 17in
London £3,500 ($8,400). 29.IV.74

An Egyptian bronze figure of a cat, 26th Dynasty, 664–525 BC, height 14¾in
New York $50,000 (£20,833). 4.v.74
From the collection of the late R. Sturgis Ingersoll

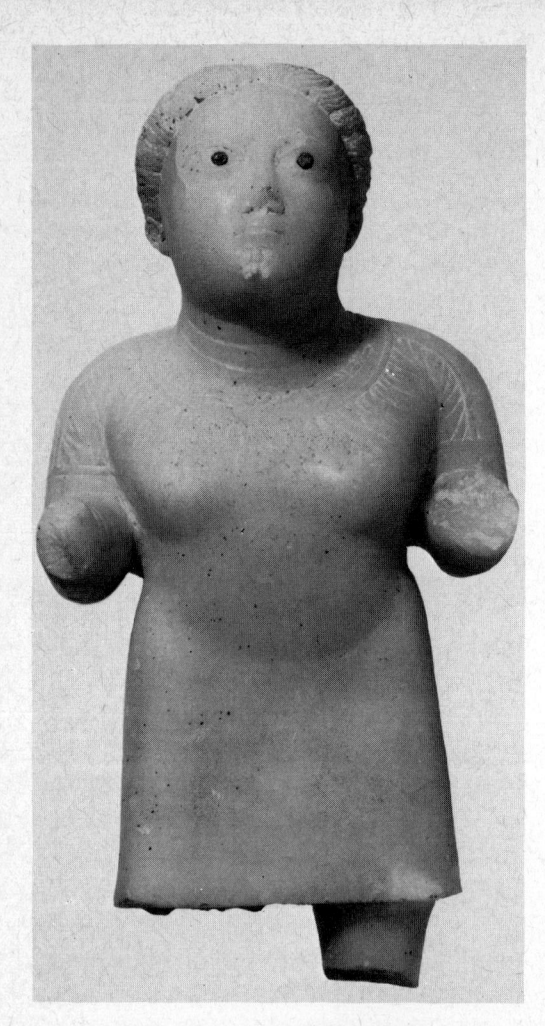

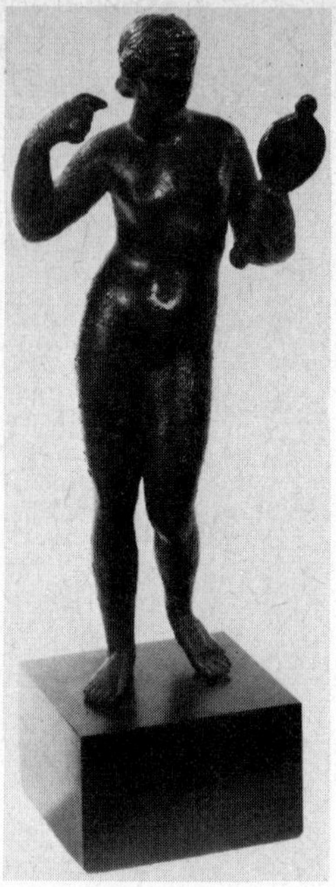

Above: from left to right
A South Arabian alabaster female figure, *circa* first century
BC/first century AD, height 16½in   London £6,000 ($14,400). 3.XII.73
From the collection of Mrs T. W. Hague
An Egyptian wood Ushabti figure, New Kingdom, reign
of Horemhab/Rameses II, 1332–1224 BC, height 9⅝in
New York $8,500 (£3,542). 4.V.74
A Roman bronze figure of Aphrodite, *circa* second century AD,
height 6in   London £4,000 ($9,600). 9.VII.74
From the collection of H. J. P. Bomford Esq

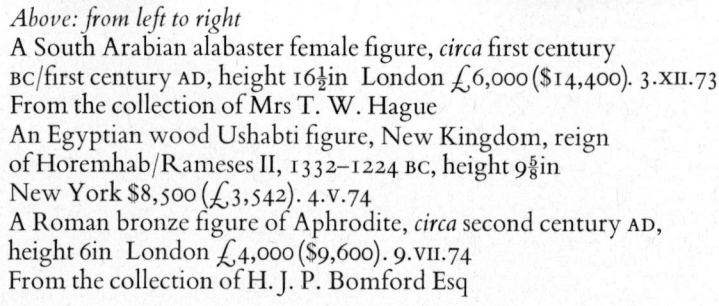

A Roman bronze bust of Hermes, *circa* third century AD, height 8⅜in   London £4,600 ($11,040). 9.VII.74

An Egyptian pink granite head of a high official, New Kingdom, height 12½in   London £5,000 ($12,000). 3.XII.73
From the collection of John Huston Esq

An Egyptian bronze figure of Bastet, Late Period, height 7in
London £1,800 ($4,320). 3.XII.73
From the collection of H. J. P. Bomford Esq

A large Egyptian bronze head of a cat, Late Period, height 8⅛in
London £5,200 ($12,480). 9.VII.74
From the collection of His Grace the Duke of Northumberland, KG, TD, FRS

A Chalcidian black-figure pottery amphora by the Phineus painter, sixth century BC, height 10⅞in
London £3,200 ($7,680). 9.VII.74

An Attic black-figure pottery amphora from the Leagros Group, *circa* 515 BC, height 17in
London £2,100 ($5,040). 9.VII.74

An Apulian pottery volute-krater, mid-fourth century BC
New York $6,000 (£2,500). 4.V.74
From the collection of James Billman Esq

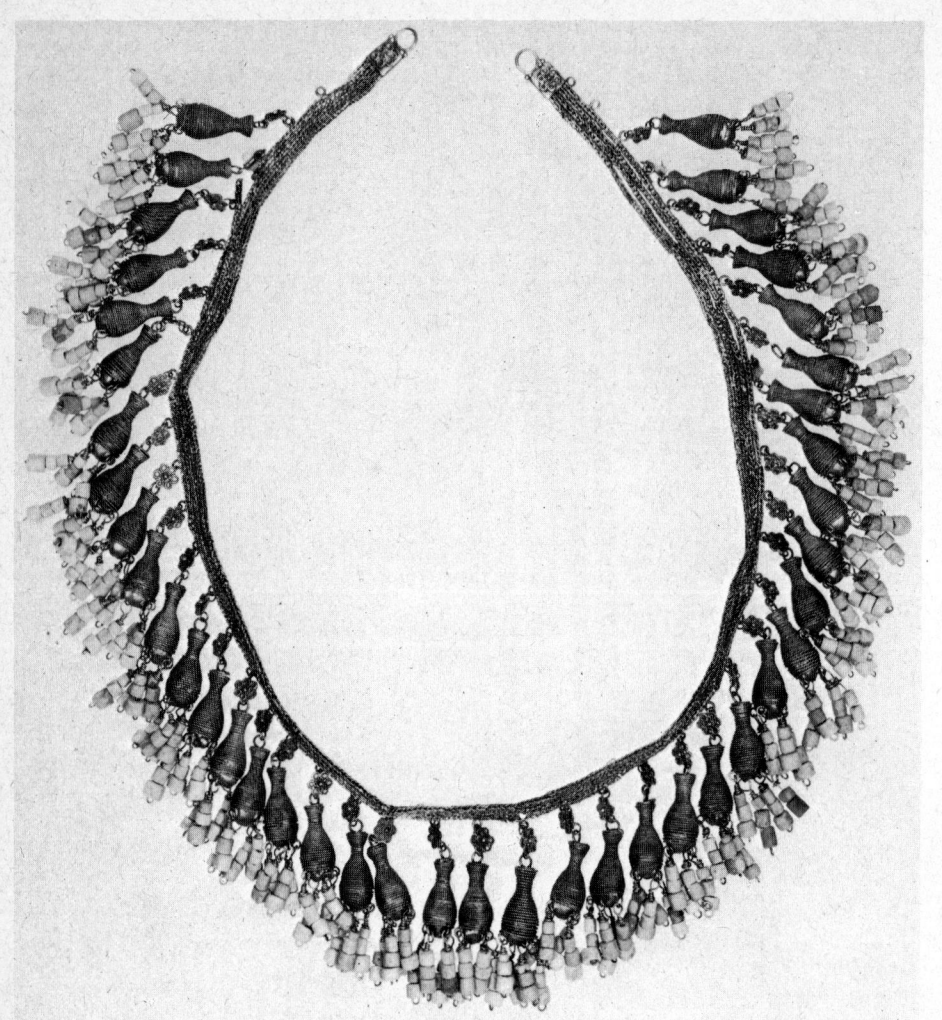

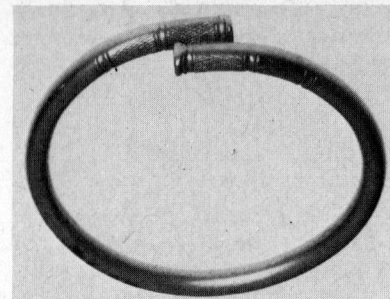

324 ANTIQUITIES

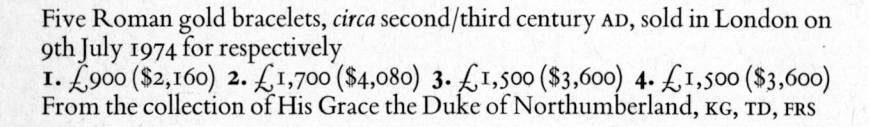

A Hellenistic gold necklace, Greece or Asia Minor, third/second century BC
London £3,800 ($9,120). 9.VII.74
From the collection of H. J. P. Bomford Esq

Five Roman gold bracelets, *circa* second/third century AD, sold in London on
9th July 1974 for respectively
1. £900 ($2,160) 2. £1,700 ($4,080) 3. £1,500 ($3,600) 4. £1,500 ($3,600)
From the collection of His Grace the Duke of Northumberland, KG, TD, FRS

A Roman fragmentary marble group, *circa* first century AD, 18¼in by 14¾in. £9,000 ($21,600)

A Hellenistic marble torso of a youth, *circa* second century BC, height 14½in. £4,000 ($9,600)
The objects illustrated on this page were in the collection of Gwen, Lady Melchett, sold in London on 9th July 1974

Fig 1 Pedestal table, the top formed by a piece of petrified wood from the collection of Charles I, mounted in steel and gilt-bronze in the Louis XVI style by F. Dammanock in 1770. After passing through the collections of the Empress Maria Theresa and Queen Marie-Antoinette it appeared at the Watson Taylor sale at Erlestoke Park in 1832 when it was sold for £115 (Musée de Versailles)

French Furniture in the Saleroom and outside, 1800-1914

By Sir Francis Watson

Amongst the numerous visitors to Erlestoke Park near Devizes during the fortnight's viewing which preceded the sale of its contents in the summer of 1832, was that great connoisseur and collector, William Beckford. He expressed the view that both the house and its contents were far more magnificent than those dispersed at his own Fonthill sale exactly a decade earlier, which had been certainly the grandest sale of the 1820s. He was, however, probably speaking with his tongue in his cheek as he often did. For, in the event, the twenty-nine day sale, starting on July 9th, did nothing to disprove the view expressed at the end of the earlier article,[1] that the years around 1830 seemed to mark a watershed in the taste for collecting eighteenth-century French furniture and the decorative arts. The occasion was the final dispersal of the collection of George Watson Taylor, whose magnificent French royal furniture sold from his Cavendish Square house in 1825 has already been discussed[2]. The sale was made necessary by the somewhat sensational failure of the owner with liabilities of nearly half a million pounds. But although the sale attracted a great deal of public attention on this account (the inn keepers at Devizes and Salisbury ran special coaches to and from Erlestoke) and in spite of the description of the furniture (by a connoisseur rather than in the auction catalogue) as 'of the most gorgeous kind, with silver fire-irons and chairs and sofas of burnished and matted gold', the prices achieved in 1832 were a good deal lower than those in the 1825 sale.

Even the splendid sale catalogue costing ten shillings, compiled by W. H. Pyne of *Walnuts and Wine* celebrity and said to be the most bulky ever produced, did not prevent disappointing results. A pair of side tables with magnificent tops of mosaic in the Florentine manner but probably made at the Gobelins factory were expected to make two thousand guineas but were in fact knocked down for only 580 guineas to Hume, the dealer who had sold them to Watson Taylor certainly for a considerably higher price. The high spot of the sale, so far as French furniture was concerned, was a table with a top of fossilised wood which had belonged to Marie-Antoinette at the Petit Trianon[3] (Fig 1). This formed lot 22 on the twelfth day of the sale and was bought by the dealer Baldock on behalf of Lord Normanton for £115, a respectable rather than a spectacular price. Lot 24 on the same day was that rare thing a *vaisseau à mat* of blue and green Sèvres porcelain (conceivably the example now in the Wallace Collection) which was also bought by Baldock for forty-two guineas, again not a special price.

1 See *Art at Auction* 1972-73, p 343
2 Ibid, p 341 ff
3 Ibid, p 343

But if these prices were not as remarkable as those of the previous two decades it was to be almost a generation before a piece of Louis XVI furniture sold at an English auction was to fetch a price comparable with that paid by Baldock for the Marie-Antoinette table. More typical of the atmosphere of the auction rooms of the period was the *bonheur-du-jour* inlaid with Sèvres porcelain attributed to Riesener and therefore presumably of fine quality, which went for a mere £5.10.0 at the Brook Greville sale in 1836, and the two drop-front secretaires of black and gold lacquer from Fonthill which fetched only eleven guineas at the Acraman sale in August 1842. These had been lots 1,520 and 1,521 in the 1823 sale when they fetched over sixty pounds for the pair.

The only type of French furniture which continued to attract some interest at auction was that made in the style of André-Charles Boulle (usually spelled with hideous inaccuracy 'Buhl' at this period). At the Duke of Sussex's sale at Christie's in 1843 a pair of Boulle commodes fetched £136.10.0 and was carried off to Paris where the taste for such furniture was even more pronounced than here. In the previous year in a sale at Christie's of furniture belonging to a Dr Petit of Paris, a large Boulle armoire had indeed been bought in at the high price of 150 guineas for it had been expected to fetch considerably more.

Even at the Strawberry Hill sale in 1842 which attracted enormous public interest, French furniture brought notably low prices, the best being forty guineas paid for a Boulle *coffre de marriage* on its stand. This was substantially less than the price of the modern ebony cabinet designed by Edward Edwards and inlaid with seventeen of Lady Diana Beauclerk's 'incomparable masterpieces in sootwater' which sold for £53.11.0, but a great deal more than a drop-front secretaire, probably by Topino, which formed lot 86. This was offered on the eleventh day and remained unsold. A pair of *encoignures* of a similar character did little better, reaching only thirteen guineas. Even an occasional table with a top inset with a plaque of Sèvres porcelain only fetched twenty-eight guineas. Yet within less than five years the banker Charles Mills was to begin forming the remarkable assemblage of Sèvres porcelain and Sèvres mounted furniture ('Severs' he pronounced it in the English fashion of the day) which was eventually to become the Hillingdon collection and the greater part of which now fills two large galleries of the Metropolitan Museum. Mills's activities were certainly contributory to the rise in price of French furniture with porcelain inlays which was a feature of the saleroom during the period from 1850 to 1870.

Yet there is something a little paradoxical about this English reaction against French eighteenth-century furniture in the 1830s, for the coming of Louis-Philippe to the French throne in 1830 marked a swing of taste in precisely the opposite direction in Paris. Ever since the Revolution the art of the *ancien régime* had been quite out of fashion. Even a sovereign so deeply embedded in the past glories of the Bourbon dynasty as Charles X had not attempted to refurnish the Tuileries in a *dix-huitième* style, but retained the Napoleonic decoration his brother had found there at the Restoration. Indeed the characteristic furniture of his reign was a continuation and simplification of the furniture of the hated Napoleonic Empire.

It is to Louis-Philippe, son of the man who had voted the death of Louis XVI, that we owe the saving of Versailles from ruin and a revival of interest in the eighteenth-century. By the mid-1830s *toilettes Pompadour* (i.e. lace draped toilet-tables) had become the height of fashion in Paris, and amongst the most sought-after furnishing materials of the period were *moiré Pompadour* and *barège Pompadour*. It is true that with furniture this veering of taste tended to take the form of a preference for pastiches to originals, as exemplified by the furniture made by Grohe for the duc d'Aumale's use at Chantilly or those elaborately curvilinear pieces inset with porcelain medallions painted with the beauties of the court of Marie-Antoinette or even those of Louis XIV's day. The elder Monbro combined the functions of furniture-maker with that of a dealer in antique furniture and we can safely suppose that the pastiches of Louis XVI furniture he supplied to the Crown were far more costly than the genuine eighteenth-century furniture he sold at the same time. Balzac, himself a passionate art collector if sadly lacking in flair, gives the best descriptions of the interiors of the period. Mme Marneffe's *petit hôtel* in the *rue Barbet-de-Jouy* in *La Cousine Bette* (published in 1846 but set a little earlier) was lit by '*des candelabres . . . création genre Pompadour*' and chandeliers *surmoulé* on Louis XIV models for economy. Although the eponymous hero of *Le Cousin Pons* (1844) complains that the snuff boxes and soft-paste Sèvres porcelain that he used to buy for ten francs during his walks around Paris in the years between 1811 and 1816 now cost 1,200 francs and that, as an impoverished musician, he can no longer afford '*un meuble de Riesener*' which now '*vaut de trois à quatre mille francs*', it is not easy to find examples at such high prices in the salerooms of the day in France. It is true that it was at just this period that Prince de Beauveau paid 1,500 francs for the famous black and gold lacquer writing table made by Weisweiler and supplied by Daguerre for Marie-Antoinette's use at Saint-Cloud in 1784 (now in the Louvre); but he bought it from a dealer on the *quai Voltaire* and not in the salerooms. The prince, however, was an exceptional collector, a man with almost as much flair as the fictional Sylvan Pons. At the Fournier sale in 1831 he had had the discernment to acquire for 1,200 francs the perfume burner by Gouthière illustrated in the previous article[4]. At the posthumous sale of his collection in 1865 Lord Hertford had to pay 31,000 francs for it, whilst the Empress Eugénie had to give over 50,000 francs for the Weisweiler table on the same occasion.

The rise in price of these two objects within three decades is indicative of the general trend of taste in these years, but at the start the rise in price was very slow, especially in England. There was hardly any sign of a movement in the French furniture market at the forty-day Stowe sale of 1848 although this was not only what Beckford used to call a 'high-puff' sale, but gained great publicity (as the Erlestoke sale had done) from the sensational bankruptcy of the Duke of Buckingham which had made the sale necessary. Much of the Duke's finest furniture was, it is true, Italian or German mixed with some very splashy modern stuff. However one of the two finest Louis XIV Boulle *armoires* in the Wallace Collection was lot 1,021 in the sale and was bought by Redfern for the fourth Marquis of Hertford for £210, hardly more than they would have fetched thirty years earlier. Other types of French furniture still brought very little. The very remarkable Louis XV *régulateur* clock (now in the Wallace Collection) with an elaborate astronomical mechanism by Stollewerck which had been made for Jean-Paris Duvernay, marquis de Monmartel (the *fermier* who did more than anyone to further Mme de Pompadour's career) fetched no more than fifty-one guineas (lot 1,153) and a handsome Louis XV *bureau plât* sold for as little as thirty-four guineas (lot 1,355) though Lord Hertford spent 175 guineas on a Boulle writing table of similar character.

Some years ago an anonymous writer in the *Times Literary Supplement* in the course of an intelligent and highly informed article, 'The Taste of Angels', dealing with the fluctuations in

4 Ibid, p 333, Fig 2

the taste for French *dix-huitième* art, suggested that the climacteric moment of its return into fashion came in 1862 at the two sales of the contents of the Earl of Pembroke's Paris house in the *Place Vendôme* at the Hotel Drouot in June 1862. On that occasion a Boulle clock sold for 25,000 francs, a Louis XV chandelier for 23,000 francs, a Boulle *console* 18,000 francs and so on. It would seem, however that the key moment really occurred over a decade earlier though the seller, the actual instrument of change, was the same.

Robert, Earl of Pembroke, sometimes referred to as the 'wicked' Earl, is almost the first of his line to remain unmentioned in the *D.N.B.* In character and tastes he somewhat resembled the fourth Lord Hertford (with some admixture of the third Marquis's taste for dissipation), a man of very considerable intellectual powers and ability who preferred to devote his life and, after inheriting the Earldom in 1827, his very considerable fortune to art collecting, rather than to politics or sport, the more usual preoccupations of the English aristocracy in the mid-nineteenth century. He resembled the 4th Marquis of Hertford too in preferring life in Paris rather than London and moved there permanently about 1850. Unfortunately all too little is known about his tastes and how he assembled his remarkable collection of French eighteenth-century art but he probably began buying around 1827, exactly the year in which Lord Hertford purchased his first two Watteaus.

The first Pembroke sale was held in his house at 7 Carlton House Terrace from 5th May to 10th May 1851. At this sale Lord Hertford made extensive purchases through his London agent Mawson. Admittedly much of what he bought was Boulle furniture, notably a sarcophagus-shaped Louis XIV commode (lot 236) for which he paid £220. But the high-spot of the sale was a Sèvres-mounted secretaire by Carlin (lot 434) for which Lord Hertford paid the hitherto unprecedented price of 650 guineas (Fig 2). That he had to pay 29,700 francs for a very similar secretaire which he bought at the Villafranca sale in Paris on 21th April 1870 (when he was within three months of his death) is an indication of the new trend of prices. Another feature of the Pembroke sale is the high price paid for French decorative objects other than furniture. Lord Hertford paid 170 guineas for a single pair of gilt-bronze candelabra of Louis XVI design (lot 227) and an almost equally high price for another pair (lot 250).

It was the sudden rise in value of the Sèvres-mounted piece which was the distinctive feature of this sale. The following year the same buyer acquired in Paris another and simpler *bureau-de-dame,* mounted with Sèvres plaques and stamped by Weisweiler, and had to pay 10,000 francs for it; but this was bought from a dealer and not in the salerooms. Four years later at the William Angerstein sale on 12th May, Mawson, acting for Lord Hertford, gave 400 guineas for a much simpler secretaire with Sèvres plaques dated 1783 but with no maker's stamp, and on 24th June 1859 in an anonymous sale at Christie's the same agent had to pay over £1,200 for a much inferior secretaire of the same character stamped by Schumann. A decade later he paid £2,100 outside the auction room for a small *table à pupitre* by Carlin mounted with Sèvres porcelain plaques, but this was one of the great masterpieces of the genre.

Nevertheless the steeply rising character of the graph of prices for this type of furniture is distinctly outlined and may perhaps be regarded as culminating about ten years later in baron Edmond de Rothschild's purchase in the mid-1870s (again outside the salerooms) of the famous commode inset with large Sèvres plaques after Watteau which the *marchand-mercier* Poirier had supplied to Mme du Barry in August 1772 for 9,750 *livres*. The price, as with the majority of Rothschild purchases of works of art, remained a closely guarded secret but in his *Causeries*

Fig 2 Drop-front secretaire mounted with plaques of Sèvres porcelain and stamped by Martin Carlin. This was purchased by Lord Hertford at the Earl of Pembroke sale in 1851 for the then unprecedented price of 650 guineas (Wallace Collection)

sur l'Art issued in 1878 Edmond Bonnaffé, a reliable witness little given to exaggeration, asserted that it cost the young banker 600,000 francs. Two years later the *Chronique des Arts* reported that the price had been nearer to 750,000 francs. Whichever source is closer to the truth it is perfectly clear that, having regard to the changing value of money, the price was far beyond anything that has been paid for any eighteenth-century French furniture in recent years even if we include the price of over half a million pounds sterling which the Louvre is rumoured to have paid last year for the two celebrated cabinets by Cressent formerly in the Ferdinand de Rothschild, Boni de Castellane and Sir Robert Abdy collections.

To mention here baron Edmond's purchases of the late 1870's is, however, to jump too far ahead in the story. Although other types of French furniture began to rise in price after 1850, none of it (not even Boulle furniture) rose at such an accelerating rate as Sèvres-mounted furniture. In 1846 a marquetry writing table said to have been made for Marie-Antoinette, sold by an anonymous nobleman at Christie's made no more than ninety-nine pounds and in the same year a secretaire with the same claim made a mere 600 francs in Paris. Nearly two decades would pass before such prices were greatly exceeded. It was not till five years after he had bought the little Sèvres-mounted *bonheur-du-jour* by Schumann that Lord Hertford paid a comparable price for a piece of pure *ébénisterie*. This was in 1863 at the James Evan Bailee sale of August 5th-8th, when Richard Wallace, acting on his father's behalf, bought a Louis XV *bureau plât* veneered with floral marquetry for 1,150 guineas. Even as late as 1868 Lord Hertford was still able to acquire for the comparatively modest price of 10,300 francs the truly magnificent *secrétaire à abattant* made by Riesener in 1784 for Marie-Antoinette's use at Trianon. This was lot 148 in the Henri Didier sale in Paris in June of that year.

Seating furniture hardly shows a different pattern. At Strawberry Hill a set of a Louis XV sofa and eight matching gilt armchairs upholstered with Aubusson tapestries sold for just £26.8.0 and another set of six armchairs brought merely eight guineas. A quarter of a century later such things were fetching very little more. The only notable price for chairs in these years was at the duc de Stacpole sale in Paris in March 1852 when a very remarkable set of chairs, sofas etc. made by Boulard, carved by the Vallois, and gilded by Chatard, delivered in August 1786 for Louis XVI cardroom at Fontainebleau, was sold for some 15,000 francs, a good deal less, of course, than the 1,500 *livres* it had originally cost.

The end of the 1860s finds us on the eve of a vast change in the history of French furniture in the salerooms. It has been necessary to tell the story of the previous forty years largely in terms of Lord Hertford's purchases simply because he was not only the major buyer in the auction rooms in those years until his death in 1870, but by far the wealthiest. His name sticks out from the marked sale catalogues of the period from amongst those of a multitude of long forgotten dealers. His only serious rivals, the almost equally wealthy Anatole Demidoff and the less wealthy but equally discerning Léopold Double, seem rarely to have bought their possessions at auction. Moreover the ambiguous, one-line descriptions of the sale catalogues of the period make identification almost impossible unless some subsidiary documentation survives, as it does in Lord Hertford's correspondence with his London agent Mawson or in a number of Richard Wallace's marked sale catalogues.

Lord Hertford died in August 1870 without apparently finding any truly worthy opponent as a collector of French furniture, though rivals existed in the field of painting and of Sèvres porcelain. For most of his lifetime the Rothschild family, whose members might have provided serious rivals, were interested in Medieval and Renaissance art rather than in that of the eighteenth century. One has only to compare baron James de Rothschild's extensive loans to the great *Musée Retrospectif* exhibition in 1865 with Lord Hertford's. But immediately after the latter's death five years later, his heir found himself in fierce competition with baron Adolphe de Rothschild for the two great chandeliers by Caffiéri, perhaps the most magnificent French *bronzes d'ameublement* in the world. They were in the possession of a dealer named Stein when they were offered to Wallace in November 1871 at a price of 150,000 francs. On the advice of a friend he was proposing to make a first offer of 80,000 francs (a high price for the period) when he learned that the baron was also negotiating for them and had recently paid 90,000 francs for a Cressent clock from Bordeaux (probably the version of the famous clock in the Wallace Collection which is now in the Wrightsman Collection). The final result was that Wallace had to pay 210,000 francs for the chandeliers, a purchase that almost anticipates baron Edmond's purchase of the Mme du Barry commode less than five years later. These two prices are indicative of the opening of a new era. French art of the eighteenth century had risen to the forefront of fashion amongst wealthy collectors. It is significant that the Goncourt brothers' *L'Art du Dix-huitième Siècle,* which was stimulated by what they considered the neglect shown by the French for the art of their immediate past, came out in book form only in 1880, the various essays having previously appeared as separate fascicules, the earliest in 1859. The writer in the *Times Literary Supplement* already quoted declared 'no one, unless he is a centenarian, can claim to remember a time when it (i.e. eighteenth-century art) was unfashionable'.

From 1870 onwards the story is one of more or less continually rising prices with occasional brief recessions (e.g. at the very end of the nineteenth century and during the 1930s when there were world-wide economic depressions). To recount the history of French furniture in the salerooms during the last hundred years with anything like the fullness it deserves would require a book rather than an article. Only a few outstanding sales can be highlighted. Fortunately during the 1870s and 1880s two collections of such outstanding importance that their sale gives tone and colour to the entire period, were dispersed at auction. They certainly exercised a marked influence not only on the taste of the day but of the succeeding decades down to the outbreak of the war in 1914. These were the sales of the contents of the palace of San Donato outside Florence and of Hamilton Palace.

Anatole Demidoff, Prince of San Donato, was a vastly rich Russian whose fortune derived from mineral resources in the Urals which had first been exploited by his grandfather, a liberated serf trained as a blacksmith. He married Princess Mathilde Bonaparte, sister of Napoleon III but his brutal behaviour quickly led to a separation after which the Tsar exiled him and ordered him to pay the princess an allowance commensurate with his wealth and her social position. Thereafter he occupied the palace and 'principality' of San Donato and the remainder of his life was governed by alternate bouts of hunting, dissipation and wildly extravagant art collecting. The contents of San Donato were so vast that it took four sales spread over the decade 1870 and 1880 to disperse them. The auctioneers were Pillet and Mannheim and the bulk of the French furniture was included in the first, a three-day sale held in March 1870, and the fourth sale which spread over six days at the end of March and early April of 1880. The first of these was one of the last sales at which Lord Hertford made purchases but it is questionable, in the political circumstances of France in that summer, whether his acquisitions reached Paris in time for him to see them before his death three months later. For one of the great Boulle *armoires* now at Hertford House he paid 11,100 francs.

Fig 3 Drop-fronted secretaire of black and gold lacquer made by J. H. Riesener in 1788 for Queen Marie-Antoinette's use at the Château de Saint-Cloud. When this appeared at the Hamilton Palace sale in 1882 it sold for 9,000 guineas. The matching commode sold at the same time for the same price (Metropolitan Museum of Art, New York)

Perhaps more surprising is the 46,500 francs he gave for the late Louis XIV mantel-clock known as *La Vénus à la Coquille*. An even higher price was fetched by a set of pieces comprising a Louis XVI commode, an upright secretaire and two matching corner-cupboards by Riesener, all veneered black and gold Japanese lacquer, though Lord Hertford did not buy them. These, as the catalogue remarked, certainly came from some French Royal palace. They were sold separately, but in the aggregate they cost the buyer 105,500 francs, an auction record at that date.

The six day sale was more remarkable for its *bronzes d'ameublement* than for its furniture though a magnificent Boulle marriage coffer claimed to have been made for the Grand Dauphin and its matching pair attained the price of nearly 75,000 francs each (the two only fetched £1,134 when they reappeared at Christie's with the Mortimer Schiff Collection in 1938). Amongst the furnishing bronzes at San Donato a pair of monumental *torchères* said to have been modelled by Falconet and made for Versailles, went for the astonishing price of 110,000 francs, a pair of granite vases with mounts by Forestier 66,000 francs, and a clock with a marble case attributed to Pigalle for 56,700 francs. Compared with these a *bureau-de-dame* certainly by B.V.R.B. which was lot 1,538 in the same sale and sold at 12,500 francs, seems chicken feed. But these were the days before Van Risamburgh had been 'discovered' and made fashionable.

The other great sale of the period was the dispersal of the contents of Hamilton Palace; made necessary by the undermining of the house by the Duke's own coal mines. It was perhaps the greatest auction sale of a single collection in modern times. Only the Spitzer sale can compare with it, or the dispersal of Mme Lelong's collection in 1903. The sale extended from 17th June to 20th July, 1882, consisted of seventeen daily sessions and the total obtained was £397,562, perhaps the equivalent of thirty to forty million pounds today (the Spitzer sale produced 9,000,000 francs for Medieval and Renaissance objects of art in 1895, and Mme Lelong's *dix-huitième* furniture and *objets d'art* £380,000). It embraced works of art of all sorts. The 10th Duke of Hamilton had married Beckford's daughter who inherited much of her father's final collections, whilst the 11th Duke, marrying a cousin of Napoleon III, lived for many years in Paris buying Renaissance objects and French furniture. Only a few of the high spots of the sale can be touched on here. Early on in the sale a secretaire, a commode and a small writing table by Riesener, all apparently matching and two not only signed (as distinct from being stamped) by Riesener in the marquetry, but bearing the mark of the *Garde Meuble de la Reine* (i.e. Marie-Antoinette), attained prices of £4,620, £4,305 and £6,000 respectively. The first two passed into the possession of Pierpont Morgan and are now in the Frick Collection at New York, and the small table, bought by Samson Wertheimer acting for Ferdinand de Rothschild, is at Waddesdon today. The last lot on the twelfth day of the sale was the celebrated *bureau plât* and matching *cartonnier* made for La Live de Jully and generally regarded as the first truly *neo-grec* furniture to have been made in France. This was bought for £3,202.10.0 by Colnaghi acting on behalf of the duc d'Aumale and can be seen in the *Musée Condé* at Chantilly today. For the Cressent commode now in the Grey Drawing Room at Waddesdon, Wertheimer went up to £6,247. On the twelfth day a group of pieces (lots 1,297 and 1,298) veneered with black and gold lacquer and also made by Riesener, two of which bore the brand of Marie-Antoinette's *Garde Meuble,* did even better than the earlier pieces which the ill-fated Queen had owned. The secretaire was bought by Fred Davis for £9,450 (Fig 3) and Samson Wertheimer paid exactly the same sum for the commode. The cabinet apparently *en suite* with the other two but actually delivered separately, was bought by Davis for £5,400. It reappeared at Sotheby's in 1971 (Fig 4) when it was sold for £72,000, considerably less in terms of the present value of money. The secretaire and commode were acquired by Cornelius Vanderbilt who bequeathed them to the Metropolitan Museum, New York at his death. These incursions into the field of collecting by two American millionaires, Morgan and Vanderbilt, are significant and mark the beginning of the transformation of the United States into a country possessing some of the most important assemblages of French furniture in existence today. A year or two later, about 1884, Duveen sold Collis P. Huntington a suite of Louis XVI chairs and sofas for an allegedly astronomical figure which has never been revealed. But the history of the collecting of French eighteenth-century furniture in the U.S.A. has yet to be written.

The prices quoted above mark a total revolution in the market for French works of art. If the declining value of money over the last hundred years is taken into consideration it is doubtful if prices have ever risen higher than these. In a sense, therefore, although French furniture has remained more or less continuously in fashion ever since 1882, there has also been a continuous declension in its true value. From that time onwards there are few new trends to be discerned; only the pressure of economic recessions caused occasional temporary set-backs in the popularity of fine French eighteenth-century furniture of all types. The historian can only point to an odd peak price here and there. Until recent years hardly any pieces of *ébénisterie* surpassed or indeed equalled the Hamilton Palace prices even in absolute terms. A Sèvres-mounted work-table and reading-stand by Carlin (now in the Huntington Library, California) sold by the Duke of Marlborough in 1883 was clearly raised to its preeminent price of £6,000 through the immediate influence of the Hamilton Palace sale of the previous year. Yet it was less than fifteen years since Lord Hertford had bought a better example of the same model for a third of that sum. In 1901 the Duke of Leeds obtained £15,000 from Charles Wertheimer at auction for a pair of Louis XV commodes signed by Joseph, but Duveen was the under-bidder and a battle of giants preceeded this exceptional price. In 1915 Duveen is said to have paid Pierpont Morgan over £50,000 for the cheaper of the two ex-Hamilton Palace pieces made for Marie-Antoinette and to have sold them to Henry C. Frick at a profit. But these are isolated instances and unusual circumstances. On the whole the Hamilton Palace sale remains a unique occasion in the annals of French furniture sales. Nevertheless a much less important piece provides a more illuminating key to the trend of the French furniture market in these years. At the Page Turner sale in 1903, a small *bonheur-du-jour* with floral marquetry, not a very grand piece, sold for 1,600 guineas. It had been bought in the same saleroom in 1868 for twenty guineas.

The only type of furniture which did not achieve records in 1882 was seat furniture, A large *canapé à confidents* made in 1784 by Blanchard (frame), Rascalon (carving) and Dutemps (gilding) for the use of Louis XV's aunts at Bellevue, merely fetched £1,176 at Hamilton Palace, though the historic details were unknown at the time of the sale. This piece is now in the Gulbenkian Museum at Lisbon. In the previous year a world record had been created at the Léopold Double sale when two suites of Louis XVI armchairs upholstered with Gobelins tapestries after Boucher fetched 110,000 francs and 100,000 francs respectively. The second and slightly less costly of these suites was the so-called *Mobilier des Dieux* (from the subjects of the tapestries) and had basically been made by Foliot for Marie-Antoinette's use at Choisy about 1770. It was purchased by the Second Empire banker Isaac de Camondo who

FRENCH FURNITURE IN THE SALEROOM AND OUTSIDE 1800–1914 337

Fig 4 Cabinet of black and gold lacquer by Riesener which sold for £5,460 at the Hamilton Palace sale in 1882. It reappeared in the auction rooms at Sotheby's in 1971 when it sold for £72,000 ($180,000)

bequeathed it to the Louvre at his death. What neither he nor the Louvre authorities knew at the time was firstly that the tapestry which was the principal cause of its exceptional price, was not what the chairs had originally been upholstered with, nor that at some time in the late eighteenth century or perhaps during the nineteenth, a sofa and three chairs had been added to the original suite to accommodate the covers. But the copies are so skilful that even M Verlet (who published the documents revealing these facts) has been unable to distinguish between originals and copies with any certainty.

The immense prices obtained by French chairs at the end of the nineteenth and in the early twentieth centuries arose from the popularity at this period of the so-called 'Louis drawing room'. To own one was a status symbol and genuine sets of eighteenth-century chairs upholstered with genuine contemporary tapestry to provide their principal furnishings were exceedingly rare but greatly in demand. So M Chauchard, the creator of the Parisian drapery store *Les Galeries du Louvre* and the patron of Millet and Meissonnier, was prepared to pay the dealer Lowengard over 350,000 francs in 1898 for a set of 20 Louis XVI armchairs and a sofa upholstered with Beauvais tapestry after Boucher (the set is now in the Louvre). And a comparable price was attained for a somewhat similar set by Sené at the Chappey sale in 1907. But these were pure scarcity prices. Smaller suites or single chairs fetched proportionately much less. The requirements of the 'Louis drawing room' also produced the paradoxical result that fine copies of Louis XVI chairs began to fetch more than genuine originals, for people preferred to see twelve matching chairs around their rooms, even though they were reproductions, to a mixed bag of chairs of several different designs. This eventually had the consequence of depressing the price of genuine eighteenth-century chairs on the market. The suite sold at the Chappey sale in 1907 had dropped by a third (and in much devalued currency) when it appeared at the Elbert Garry sale in New York in 1928 and at the Rasmussen sale in 1938 it was bought in at less than half the 1928 price.

But such incidents were relatively rare. If prices have probably never exceeded those of the Hamilton Palace sale of 1882, the market for French eighteenth-century furniture has remained conspicuously buoyant if not always booming since its return into fashion about 1870 after more than a generation in the doldrums. And there are few items that come regularly into the auction rooms that have had such a continuously long run of good fortune.

Furniture, Decorations and Textiles

A Queen Anne black- and gilt-japanned bureau-cabinet. First quarter of the eighteenth century, height 8 ft, width 3 ft 4¾ in
Los Angeles $90,000 (£37,500).
19.XI.73
From the collection of Miss Merle Oberon
Formerly in the collection of the late Queen Mary and the late Duke of Windsor

A French Gothic oak pew bench of four seats, the three uprights with crocketed finials, the front of the boxed seats with panels of horizontal linenfold, height 5ft 10in, width 7ft 4in
London £2,400 ($5,760). 24.V.74

A German Gothic oak cupboard in two parts with fourteen panels of finely carved linenfold embellished with chip borders and unusual florid ends, height 6ft 2in, width 5ft 9in
London £3,000 ($7,200). 24.V.74

A mid-seventeenth-century oak Dutch beeldenkast richly carved with scrolling foliage, cherubs, birds, flowers and at the centre of the cornice the Sacrifice of Isaac, height 8ft 3in, width 5ft 4in
London £4,400 ($10,560). 15.III.74

A mid-sixteenth-century French walnut side cabinet, carved throughout to show perspective views, height 5ft 8½in, width 4ft 4½in
London £3,200 ($7,680). 26.x.73

FURNITURE, DECORATIONS AND TEXTILES 343

A seventeenth-century hanging oak food cupboard, probably French, *circa* 1620, height 2ft 8in, width 2ft 2½in
London £1,500 ($3,600). 24.V.74

A late Gothic oak hutch table, height 2ft 8in, width 3ft 7½in
London £4,800 ($11,520). 24.V.74

FURNITURE, DECORATIONS AND TEXTILES

A mid-eighteenth-century Venetian white-painted and gilt commode, height 2ft 11in, width 4ft 7½in
London £4,200 ($10,080). 26.X.73

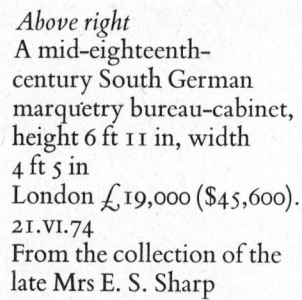

Above right
A mid-eighteenth-century South German marquetry bureau-cabinet, height 6 ft 11 in, width 4 ft 5 in
London £19,000 ($45,600). 21.VI.74
From the collection of the late Mrs E. S. Sharp

Left A mid-eighteenth-century Venetian walnut bureau-bookcase, height 9ft 1½in
Florence L21,500,000 (£14,191; $33,960). 9.IV.74

Right An early eighteenth-century Dutch East Indies padoukwood bureau-cabinet, height 7ft 2in, width 3ft 4in
London £4,200 ($10,080). 16.XI.73

A Louis XVI royal commode in ebony, ormolu and inlaid marbles, signed G. Benéman. The side doors inset with panels of *pietra dura*, after Casanova, depicting mounted huntsmen and hounds in landscapes, the men in Louis XV costume; the centre door inset with a seventeenth-century *pietra dura* panel of a vase of flowers in griotte, lapis lazuli and Sienna marbles. The mount of the centre drawer composed of branches of laurel with coronets and victor's wreaths with crossed flags and Roman military trophies; the mounts on the flanking drawers and at the sides centred by the royal monogram of interlaced 'L's with the cockerel of France on either side and sprays of lilies symbolising the House of Bourbon. The top with a grey and white marble of conforming shape, signed at each of the corners G. *Benéman,* height 3 ft, width 4 ft 5 in
London £150,000 ($360,000). 21.VI.74
From the collection of Mrs John Allnat
Formerly in the collection of the Earls of Powis
From the bedchamber of Louis XVI at St Cloud
The back of the commode bears a partially illegible inventory mark and a figure 8 beneath a Royal crown. The *ébéniste*'s stamp is not accompanied by the JME as this was not required on Royal commissions. Jean Guillaume Benéman succeeded J. H. Riesener as principal cabinet-maker to the *Garde Meuble de la Couronne* in 1785 and worked until 1804

346 FURNITURE, DECORATIONS AND TEXTILES

A Louis XV ormolu-mounted marquetry *table à écrire*, attributed to Pierre Roussel. Mid-eighteenth century, height 28¾in, width 24in
New York $32,000 (£13,333). 13.x.73

A Louis XVI ormolu-mounted marquetry *table à écrire*, signed *L. Boudin, JME*. Last quarter of the eighteenth century, height 29in, width 19¼in
New York $15,000 (£6,250). 13.x.73

Left A Louis XV-XVI marquetry *table à écrire*, signed *C. Topino, JME*. Third quarter of the eighteenth century, height 29¾in, width 18½in
New York $30,000 (£12,500). 13.x.73

Right A small Empire *guéridon* table in ormolu, bronze and mahogany with a Sèvres porcelain top, height 2ft 5½in, width 1ft 5in
London £4,000 ($9,600). 26.x.73
The porcelain plaque was painted by Mlle Xhrouet, who worked from 1772 to 1788

A Régence Boulle *bureau plât*, height 2 ft 6 in, width 5 ft 11 in
London £16,000 ($38,400). 21.VI.74

A large Régence ormolu-mounted kingwood commode, stamped *FL*, height 3 ft, width 6 ft 3 in
London £16,000 ($38,400). 26.X.73

348 FURNITURE, DECORATIONS AND TEXTILES

A Louis XVI ormolu-mounted commode, signed *M. Carlin, JME*.
Third quarter of the eighteenth century, height 2ft 10in, width 4ft 3½in
New York $37,000 (£15,416). 13.X.73

A late Louis XV ormolu-mounted *bombé* commode, stamped *F.A. Mondon, JME*, and *E.H.B.* underneath, height 2ft 10in, width 4ft 2in
London £12,500 ($30,000). 26.X.73
François-Antoine Mondon, son of the famous François Mondon, was received Master in 1757
The initials E.H.B. traditionally stand for the *Ecuries de L'Hôtel de Bourbon*

FURNITURE, DECORATIONS AND TEXTILES 349

A Louis XV ormolu-mounted black lacquer commode, indistinctly signed. Mid-eighteenth century, height 2ft 10¼in, width 4ft 1in
New York $29,000 (£12,083). 16.III.74
The signature appears to be that of Claude Chevallier, JME 1738

One of a pair of small Régence kingwood commodes, height 2ft 8in, width 3ft
London £8,000 ($19,200). 26.X.73

Left A carved oak wainscot chair. School of Thomas Dennis, Ipswich, Massachusetts, 1650–75
New York $24,000 (£10,000). 26.I.74
From the collection of Philip Leffingwell Spalding Esq

Right A Queen Anne walnut balloon-seat side chair. Philadelphia, 1735–45
New York $25,000 (£10,410). 11.V.74
From the collection of Richard S. du Pont Esq

A Pilgrim Century Hadley chest. Hadley, Massachusetts, 1690–1705, height 3ft 6in, width 3ft 8in
New York $12,000 (£5,000). 17.XI.73

A Chippendale mahogany serpentine card table. Goddard-Townsend school, Newport, Rhode Island, 1770–80, height 2ft 4½in, width 2ft 7½in
New York $40,000 (£16,666). 11.V.74
From the collection of Richard S. du Pont Esq

A Chippendale mahogany block-front kneehole chest-on-chest. Massachusetts, probably Boston, 1760-80, height 7ft 6in, width 3ft 6½in
New York $50,000 (£20,800). 26.1.74

352 FURNITURE, DECORATIONS AND TEXTILES

Right One of a pair of carved mahogany card tables by Duncan Phyfe. New York, *circa* 1815, height 2ft 6¾in, width 3ft 1in
New York $20,000 (£8,333). 11.v.74
From the collection of Richard S. du Pont Esq

Below right A Chippendale carved mahogany five-legged games table. New York, 1760-80, height 2ft 4in, width 2ft 10in
Los Angeles $40,000 (£16,667). 20.xi.73
From the collection of Mr and Mrs Elling of San Francisco

Below left A Chippendale carved mahogany hairy-paw-foot card table attributed to Benjamin Randolph or Thomas Affleck. Philadelphia, *circa* 1770, height 2ft 4¾in, width 2ft 8in
New York $90,000 (£37,500). 11.v.74
From the collection of Richard S. du Pont Esq

A Pilgrim Century carved and painted press cupboard. Essex County, probably Ipswich, Massachusetts, dated 1683, height 4ft 11in, width 4ft 1½in
New York $62,000 (£25,833). 26.I.74
From the collection of Philip Leffingwell Spalding Esq

A George II palissanderwood secretaire bookcase by William Vile, height 8ft 9in, width 7ft 7in
London £21,000 ($50,400). 27.VI.74
Formerly in the collection of the Earls of Cadogan

William Vile (died 1767) worked for George, Prince of Wales, before his accession to the throne in 1760 and for the next five years he was favourite and principal cabinet-maker to the King. He worked in a strongly individual style favouring 'ovals of laurels' and swags and pendants of flowers, always of the highest craftsmanship

Left A late George II carved walnut card table by Thomas Johnson, height 2ft 6in, width 3ft
London £15,000 ($36,000).
27.VI.74
Thomas Johnson flourished 1755-1778. The design for this table is probably based on two designs for tables from a *Collection of designs* 1758, plate 19

Below A late George II carved mahogany library table, height 2ft 8in, width 4ft 9in
London £19,000 ($45,600).
27.VI.74

Opposite page
An early George III mahogany secretaire-cabinet known as the D'Arcy Cabinet, height 6ft ½in, width 2ft 4in
London £29,000 ($69,600). 27.VI.74
Formerly in the collections of Robert D'Arcy, 4th Earl of Holderness, Secretary of State to George III, of Hornby Castle, Yorkshire, and the Hon Augusta Leigh, half-sister of Lord Byron

One of a pair of George III satinwood and mahogany marquetry commodes. Last quarter of the eighteenth century, height 2ft 9in, width 4ft 3in
New York $42,000 (£17,500). 29.IX.73
From the collection of the late Edwin C. Vogel of New York. Formerly in the collection of the late Viscount Leverhulme

FURNITURE, DECORATIONS AND TEXTILES 357

Above An ormolu-mounted kingwood *bureau plât* by F. Linke, *circa* 1870, width 6ft 6in
London £4,800 ($11,520). 26.VI.74

Left A French ormolu-mounted kingwood display cabinet, late nineteenth century, height 5ft 5in, width 3ft 3in
London £2,200 ($5,280). 26.VI.74

FURNITURE, DECORATIONS AND TEXTILES

1. William and Mary walnut armchair £1,750 ($4,200) 29.III.74. 2. Comb-back writing-arm Windsor chair, attributed to Ebenezer Tracy, Connecticut, 1765-1800 $9,250 (£3,854) 11.V.74. 3. One of a pair of William and Mary painted wing armchairs £1,900 ($4,560) 23.XI.73. 4. Sixteenth-century yew-wood Turner's armchair, possibly German £650 ($1,560) 2.XI.73. 5. One of a set of eight Chippendale carved mahogany side chairs and a corner chair, Salem or Marblehead, Massachusetts, 1760-80 $25,000 (£10,410) 26.I.74. 6. One of a set of Queen Anne maple rush seat chairs, comprising one arm chair and five single chairs, Massachusetts, 1720-40 $18,000 (£7,500) 17.XI.73. 7. George I library chair $5,500 (£2,292) 22.IV.74. 8. George II carved mahogany armchair. $8,500 (£3,542) 29.IX.73. 9. A settee from a suite of Japanese heavily carved hall furniture, c. 1900 £320 ($768) 30.I.74. 10. One of a set of eight late George II dining chairs £4,200 ($10,080) 23.XI.73.

FURNITURE, DECORATIONS AND TEXTILES

1. One of a pair of Louis XV ormolu, painted metal and Meissen porcelain candelabra, 1ft 3in £4,200 ($10,080) 26.X.73. 2. A Dutch marquetry barometer, Bianchi & Compi., Amsterdam, last quarter of the eighteenth century, 4ft 9in $2,700 (£1,125) 7.VI.74. 3. One of a pair of gilt-bronze and ivory candelabra, French, late nineteenth century, 2ft £850 ($2,040) 20.III.74. 4. An American album quilt, probably Maryland, dated 1847 $1,900 (£791) 11.V.74. 5. A fraktur: Taufschein of Elizabeth Erlin, probably Pennsylvania, signed and dated 1787, from the collection of Edgar William and Bernice Chrysler Garbisch, 8 by 12¾in $5,000 (£2,080) 24.I.74. 6. A K'ang Hsi twelve fold Coromandel lacquer screen, each fold 7ft 9in £4,200 ($10,080) 25.I.74. 7. A mid-eighteenth-century Chinese mirror painting in a contemporary English giltwood frame, 2ft 1in £3,600 ($8,640) 23.XI.73. 8. One of eight panels of early nineteenth century painted wallpaper, 8ft $6,250 (£2,604) 23.III.74

FURNITURE, DECORATIONS AND TEXTILES 361

A pair of William and Mary male and female wooden dolls and their original caned beechwood and elmwood armchairs. The dolls' heads with delicately painted eyes and eyebrows, scarlet lips and well rouged cheeks, the bodies with well modelled hands and legs joined at the hips and knees, height of dolls 22in, height of chairs 21in
London £16,000 ($38,400). 19.IV.74
This pair of dolls, remarkably preserved and with their original chairs, is further distinguished by the variety and extent of their wardrobe. The dolls were known traditionally as Lord and Lady Clapham

FURNITURE, DECORATIONS AND TEXTILES

FURNITURE, DECORATIONS AND TEXTILES

Above A Louis XIV yellow ground Beauvais tapestry by Philip Behagle after Jean Berain, entitled *Les grotesques des dieux chinois. Circa* 1700, height 10ft 3in, width 12ft 4in
London £14,200 ($34,080). 21.VI.74

Opposite page
A Brussels tapestry depicting the Holy Family. Second quarter of the sixteenth century, height 6ft 2 in, width 6ft 3in.
New York $24,000 (£10,000). 2.XI.73

364 FURNITURE, DECORATIONS AND TEXTILES

A Gobelins mythological tapestry depicting the Rape of Europa, inscribed *Cozette 1787*, 9ft 10in by 9ft 10in
New York $14,500 (£6,042). 2.III.74
From the collection of Principia College, Elsah, Illinois
This tapestry belongs to the series *Les Amours des Dieux* and is after a design by J. B. Pierre

Opposite page A Brussels Teniers tapestry depicting a winter scene of skating and a pig killing. Early eighteenth century, height 11ft 8in, width 10ft 10in
New York $22,000 (£9,167). 2.III.74
From the Estate of Mr and Mrs Frank Buttram

366 FURNITURE, DECORATIONS AND TEXTILES

A large Tabriz silk garden carpet, the field composed of numerous rectangular tiles enclosing stylised plants and mihrabs in shades of rust, gold, red, blue and ivory, with a main wine-red border flanked by ivory and gold floral meander borders, 15ft 7in by 10ft 3in New York $42,000 (£17,500).
1.XII.73

FURNITURE, DECORATIONS AND TEXTILES 367

A Hereke silk and metal thread
prayer rug of Persian design,
3ft by 4ft 1in
New York $16,000 (£6,666).
1.II.74

368 FURNITURE, DECORATIONS AND TEXTILES

Above left
Two lengths of sixteenth-century Turkish velvet brocade, 4ft 5in by 4ft 2¾in $2,000 (£833)
Above right
Two lengths of sixteenth-century Turkish satin brocade, part of a chasuble, 4ft 5in by 30¾in $2,300 (£958)
Left
A length of sixteenth-century Turkish satin brocade, 4ft 5½in by 26in $2,100 (£875)
The textiles illustrated on this page were part of the collection of Vojtech Blau Esq sold in New York on 2nd November 1973

Musical Instruments

A bass viola da gamba by Barak Norman, London 1700, bearing its original label *Barak Norman, at the Bass Violl in St Pauls Ally, London, Fecit* 1700. Length of back 26 15/16 in
London £2,600 ($6,240). 6.VI.74
The label of Alexander Livingstone is a particularly good example of its kind. The text is flanked on each side by illustrations of a violin, a viol, a recorder, an oboe, a flageolet and an open music book inscribed 'Nolens Volens'
From the collection of Miss Margaret Harrison

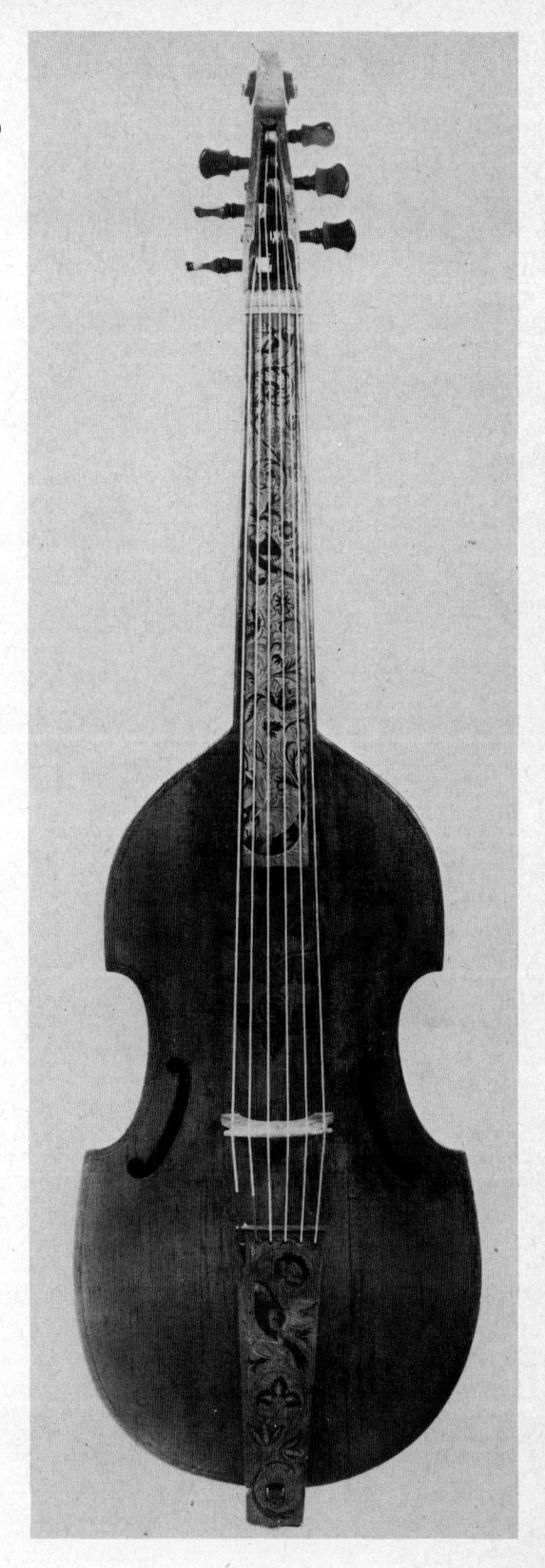

Opposite page left
The Corbett Stradivari
A violin by Antonio Stradivari, Cremona 1706, labelled
Antonius Stradivarius Cremonensis faciebat Anno 1706.
Length of back 14in
London £62,000 ($148,800). 6.VI.74
This violin takes its name from the first known owner, William Corbett, who was a distinguished English violinist and composer of the first half of the eighteenth century

Right
The Consolo Guarneri del Jesu
A violin by Joseph Guarneri del Jesu, Cremona 1733, bearing its original label. Length of back 13$\frac{7}{8}$in
London £58,000 ($139,200). 25.IV.74
From the collection of Miss Elaine Weldon

A Spanish guitar by Juan Pages, Cadiz 1795, labelled
Joan Pages me hizo en Cadiz, Ano de 1795.
Length of body 17$\frac{7}{8}$in
London £800 ($1,920). 25.IV.74

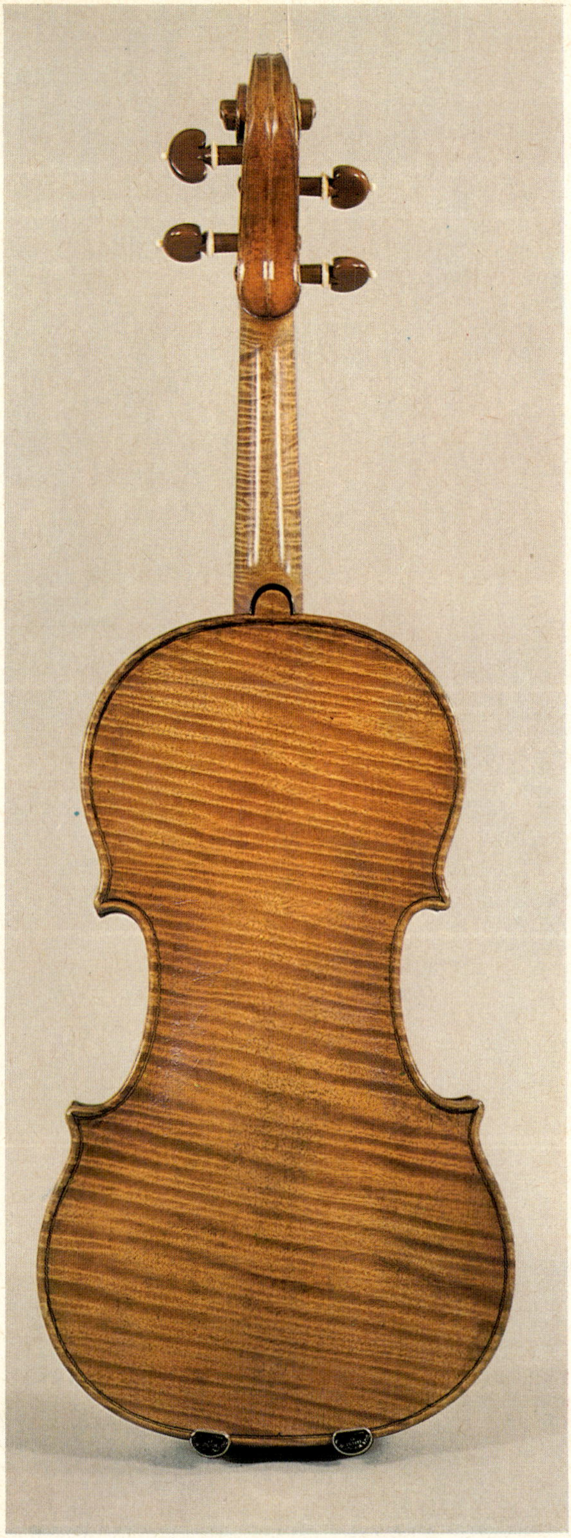

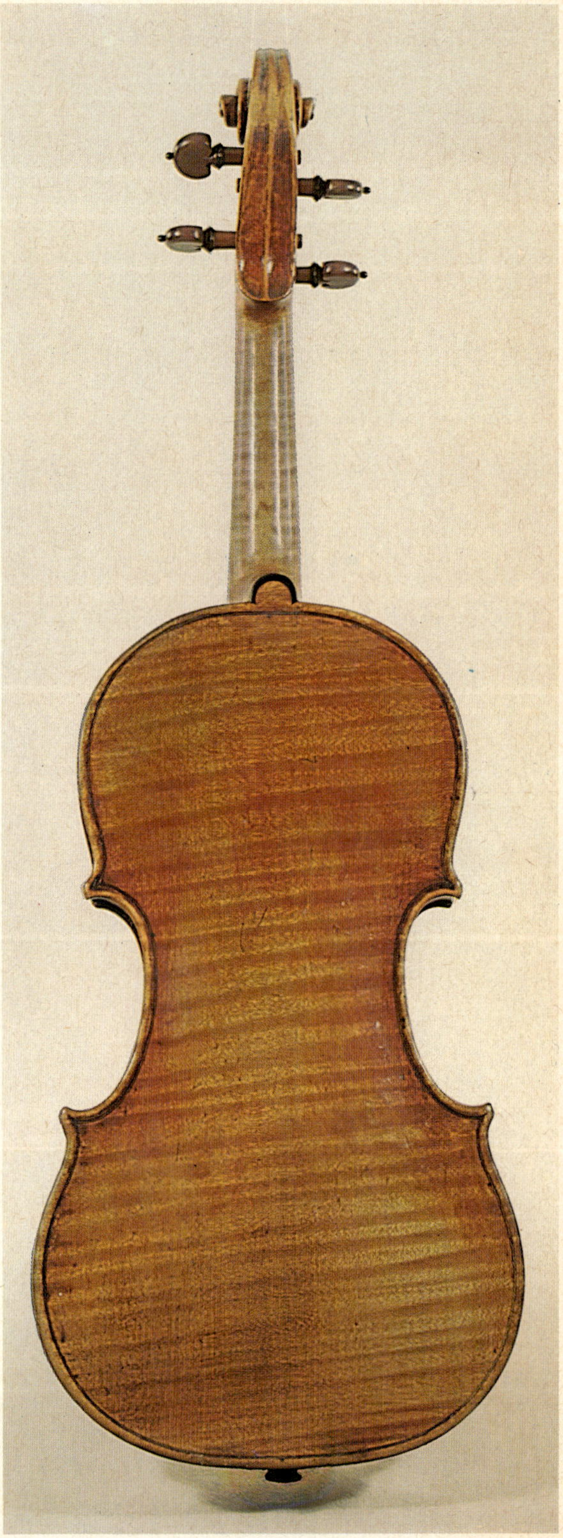

372 MUSICAL INSTRUMENTS

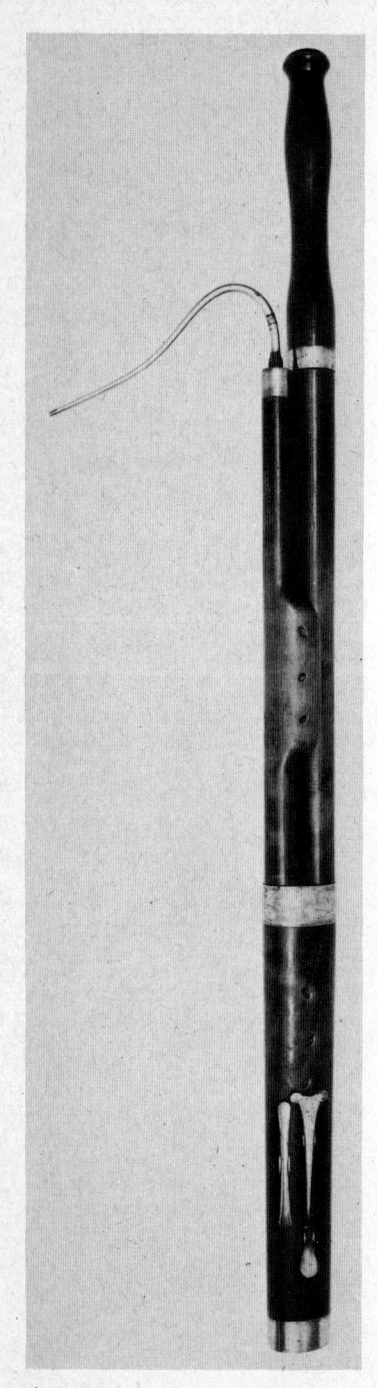

A four-keyed bassoon by
William Milhouse, Newark,
stamped *Milhouse, Newark*. Circa
1760. Length 48 11/16 in
London £1,100 ($2,640). 25.IV.74
From the collection of
Eric Halfpenny Esq, FSA

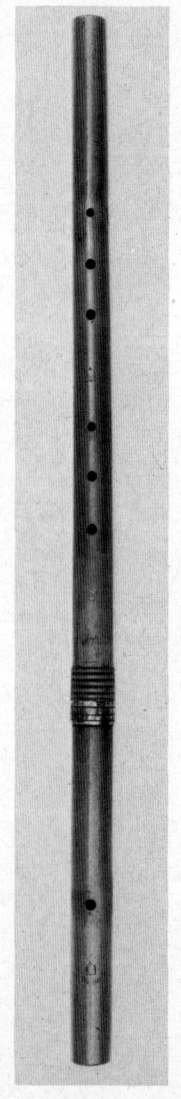

A Renaissance bass flute of
boxwood, stamped on the head
joint *IA NENI(?)*. Probably
Italian, late sixteenth century.
Length 35 13/16 in
London £4,200 ($10,080).
22.XI.73
From the collection of
Eric Halfpenny Esq, FSA

A two-keyed boxwood oboe by
William Milhouse, London, circa
1800, stamped on the bell joint
*W. Milhouse, London, 337,
Oxford St*. Length 22½ in
London £1,050 ($3,520). 25.IV.74
From the collection of
Miss D. Gilbert

Ceramics

377 ENGLISH POTTERY
382 ENGLISH PORCELAIN
388 AMERICAN POTTERY
389 CONTINENTAL POTTERY
390 MAIOLICA
392 CONTINENTAL PORCELAIN
397 VICTORIAN CERAMICS

A Medici blue and white porcelain bowl, 'Duomo' mark and the letter F flanked by two dots, Florentine, late sixteenth century. Width 5⅛in, greatest height 1⅞in
New York $180,000 (£75,000). 1.XI.73
From the collection of the Elizabeth Seton College, Yonkers, New York.

374 THE MEDICI BOWL FROM SETON COLLEGE

The Medici Bowl from Seton College

By Joseph J. Kuntz

Magic, myth, alchemy, the Medici name and the smallest known object produced by the short-lived workshops set up by Francesco I in the last quarter of the sixteenth century, all combined to bring the world auction record for Western ceramics almost exactly four hundred years after the object was made. The blue and white soft-paste porcelain bowl is one of a small group of objects which forms a category of the utmost rarity among decorative art objects – so rare, in fact, that a *catalogue raisonné,* compiled by Giuseppe Liverani in 1936, listed only fifty-nine examples, fourteen of which had not been seen since the nineteenth century. When sold at Sotheby Parke Bernet in New York in November 1973, it reached the extraordinary figure of $180,000 (the previous world record at auction for a Western ceramic object was $100,000 for a Meissen coffee-pot sold at Sotheby's in London last year). It is ironic that after four centuries the only decorative art objects of comparable or greater value in financial terms are the Chinese porcelain ones which the Medici greatly admired and endeavoured to copy. The last example of Medici porcelain offered at public auction was a plate, one of the lost Liverani pieces, which fetched £1,100 at Sotheby's twenty-five years ago.

The Seton College bowl was not among the objects listed by Liverani in 1936 (one or two others have, in fact, come to light since his catalogue was published). It was known to have appeared in the Davanzati Palace sale held by the American Art Galleries in New York, in which the bowl was given scant notice. The catalogue of that sale was large and generously illustrated, the bowl however received only a four-line description, a rather hazy foot-note and no photograph; perhaps its small size and misshapen form did not lend themselves to the photographic talents of the day, or perhaps it was not considered of any consequence. It fetched only $200.

The first impression which the bowl gives today is of an extraordinary purity and simplicity. Barely five inches wide and slightly irregular in shape, having sagged during firing, painted only in blue, it is decorated with an extremely restrained design of blossoms and foliage, and marked with that most beautiful of all ceramic marks, the lantern of the Duomo and the letter F for Firenze.

The origins of European porcelain are not well known or documented, but it would appear that the few documented experiments in the late fifteenth and in the first half of the sixteenth century ended in achieving only variations of maiolica or glass, never porcelain. Chinese hard-paste porcelain had been known in Europe probably since the end of the thirteenth century, when Marco Polo returned to Venice from his travels in the Orient.

Fourteenth- and fifteenth-century inventories of noble households list objects that were almost certainly Chinese porcelain and there are records of gifts of Chinese porcelain from Near-Eastern potentates to Italian rulers during the fifteenth century. At the end of the fifteenth century and the beginning of the sixteenth, the decorative motifs of Ming blue and white porcelain were sufficiently familiar and they were admired to the extent of finding their way into the decoration of maiolica, particularly at Faenza.

It would seem however that Venetian workshops, already famous for their great achievements with glass, first attempted to make porcelain in about 1500. What was produced was in fact opaque white glass painted with enamel colours. In 1561-62 Duke Alfonso II d'Este commissioned two brothers from Urbino to make porcelain, but no examples of their experiments are known to have survived; it would again appear that these wares were in fact disguised maiolica or *porcellana contrafatta*.

The Grand Duke Francesco I de' Medici (1574-87) inherited from his father, Cosimo I, the workshops which the latter had set up near Palazzo Pitti in the Boboli Gardens and which produced tapestries, engraved crystal and the famous *pietra dura* mosaics. It appears that by 1575, after at least ten years of attempts, Francesco's workshops produced the first example of porcelain in the West, albeit soft-paste and not hard-paste porcelain. While names of supervisors, designers and potters connected with the workshops are known, we do not know who was personally responsible for the great discovery. A manuscript in the Biblioteca Magliabecchiana in Florence gives the ingredients for the porcelain as a mixture of glassy materials and white clay (possibly kaolin) from Vicenza. The glassy materials include white sand, a frit made of rock crystal and perhaps shards from other wares.

The shape of the Seton College bowl is in no way unusual. Numerous extant Medici porcelain objects, particularly the more ambitious types, exhibit technical defects: sagging, slanting forms, bubbles in the glaze, or a tendency for the cobalt blue to turn grey are quite common faults. One could reasonably assume, therefore, that an enormous number of trials must have been abortive and the proportion of wasted pieces substantial. This may well be a major factor in the short-lived period of production which appears to have ended in 1587, with the possible exception of a few pieces which were made during the two following decades.

Various types of decoration were used on Medici porcelain, principally from European, Chinese and Near Eastern sources; the painting on the present example falls into the last category. While the bowl is misshapen, it has remained in perfect condition; the painting is of the highest quality, a deep clear blue not marred by the tendency to go grey which we mentioned and seems to appear on so many examples.

For nearly fifty years the whereabouts of this bowl were unknown; it was rediscovered by one of Sotheby Parke Bernet's experts on a visit of inspection to view 'some Italian pottery'. In all this time it had occasionally been used as a sugar bowl at tea parties. As with so many Renaissance works of art, both major and minor, brought to America at the beginning of this century, the bowl has now returned to Europe, becoming the fifth piece of Medici porcelain that has been traced, apart from the known examples in public collections.

ENGLISH POTTERY 377

A Staffordshire salt-glazed figure of a piper, height 9¼in
London £3,400 ($8,160). 17.IV.74

A pair of Ralph Wood figural spill vases, modelled as an elephant (illustrated) and as a bull-baiting group, *circa* 1770, height 8in
New York $5,200 (£2,167). 13.XI.73

A pair of Ralph Wood figures of a stag (illustrated) and hind at lodge, length 6¼in
London £3,200 ($7,680). 30.X.73

A slipware dish by Ralph Toft, decorated with a three-quarter length portrait of a woman holding a tulip, the rim decorated with a trellis diaper and the name RALPH TOFT below the portrait, diameter 16¾in
London £7,500 ($18,000). 23.v.74
Formerly in the Edkins Collection sold at Sotheby's 21st May 1891 for £35, and the Pitt-Rivers Collection

A London delftware 'William III' equestrian portrait charger, diameter 17¼in
London £3,000 ($7,200). 23.V.74

An English delftware George I portrait charger, Bristol or Brislington, diameter 13¼in
London £1,500 ($3,600). 23.V.74

Left
A Whieldon Chinese court figure, height 5¾in
London £1,150 ($2,760). 17.IV.74

Right
An English delftware shoe, the instep with the initials
E:C above the date 1727, probably London, length 4¾in
London £620 ($1,488). 8.I.74
From the collection of Mrs M. P. Annesley

Below left
An early Lambeth delft wet drug jar, painted in blue on one side with a 'man-smoking-a-pipe' label containing the name of the drug, S:DIACODION, height 8¼in
London £680 ($1,623). 8.I.74

Below right
A Lambeth delft posset pot and cover, diameter 5½in
London £900 ($2,160). 30.X.73

A Wedgwood and Bentley black basaltes library bust of Homer, taken from a plaster cast by Hoskins and Grant perfected by Hackwood. The bust impressed *HOMER* and *Wedgwood & Bentley*, the socle impressed *WEDGWOOD & BENTLEY*, height 21in
New York $4,700 (£1,958). 7.v.74

Below left
A Wedgwood and Bentley black basaltes wall plaque, unmarked, 1768-80, diameter 15in
New York $2,100 (£875). 29.v.74
From the collection of Louise C. Morgan

Below right
A Wedgwood and Bentley shield shaped urn and cover, the body covered with a powdered cobalt and manganese ground simulating porphyry, applied medallion mark, height 14¾in
London £1,450 ($3,480). 8.i.74

Above: A Chelsea billing doves tureen and cover, both pieces with red anchor marks and numerals 12, length 17in £9,500 ($22,800)
Below: A Chelsea boar's head tureen, cover and stand, the interior of the tureen with red anchor mark, length of tureen 14½in £32,000 ($76,800)
Both pieces from the collection of the late Mr & Mrs James McG. Stewart, sold in London on 13th November 1973

A Chelsea figure of a 'Little Hawk Owl', raised anchor mark, height 6¾in
London £4,000 ($9,600). 14.v.74
From the collection of James A. MacHarg Esq

384 ENGLISH PORCELAIN

Left
A pair of Worcester figures of a gardener and his companion, modelled by Tebo, First Period, heights 6¾in and 7in
London £8,200 ($19,680).
13.XI.73
From the collection of the late Mr & Mrs James McG. Stewart

Right
A Chelsea white figure of *The Gardener's Companion*, finely modelled by Joseph Willems, adapted from an engraving after Boucher, raised anchor mark and period, height 8¾in
London £4,000 ($9,600).
14.V.74
From the collection of James A. MacHarg Esq

Right
A Chelsea figure of *Isabella*, probably modelled by Joseph Willems, raised anchor mark, height 9½in
London £3,200 ($7,680)
10.XII.73
From the collection of Lady Lloyd

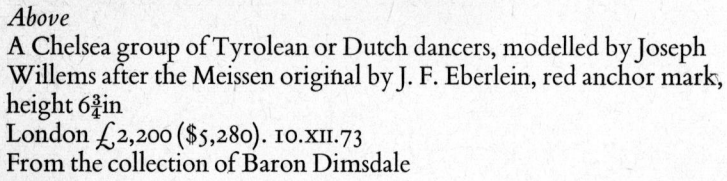

Above
A Chelsea group of Tyrolean or Dutch dancers, modelled by Joseph Willems after the Meissen original by J. F. Eberlein, red anchor mark, height 6¾in
London £2,200 ($5,280). 10.XII.73
From the collection of Baron Dimsdale

ENGLISH PORCELAIN

A Worcester teapot and cover, decorated with a 'Valentine' pattern after a Chinese original, First Period, height 4¾in
London £860 ($2,064). 2.x.73

A documentary Lowestoft blue and white flask, painted in underglaze-blue with the inscription *Iohn Toake Yarmouth 1782*; height 5¾in
London £1,000 ($2,400). 23.x.73

A Longton Hall mug, transfer-printed in Liverpool by J. Sadler, signed, after an engraving by Thomas Billinge of a bust portrait of Queen Charlotte, height 4¾in
London £580 ($1,392). 2.x.73
From the collection of T. Windsor Esq

A Chelsea white Chinaman and parrot teapot and cover, incised triangle mark, height 7in
London £15,500 ($37,200). 13.XI.73
From the collection of the late Mr & Mrs James McG. Stewart
This is one of only four known examples, one of which, the Kaufman teapot, was sold in these rooms on 3rd April 1973 for £3,500 ($8,750)

A Lowestoft coffee pot and cover, painted by the *Tulip Painter*, height 9in
London £1,200 ($2,880). 23.x.73

A Worcester blue-scale dish, probably painted by J. H. O'Neale, seal mark, First Period, diameter 11½in
London £5,500 ($13,200). 13.XI.73   From the collection of the late Mr & Mrs James McG. Stewart

The celebrated Worcester 'Wigornia' cream boat, of hexagonal shape, moulded in coloured relief with a continuous Chinese landscape. The word Wigornia and a scroll in crisp relief on the underside of the base, height 2½in
London £20,000 ($48,000). 13.XI.73
From the collection of the late Mr & Mrs James McG. Stewart

Opposite page below:
Part of the Stowe Service of 56 pieces
London £18,670 ($44,808). 12.III.74
This service was made for Richard Nugent-Temple-Grenville, 2nd Marquess of Buckingham, who married Lady Anna Eliza *de jure* Baroness Kinloss, daughter and sole heiress of James Bridges, 3rd Duke of Chandos. Richard succeeded to the Marquessate on the death of his father, the 1st Marquess, in 1813. In 1822 he was created Earl Temple of Stowe and Duke of Buckingham and Chandos. The arms of the 2nd Marquess are shown with those of his wife in pretence, and therefore the service is dated after their marriage in 1796. They are surmounted by a marquess's coronet, and this dates the service between his succession in 1813 and becoming Earl Temple and Duke of Buckingham and Chandos in 1822. The service comprises items with impressed and other marks from both the Barr Flight and Barr (1807-1813), and Flight Barr and Barr periods (1813-1840)

388 AMERICAN POTTERY

Left
A nineteenth-century Pennsylvania glazed redware figure of a seated minstrel with a dog, height 6½in $3,100 (£1,292)

Right
A nineteenth-century Pennsylvania glazed redware flower pot with stand, inscribed in script around the rim *Tacy Lewis Newtown Township Delaware County, 10th Mo. 5th 1824*, height 10in $2,400 (£1,000)

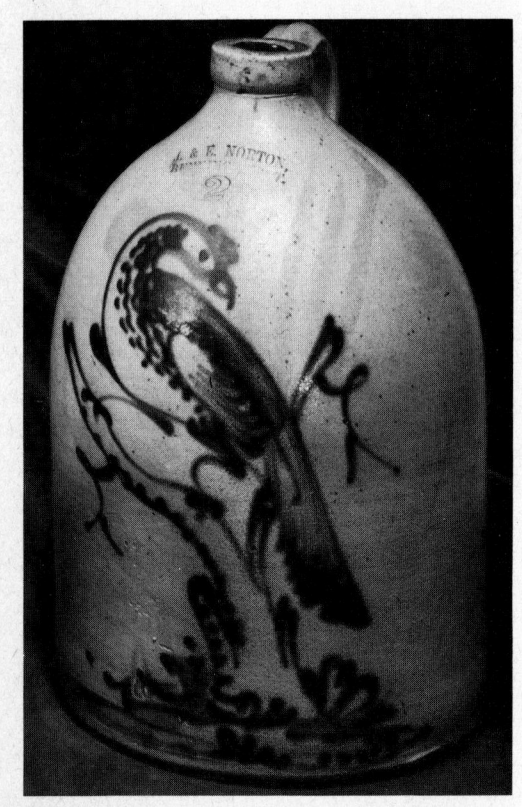

A glazed stoneware jug painted in bright blue with an exotic bird below the impressed numeral 2 and the mark *J. & E. NORTON, BENNINGTON VT.*, 1850-59, height 13½in $300 (£125)

A glazed stoneware water cooler painted in blue with a reclining stag, impressed *J. & E. NORTON, BENNINGTON VT.* mark and numeral 5 on exterior, 1850-59, height 14¾in $1,500 (£625)

The objects illustrated on this page were in the collection of the late Jacqueline D. Hodgson, sold in New York on 22nd January 1974

CONTINENTAL POTTERY

One of a pair of eighteenth-century faïence tureens and covers modelled in the form of a tortoise, possibly Schrezheim, length 12¼in
Florence L7,000,000 (£4,620; $11,056). 9.IV.74

A German faïence duck tureen and cover, possibly Glienitz, *circa* 1760, length 6⅞in
New York $7,000 (£2,917). 12.X.73
Formerly in the collection of Mme Jacques Balsan

A Strasbourg blackcock tureen and cover, *circa* 1750, length 20¾in
London £8,500 ($20,400). 23.IV.74
Formerly in the collection of the Marquess of Lansdowne, sold in these rooms on the 5th December 1972 for £7,500

A Castel Durante portrait dish depicting a bearded young man, behind his head a scrolling label inscribed *ASTOLFO*, first half of the sixteenth century, diameter 14in
London £4,600 ($11,040). 2.VII.74
Formerly in the Somzee, Pannwitz and Pringsheim Collections

A late fifteenth-century Faenza albarello, height 10¼in
London £4,200 ($10,080). 2.VII.74

392 CONTINENTAL PORCELAIN

From left to right
One of a pair of Chantilly *seaux-à-verre*, hunting horn mark in red enamel on one, height 3¾in. London £950 ($2,280). 2.VII.74
One of a pair of du Paquier bud vases, *circa* 1730, height 3⅞in
New York $6,500 (£2,708). 20.VI.74. From the collection of Mrs Leopold Gellert
A Capodimonte teabowl and saucer, painted by Giuseppe della Torre with *battaglie*, fleur-de-lys marks in pale blue
London £3,200 ($7,680). 4.XII.73

From left to right
An early Meissen chinoiserie tankard and cover, painted in the manner of Johann Gregor Höroldt, *circa* 1728, height 8½in
New York $13,000 (£5,400). 20.VI.74. From the collection of Mrs Leopold Gellert
A Cassel hot water jug and cover, lion rampant mark in underglaze-blue and incised *S:72*, *circa* 1756, height 6½in
New York $2,000 (£833). 20.VI.74. From the collection of Mrs Leopold Gellert
A Böttger stoneware tankard with copper-gilt mounts, the body of dark grey material polished and wheel-engraved with a mirror monogram below an electoral crown, *circa* 1715, height 9in
London £3,500 ($8,400). 4.VI.74

A pair of Fulda figures of a boy and his companion modelled by Georg Ludwig Bartholome, cross marks in underglaze-blue, *circa* 1775-80, height 5¼in. New York $3,750 (£1,562). 12.X.73
Left One of a pair of Meissen ormolu-mounted vases of inverted baluster shape and hexagonal section, painted in Kakiemon style, caduceus mark in underglaze-blue, the rococo ormolu mounts hallmarked with a crowned C, height 12in
London £3,000 ($7,200). 2.VII.74

A Meissen *Commedia dell'Arte* figure of Mezzetin modelled by J. J. Kaendler, letter M in iron-red, *circa* 1739, height 7¼in
New York $21,500 (£8,958). 12.X.73
From the collection of
Mrs Millard Waldheim

A Meissen *Commedia dell'Arte* figure of Pantaloon modelled by Reinicke and J. J. Kaendler, crossed swords mark in blue, height 5¼in   London £1,150 ($2,760). 4.VI.74
From a series of small *Commedia dell'Arte* figures commissioned from the Meissen factory by Johann Adolf II, Duke of Weissenfels. They were modelled by Peter Reinicke with the help of Kaendler whose assistant he had become in 1743. The source of most of the figures was Luigi Riccoboni's *Histoire du Théatre Italien*, first published in 1728. *Pentalon Ancien* (sic), plate 3 of Riccoboni's book, differs from this model in that his right hand is on his breast

A Vienna *hausmaler* bowl, decorated by Ignaz Bottengruber with scenes from classical mythology after a woodcut by Theodor de Bry, initial K incised, *circa* 1730, diameter 7⅜in
London £6,000 ($14,400). 9.x.73

A pair of Zürich figures of a huntsman and his companion, symbolic of Autumn from a set of 'The Four Seasons', modelled probably by J. J. Meyer, one with incised mark FK for 1768, height 8½in
Zürich SF85,000 (£12,140; $29,136). 7.v.74
From the collection of Alfred Schwarzenbach Esq

A Böttger porcelain figure of a pagod in a pavilion, as a pastille burner, *circa* 1715, height 6¾in
London £26,000 ($62,400). 4.VI.74.
The inspiration for this and other Meissen pagoda figures derives from Chinese biscuit models of the K'ang Hsi period. Only one other example of this masterpiece is recorded, that in the State Collections at Dresden

Left
One of a pair of mid-nineteenth-century ormolu-mounted Sèvres vases, height 24½in
London £3,600 ($8,640). 20.VI.74

Below right
A mid-nineteenth-century Meissen double-handled urn, crossed swords mark in underglaze-blue and incised *G103* height 39⅛in
New York $5,000 (£2,083). 11.I.74
From the collection of the late Edward A. Parsons

Below left
A Coalport *bleu-céleste* vase and cover, painted probably by James Rouse, gilt ampersand mark, the cover with original paper label of Daniell, 129 New Bond St, *circa* 1861, height 34¼in
London £1,950 ($4,680). 6.VI.74
From the collection of His Grace the Duke of Northumberland, KG, TD

VICTORIAN CERAMICS

1. One of a pair of Vienna chinoiserie vases, impressed marks including shield and code for 1859, height 21in £980 ($2,352) 14.III.74. **2.** A Charles and Nell Vyse pottery group of Punch and Judy, incised *C. Vyse, Chelsea*, number 27, issued 1928, height 12½in £480 ($1,052) 20.IX.73. **3.** One of a set of four Mettlach stoneware plaques of 'The Seasons', by C. Warth, signed and dated 1882 and with impressed Castle mark, each 16¼in by 10¾in £600 ($1,440) 22.XI.73. **4.** A Wedgwood fairyland lustre vase, gilt printed mark and incised 2465, *circa* 1925, height 16½in £720 ($1,728) 20.XII.73. **5.** One of a pair of Mintons *pâte-sur-pâte* pilgrim flasks, by Marc Louis Solon, signed, gilt Mintons globe mark, impressed *Mintons* and date code for 1890, height 10½in £1,550 ($3,720) 6.VI.74. **6.** A large exhibition pot lid depicting the first version of *The second appeal* £820 ($1,968) 20.XII.73. **7.** A Royal Doulton stoneware pilgrim bottle and cover, by Richard Garbe, RA, signed in the mould, impressed crowned circle mark, *circa* 1930, height 13½in £350 ($840) 4.IV.74. **8.** A Vienna dish, titled on the reverse, shield mark in blue, *circa* 1870, diameter 19½in £600 ($1,440) 20.VI.74 **9.** A porcelain plaque by E. Schade after August-Karl-Friedrich von Kloeber, signed and dated 1856, 11¼in by 10¾in £550 ($1,320) 20.VI.74. **10.** The Burne-Jones, William de Morgan *Orpheus* plate, painted with a design after Edward Burne-Jones, impressed *J. H. Davis*, *circa* 1875, diameter 12 in £650 ($1,560) 4.IV.74

One of a pair of large Minton earthenware blackamoor figures and stands, impressed *Minton* and date code for 1865, height 71 ½in
London £3,600 ($8,640). 6.VI.74

Chinese Ceramics and Works of Art

An archaic bronze wine vessel *(yu)*, early Western Chou Dynasty, height 10⅞in, width 7¾in
£32,000 ($76,800)
An archaic bronze wine vessel *(ku)*, Shang Dynasty, height 12in
£15,000 ($36,000)
The wine vessels illustrated on this page were sold in London on 27th November 1973
From the collection of the late Edward G. Robinson

A melon-shaped silver-gilt box and cover, the sides divided into eight lobes, the sections worked in *repoussé* with birds and scrolling vines in gilt relief on a very finely granulated silver ground, T'ang Dynasty, height 3in, width 2in
London £13,000 ($31,200).27.XI.73

A glazed pottery figure of a dog, Han Dynasty, height 9½in
New York $11,000 (£4,580).7.II.74

A three-colour tripod dish, the centre deeply incised with a ring of six heart-shaped panels, the everted rim with lipped edge glazed in green and in amber on the underside, the three paw feet ringed with amber glaze on the otherwise unglazed base, T'ang Dynasty, width 9½in
London £38,000 ($91,200). 1.IV.74

402 CHINESE CERAMICS

A glazed pottery equestrian figure with hound, T'ang Dynasty, height 16½in
New York $92,500 (£38,538). 7.II.74

A large chestnut-glazed pottery figure of a Fereghan horse, T'ang Dynasty, height 22¾in
New York $72,000 (£30,000). 20.XI.73
From the collection of Vance Kirkland Esq

An early Ming blue and white flower-shaped bowl, six-character mark of Hsüan Tê within a double circle, and of the period, width 8in
Hong Kong £190,000 ($456,000). 16.XI.73

Opposite page above
A Ming blue and white saucer dish, the interior painted with a central medallion of the Three Friends, six-character mark of Ch'êng Hua within a double circle, and of the period, width 7⅞in
Hong Kong £160,000 ($384,000). 16.XI.73

Below
Two Ch'ing copies of the Ming pattern which originated in the reign of Hsüan Tê (1426-1435).
Left Seal mark and period of Ch'ien Lung (1736-95), 7in, Hong Kong £1,900 ($4,560). 16.XI.73
Right One of a pair, six-character marks and period of T'ung Chih (1862-1873), 7in, Hong Kong £550 ($1,320). 16.XI.73

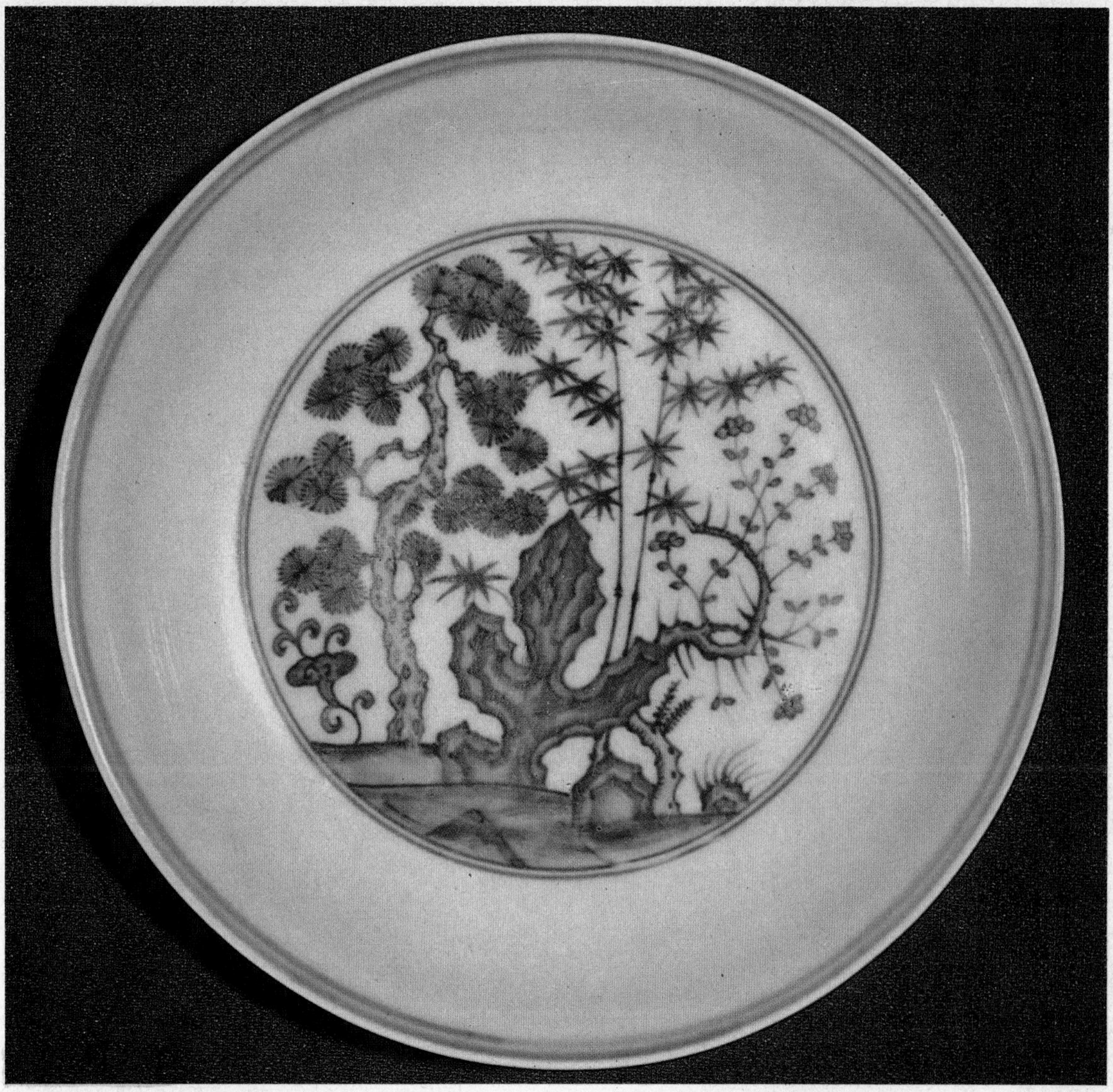

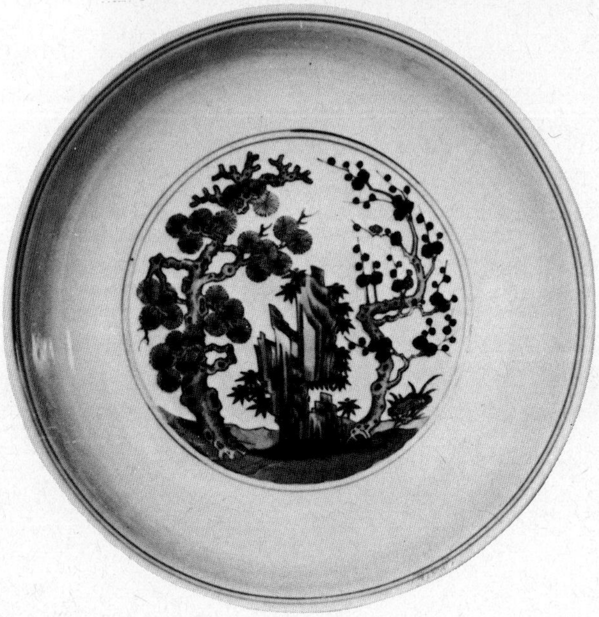

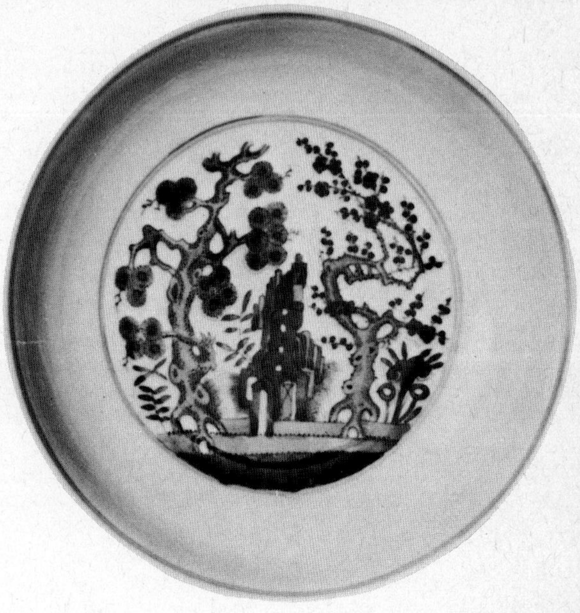

406 CHINESE CERAMICS

An early Ming blue and white bottle, decorated with a single superbly drawn dragon, Yung Lo, height 16¼in
London £420,000 ($1,008,000). 2.IV.74

A Ming blue and white *mei p'ing* and cover, Yung Lo, height 10¾in
London £160,000 ($384,000). 2.IV.74

An early blue and white *mei p'ing*, second half of the fourteenth century, height 16½in
London £170,000 ($408,000). 2.IV.74
From the collection of Ernst Schaefer

A sixteenth-century blue and white potiche, six-character mark of Chia Ching in underglaze-blue with a double circle, and of the period, height 10¼in
London £52,000 ($124,800). 2.IV.74
From the collection of Richard de la Mare Esq

An early fourteenth-century underglaze-red decorated vase, height 11½in
London £65,000 ($156,000). 2.IV.74

A fifteenth-century red-ground stemcup, Ch'êng Hua, height 4⅛in
London £48,000 ($115,200).
27.XI.73
Formerly in the collection of Sir Frank Swettenham, GCMG, sold in these rooms, 7th November 1946, £30; the collection of W. W. Winkworth Esq; and in the collection of Mrs Walter Sedgwick, sold in these rooms, 2nd July 1968, £1,900

A Ming red-ground saucer dish, *circa* 1500, width 8⅝in
London £26,000 ($62,400).
2.IV.74
From the collection of Mrs C. H. Lauru to whom this dish was presented by the priest of the Spirit Temple of Pai Chia T'an, from the furnishings of the temple. The gift was made with the approval of the princely family of Yi and of the village elders in recognition of her help to a child of the village

412 CHINESE CERAMICS

A Ming green-ground ovoid jar decorated with dragons in pursuit of 'flaming pearls', six-character mark and period of Wan Li, height 6⅞in
London £88,000 ($211,200). 27.XI.73
From the collection of Jonathan Leaver Esq
Previously sold in these rooms, 11th May 1965, £550

A large glazed pottery figure of an official, Ming Dynasty, height 44in
New York $28,000 (£11,667). 29.v.74
From the collection of Louise C. Morgan

414 CHINESE CERAMICS

A pair of blue and white *mei p'ing* vases, six-character mark and period of Ch'ien Lung, height 12¾in
New York $62,500 (£26,040). 24.v.74

A blue and white pilgrim flask painted in fifteenth-century style, early eighteenth century, height 12in
London £30,000 ($72,000). 2.IV.74
From the collection of Richard de la Mare Esq

A pair of Chinese taste *famille verte* stemcups, six-character marks of K'ang Hsi in underglaze-blue inside the footrims, and of the period, height 3in
London £160,000 ($384,000). 2.IV.74

A finely enamelled hexagonal *famille rose* bowl, six-character seal mark of Yung Chêng in underglaze-blue, and of the period, width 8¾in
London £95,000 ($228,000). 2.IV.74

A pair of Chinese taste *famille rose* chrysanthemum vases, six-character marks of Yung Chêng in underglaze-blue within double circles, and of the period, height 10¾in
London £75,000 ($180,000).2.IV.74

418 CHINESE CERAMICS

An imperial ruby-ground bowl, four-character mark *k'ang hsi yü chih*, in puce enamel within a double square, and of the period of K'ang Hsi, width 4⅜in
London £65,000 ($156,000). 27.XI.73

An imperial *famille rose* blue-ground bowl, four-character mark *k'ang hsi yü chih* in pink enamel within a double square, and of the period of K'ang Hsi, width 5¾in
London £65,000 ($156,000). 2.IV.74

CHINESE CERAMICS 419

A pair of *famille verte* figures of Asil game cocks, K'ang Hsi, mounted on Louis XV ormolu bases
London £48,000 ($115,200). 6.XI.73

A pair of *famille rose* figures of monkeys, their bodies finely flecked in brown with paler undersides, the ears and muzzles in pink, the noses and cheeks in iron-red and the eyes in yellow with black pupils, Ch'ien Lung, height 9¼in
London £34,000 ($81,600). 5.III.74

A pair of *famille rose* figures of pheasants, Ch'ien Lung, height 15in
London £62,000 ($148,800). 6.XI.73

A pair of brilliantly enamelled *famille rose* figures of pheasants, Ch'ien Lung, height 13in London £60,000 ($144,000). 5.III.74

A *famille rose* figure of an elephant, Ch'ien Lung, height 22¾in
London £50,000 ($120,000). 6.XI.73

424 CHINESE CERAMICS

An armorial dish of saucer shape, the centre decorated with the arms of the Portuguese Almeidas family, *circa* 1600, 7½in
London £1,800 ($4,320). 27.VI.74

A plate from George Washington's 'Order of the Cincinnati' service, *circa* 1786, 9⅝in
New York $12,000 (£5,000). 24.I.74

'O the roast beef of Old England, &C.' A *famille rose* punch bowl enamelled on each side after the print by William Hogarth, Ch'ien Lung, 15¾in
London £9,000 ($21,600). 6.XI.73

CHINESE CERAMICS 425

A *famille rose* vase finely painted in sepia with a portrait of George Bernard Shaw, the reverse with a long dedicatory inscription which translated reads: *Mr Bernard Shaw, Born 1856 in Ireland, is the most prominent thinker, statesman and man of letters of the present age. His essays and novels amount to millions of words and he has written more than forty plays. Wherever there is a language in the world, there is a translation of his works. His age is now approaching eighty and the brilliancy of his reasoning and discussion, as well as that of his spirit and energy, is still increasing incessantly. He is, indeed, a man of wisdom, of benevolence and of long age! by his follower, S. I. Hsiung.*
Circa 1916, 8¼in
London £800 ($1,920). 30.1.74
From the collection of Major R. Limbert

Left
A large *rouge-de-fer* and gilt Canton vase, mid-nineteenth century, 34¾in
London £1,300 ($3,120). 28.11.74

Far left
One of a pair of Canton *famille rose* vases, second half of the nineteenth century, 35½in
London £2,600 ($6,240). 30.1.74

426 CHINESE WORKS OF ART

A white jade covered vase, Ch'ien Lung period, height 11in
New York $75,000 (£31,250). 21.XI.73
Formerly in the collections of Captain and Mrs Dudley W. Knox, and Admiral Bowman McCalla, to whom it was presented by the Emperor of Japan, *circa* 1900, for services rendered for which no medal could be awarded.
Admiral Bowman McCalla lead the American relief expedition for the assistance of the legations at Peking during the Boxer Rebellion

Japanese Works of Art

A *Ko-Kutani* bottle decorated with a design of a cock and hen, late seventeenth century, 38.8cm London £8,500 ($20,400). 17.X.73

428 JAPANESE CERAMICS

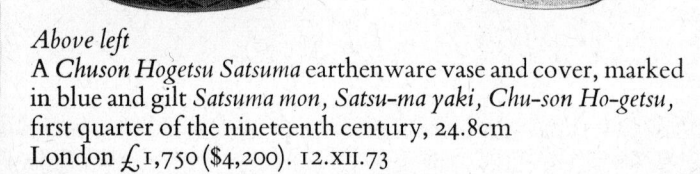

Above left
A *Chuson Hogetsu Satsuma* earthenware vase and cover, marked in blue and gilt *Satsuma mon, Satsu-ma yaki, Chu-son Ho-getsu*, first quarter of the nineteenth century, 24.8cm
London £1,750 ($4,200). 12.XII.73

Above right
One of a pair of *Imari* covered jars, *circa* 1700, 62.3cm
New York $5,200 (£2,167). 28.XI.73

A large *Kakiemon* jar and cover of baluster form, decorated in coloured enamels after a Dutch design with two figures under a flowering plum tree, late seventeenth century, 60.8cm
London £13,500 ($32,400). 20.II.74

Right
A large *Kakiemon* vase painted in coloured enamels with a continuous scene of peonies, late seventeenth century, 36cm
London £3,300 ($7,920). 17.X.73

Above
A lacquered wood figure of a *rakan* from the Rakan-Ji, Tokyo, *circa* 1690, height 86.7cm
New York $7,250 (£3,021). 27.XI.73
From the collection of the Honolulu Academy of Art

Right and below
A set of *suzuribako* and writing table, the table is lacquered completely *togidashi* with a scene of the Battle of the Uji Bridge, the *suzuribako* is lacquered in the same technique with a figure of Kajiwara Kagesuye, both unsigned, nineteenth century, table 62.2cm by 34.2cm, *suzuribako* 24.4cm by 22.2cm
New York $12,500 (£5,208). 27.XI.73

A gold lacquer three-tiered *jubako*, nineteenth century, 17.1cm by 21.2cm
Los Angeles $5,250 (£2,187). 12.III.74

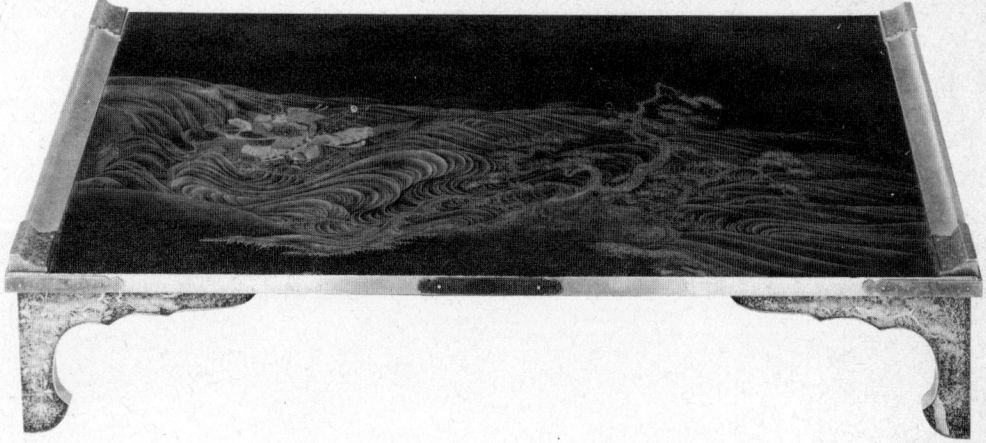

さらし賣
佐野川市蔵

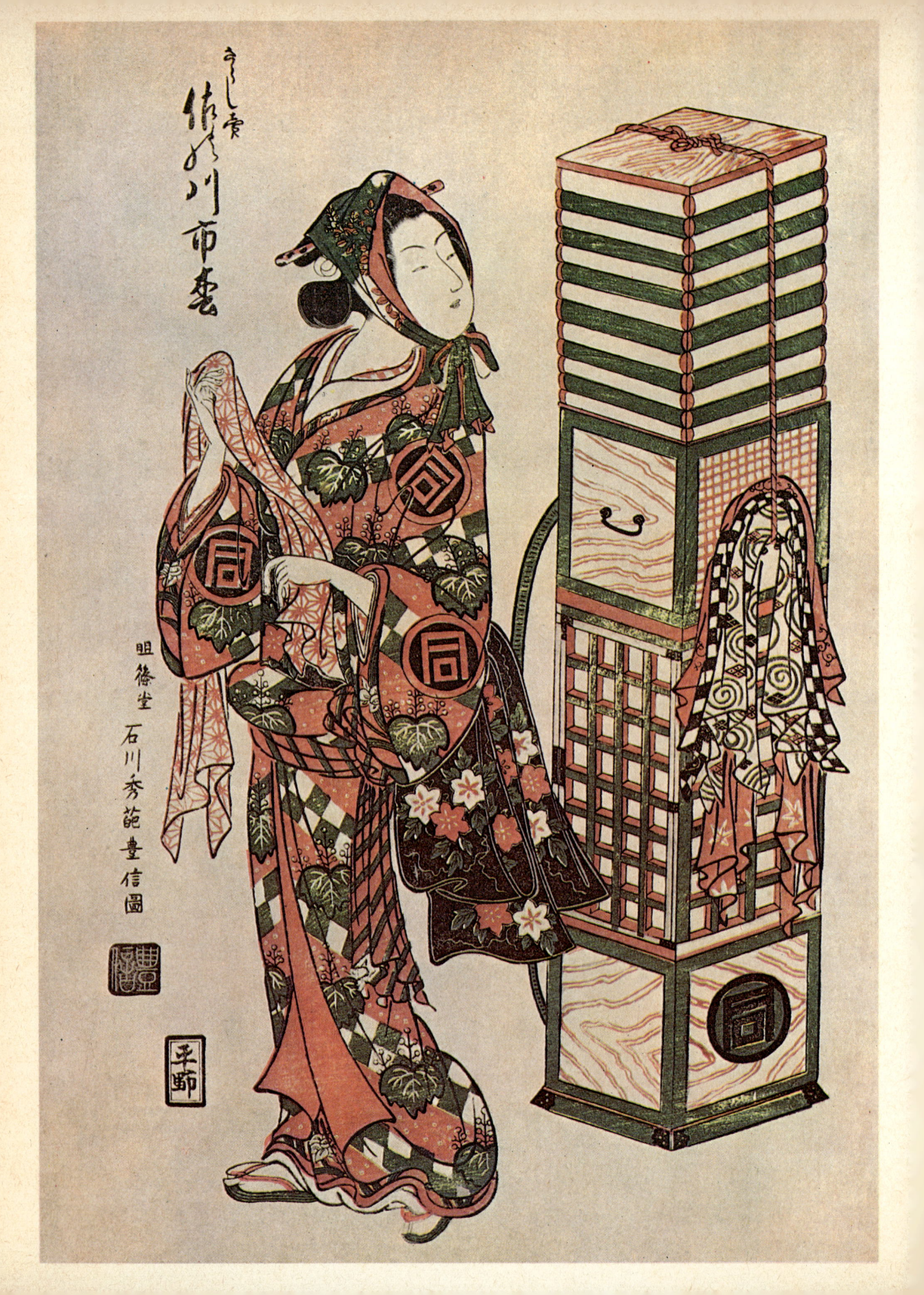

明篠堂
石川秀範豊信圖

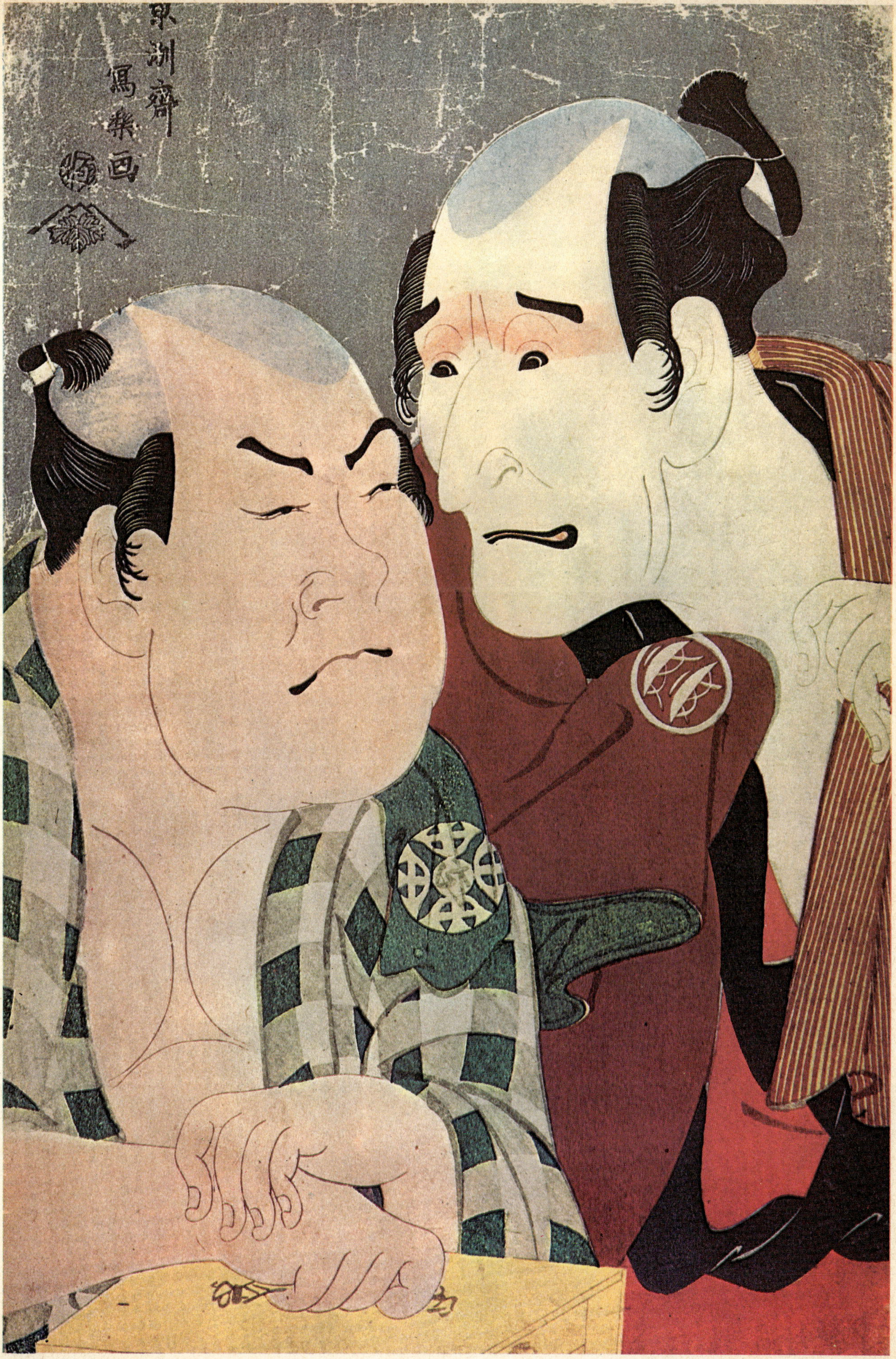
東洲齋寫樂画

KATSUSHIKA HOKUSAI
A drawing known as 'The Rape', but in fact a preliminary study for a book illustration of Soko protecting Lady Fujiyo from danger, from Vol 29 of *Shimpen Suiko Gaden*, published *circa* 1825, 29.8cm by 31.5cm
London £28,000 ($67,200). 26.III.74
From the collection of Henri Vever

TOSHUSAI SHARAKU
Brush drawing of the *sumo* wrestler Tanikaze standing beside the notorious Daidozan, ink and slight colour on thin paper, signed, 33.3cm by 24.3cm
London £24,000 ($57,600). 26.III.74
From the collection of Henri Vever

Opposite page
KITAGAWA UTAMARO
An *oban* of a half-length figure of a young woman, silver mica ground, signed, 38cm by 25.1cm
London £16,000 ($38,400). 26.III.74
From the collection of Henri Vever

Page 430
ISHIKAWA TOYONOBU
A large *oban*, *benizuri* (rose and green), signed, 42.9cm by 30.2cm
London £22,000 ($52,800). 26.III.74
From the collection of Henri Vever

Page 431
TOSHUSAI SHARAKU
An *oban* of Nakamura Konozo as the 'homeless boatman', signed, 37.5cm by 25.5cm
London £32,000 ($76,800). 26.III.74
From the collection of Henri Vever

婦人相學十躰
浮氣之相
相見
歌麿画

434 JAPANESE ARMS

A gilt-mounted *tachi-do* with a *saotome koshozan-suji-bachi*
New York $17,000 (£7,083). 29.XI.73

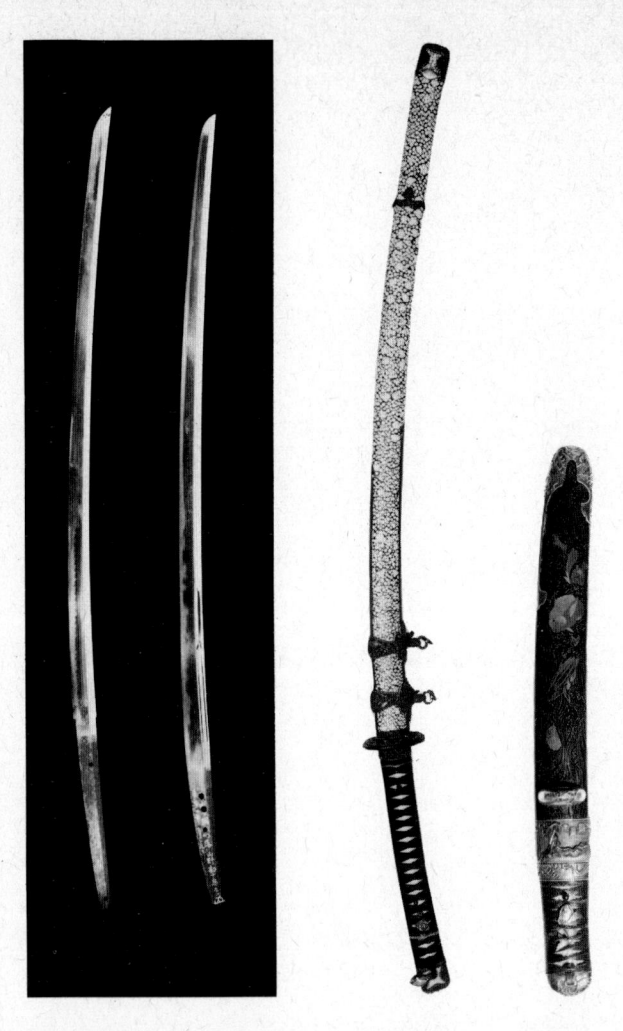

From left to right
A *Shinto Katana* by Fujiwara Naganobu, dated 1857. Length 84.8cm
London £5,600 ($13,440). 11.XII.73
From the collection of Colonel F. M. Hill, CBE

A *Koto Tachi* signed *Bishu Osafune Tsuneiye* and dated *Oei* 28th year (1421). Length 69.7cm
London £2,400 ($5,760). 11.XII.73

A *Tachi* mounted in a polished shark-skin scabbard with finely carved copper mounts by Hisataka, signed *Noshu Akasaka ju Kaneshige* and dated *Taiei* 2nd year (1522). Length 86.8cm
London £2,700 ($6,480). 11.XII.73
From the collection of L. W. Avery Esq

A *Shinshinto Aikuchi* signed *Maizuru Tomohide saku* and mounted in a fine lacquer scabbard with silver mounts. Length 23.2cm
New York $2,400 (£1,000). 3.IV.74

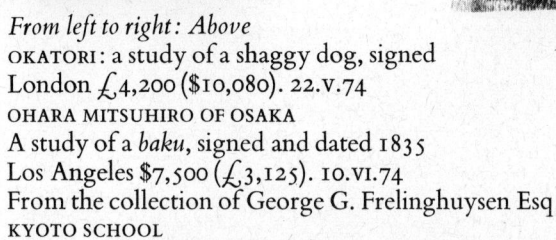

From left to right: Above
OKATORI: a study of a shaggy dog, signed
London £4,200 ($10,080). 22.V.74
OHARA MITSUHIRO OF OSAKA
A study of a *baku*, signed and dated 1835
Los Angeles $7,500 (£3,125). 10.VI.74
From the collection of George G. Frelinghuysen Esq
KYOTO SCHOOL
A study of a sleeping boar, unsigned, late eighteenth century
London £2,400 ($5,760). 22.V.74
Right
KOGETSU
A model of a pear and wasp, signed
New York $4,200 (£1,750). 16.I.74
From the collection of Ambassador and Mrs
William J. Sebald
TAMETAKA
A large study of a ghostly *nue*, signed
London £7,500 ($18,000). 27.III.74
From the collection of Henri Vever

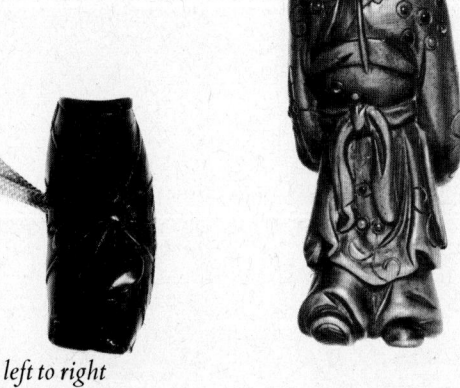

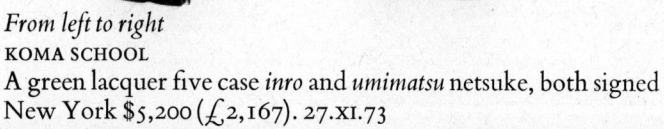

From left to right
KOMA SCHOOL
A green lacquer five case *inro* and *umimatsu* netsuke, both signed
New York $5,200 (£2,167). 27.XI.73
KOKEISAI SANSHO
A wood netsuke depicting a conjurer, signed, late nineteenth century
Los Angeles $4,100 (£1,708). 10.VI.74

A study of a heraldic lion, the plinth carved with a seal character *Raku*, eighteenth century
London £3,000 ($7,200). 27.III.74 From the collection of Henri Vever

Fig 4 A five case *inro*, decorated on *fundame* ground with a scene of a stag and doe on rocky ground, the interior is of *nashiji*, signed *Sosen fude, Koma Kansai saku*
London £2,000 ($4,800). 28.III.74

Fig 3 A two case *inro* of rounded form, with a shaded gold ground and on either side a design of bamboos bending in the wind, the interior is of *nashiji*, signed and dated *Gyonen rokuju go Kobayashi Yasutaka* with *kakihan*
London £1,300 ($3,120). 28.III.74

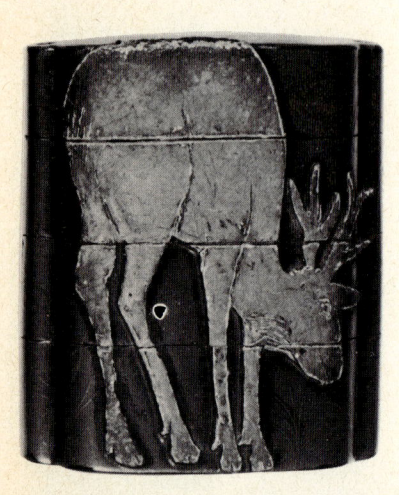

Fig 1 A three case *inro*, decorated with a grazing deer and trees in oxidised pewter, mother-of-pearl and gold *hiramakie*, the interior is of *kinji*, with scratched signature inside upper case *Hokkyo Korin tsukuru*
London £50 ($120). 28.III.74

Fig 2 A three case *inro*, decorated on the *roiro* ground with a broad river winding between undulating banks, the interior is of *kinji*, with the scratched signature *Hokkyo Korin tsukuru* with *kakihan*
London £160 ($384). 28.III.74

The Harari Collection of *Inro*

By Neil Davey

Among the many arts peculiar to Japan, that of the lacquerer must stand out as being one of the most accomplished. Originally 'taken' from China, as were a number of their arts, the Japanese love of design soon showed itself in this highly difficult technical skill and turned what in China had been a craft into a very sophisticated art form. The most brilliant examples of this art are the *inro*, small boxes of interlocking compartments used for seals and medicines, which were worn slung from the belt (*obi*) by a thin cord.

The Harari collection of *inro*, sold in London in March, comprised a wide variety of types and styles forming a very interesting group of study pieces as well as expressing the collector's personality. Ralph Harari was a man of great taste whose love of works of art was eclectic. His first interest in Japanese art was for paintings and drawings, more particularly he collected the work of Katsuchika Hokusai, his collection of the drawings of this artist is now in the Ashmolean Museum, Oxford. It was fitting that when he discovered *inro*, Mr Harari should have recognised an extension of the work of well-known painters – albeit in a different medium and in miniature form – as some *inro* were in fact executed by them.

Among the styles represented in the collection, which included works by the majority of known schools of lacquerers, was an interesting group of *inro* in the manner of Ogata Korin (1658-1716). A number of *inro* and other lacquer wares bearing the signature of Korin are known, although it is extremely doubtful whether he actually made any of them. He was a highly gifted painter, working with the celebrated Kano school and it is known that he studied laquer painting under Koetsu Honnami. Most of the works ascribed to him, however, were probably made by lacquerers working from his designs and under his direction. These *inro*, consisting mainly of gold or black lacquer, profusely inlaid in pewter and mother-of-pearl, show great inventiveness and freedom from the rigid traditional styles. The examples illustrated on figures 1 and 2 are typical of the style of Korin and his school.

Ralph Harari's fascination with Japanese painting can be recognised in two *inro* of the Koma school of lacquerers made in the nineteenth century (Fig 3 and 4). The first shows two bamboo paintings, realistically rendering the style of *sumie* (ink painting) and inscribed to the effect that the two scenes are after paintings by masters of the Kano school. The shaded gold ground has been cleverly worked to simulate the gold leaf ground used by members of that school. The second example shows a charming scene of a stag and a doe, again in the manner of a brush painting, this time from a design by the eighteenth-century painter Mori Sosen, well known for his studies of deer and monkeys which were executed in a soft naturalistic style.

Painters who turned to lacquering were also well represented in the collection. Particularly important were Ogawa Haritsu, known by his art name of Ritsuo (1663-1747), and the later

Fig 5 A two case *inro*, decorated on the *roiro* ground with an owl perched on a gnarled branch, all in gold *takamakie*, inlaid pottery and malachite, signed with a seal *Kwan*
London £260 ($624). 28.III.74

Fig 6 A three case *inro* in the form of a Chinese ink-cake, the interior is *nashiji*, scratched signature *Zeshin*, with nut *ojime*
London £5,000 ($12,000). 28.III.74

artist, thought by many to be one of the greatest lacquerers of all times, Shibata Zeshin (1807-1891). Ritsuo was a student of the Tosa school of painting and a disciple of Koetsu Honnami, as well as being a gifted poet; he developed a bold, uninhibited style of lacquer work. He embellished his works with inlay and appliqué of pewter, mother-of-pearl and glazed pottery. The last had the particular effect of strengthening the design by adding colours difficult to produce with lacquer. The *inro* illustrated (Fig 5) is typical of his style, the strong black ground decorated with a pottery owl on a creeper-clad branch in gold lacquer with further details of pottery.

Zeshin was a superb artist with a fine sense of line, equally skilful with a brush or the tools of the lacquerer. The example illustrated (Fig 6) shows the art of Zeshin the lacquer worker rather than the painter and is in the style for which he was famous. It depicts a Chinese ink cake, brilliantly carved in black lacquer with a ferocious tiger beside a gnarled pine tree, the reverse similarly carved with the boy hero Yoko, stalking the beast before slaying it.

These few examples illustrate the close connection which existed between painters and lacquerers in Japan; they also belie the arduous process needed to paint or build up by layers a picture or a design on a miniature object such as the *inro*. This is an art form which others have attempted to imitate throughout the centuries with little or no success. It has recently enjoyed a revival of interest in the West. Ralph Harari did much with his collection to further our knowledge and awareness of it.

Glass and Paperweights

Left A stippled wine glass by A. Schouman, signed and dated 1747, height 7⅞in London £3,400 ($8,160). 3.VI.74
Aert Schouman (1720–1792), a well-known painter and engraver, was born in Dordrecht and worked at The Hague. He was a friend and pupil of Greenwood
Right A documentary stippled goblet by Frans Greenwood, the round-funnel bowl stipple-engraved with a half-length portrait, in the manner of Gerard Dou, with the signature and date *F. Greenwood, fecit 1742*, height 11 5/16 in London £4,200 ($10,080). 3.VI.74
Frans Greenwood born 17th April, 1680, of English parents in Rotterdam, was probably a merchant in Rotterdam before he entered the Civil Service in 1726. He married Maria van de Hoolaart and had a son Cornelis who became a painter. Greenwood died on August 12th, 1761

440 GLASS AND PAPERWEIGHTS

A Silesian wheel-engraved goblet probably by Christian Gottfried Schneider, Warmbrunn, *circa* 1760, height 7¾in
London £950 ($2,280). 3.VI.74
From the collection of R. H. Tappin Esq

A late seventeenth-century Nuremberg engraved goblet, height 9¼in
London £2,300 ($5,520). 3.XII.73

A Silesian goblet probably by Christian Gottfried Schneider of Warmbrunn, engraved with a portrait of Frederick the Great, *circa* 1740, height 9⅞in
London £1,250 ($3,000). 3.XII.73

A commemorative goblet, engraved with a three-masted sailing vessel inscribed *Prosperity to the East India Company, Duke of Cumberland*, height 8in
London £1,950 ($4,680). 22.X.73

A finely-gilt blue-glass decanter and stopper, *circa* 1760, height 10¾in
London £1,250 ($3,000). 4.II.74
From the collection of H. Jacob Esq

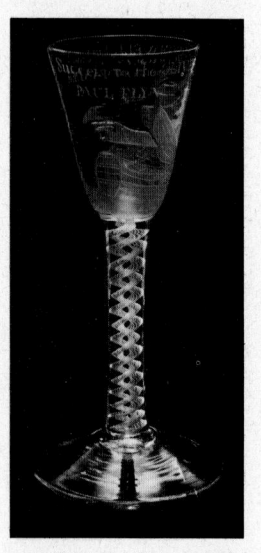

An engraved privateer glass inscribed in diamond point *Success to the OLIVER CROMWELL Privateer, PAUL FLYN COMMANDER*, height 6 3/16 in
London £1,100 ($2,640). 3.VI.74
From the collection of J. W. Hele Esq

GLASS AND PAPERWEIGHTS 441

An Apsley Pellatt sulphide plaque enclosing a *crystallo-ceramie* bust portrait of King George IV, the top surmounted by a metal crown, 5¾in by 3⅝in
London £420 ($1,008). 3.XII.73

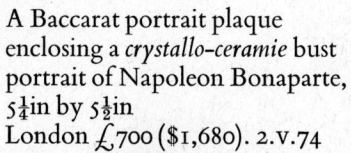

A Baccarat portrait plaque enclosing a *crystallo-ceramie* bust portrait of Napoleon Bonaparte, 5¼in by 5½in
London £700 ($1,680). 2.V.74

A Webb plum-coloured cameo-glass vase signed *Geo. Woodall*, the base marked *AURORA*, *Thos. Webb & Sons*, circa 1885, height 8¾in
London £5,200 ($12,480). 20.VI.74

A cameo-glass vase, the translucent-pink glass overlaid in opaque white and finely carved, circa 1885, height 18¼in
London £1,020 ($2,448). 14.III.74

A Webb ivory-cameo eastern taste vase, marked *WEBB*, circa 1880, height 8¼in
London £270 ($648). 20.VI.74
From the collection of Mrs H. Aubrey-Gentry

442 GLASS AND PAPERWEIGHTS

A Baccarat early pansy and garland weight, 3⅛in
London £4,200 ($10,080). 2.v.74
Formerly from the Paul Jokelson Collection, sold in these rooms, 20th May, 1963 £300

A Baccarat blue pom-pom weight, 2⅞in
London £2,000 ($4,800). 2.v.74

A Baccarat flat bouquet weight, 3⅛in
London £2,100 ($5,040). 3.xii.73

A St Louis blue salamander weight, 3¼in
London £2,400 ($5,760). 3.xii.73
This type of salamander appears to be unrecorded in blue glass

A Baccarat faceted 'horse' weight, 3⅛in
London £3,200 ($7,680). 2.v.74
Very few weights of this unusual technique are known. It is particularly rare to find the horse in a standing position; weights with a galloping blue horse and with a trotting pink horse are known

A St Louis tricolor marbrie weight, 3⅛in
London £2,100 ($5,040). 3.xii.73
This combination of colours appears to be unrecorded

Art Nouveau and Art Deco

From left to right
An Art Deco vase by André Thuret, engraved *André Thuret, circa* 1930, height 11¼in £420 ($1,008)
A Tiffany feathered vase, engraved *Louis C. Tiffany, LCT D 708, circa* 1900, height 10½in £700 ($1,680)
A 'Jack-in-the-Pulpit' peacock iridescent glass vase by Louis Comfort Tiffany, engraved *1932 JLC Tiffany Favrile, circa* 1900, height 19½in £3,600 ($8,640)
A Tiffany lava/Cypriote glass vase, engraved *Louis C. Tiffany L.C.T.D 140, circa* 1900, height 7⅜in £1,600 ($3,840)
An angular *pâte-de-cristal* vase by Gabriel Argy Rousseau, signed, *circa* 1925, height 6⅜in £400 ($960)
Sold in London on 3rd April 1974

Three decorated gesso and mother-of-pearl panels by Frederick Marriott

Above: The Angel of Night, monogrammed *FM* and dated 1904, 14in by 9¾in £2,400 ($5,760)
Above right: Oberon, set with opals, monogrammed *FM* and dated 1905, 9¾in by 14in £2,200 ($5,280)
Below right: Titania, set with opals, monogrammed *FM* and dated 1903, 9¾in by 14in £2,000 ($4,800)
Sold in London on 3rd April 1974

A Tiffany Studios peacock feather lamp, the domed shade marked *Tiffany Studios New York 1472-2*, the oil container marked *Tiffany Studios New York 7877*, circa 1900, height 25⅞in London £10,000 ($24,000). 5.VII.74

A Tiffany Favrile glass and bronze wisteria lamp, base impressed *Tiffany Studios, New York, 1073*, height 26½in New York $27,000 (£11,250). 26.X.73

446 ART NOUVEAU AND ART DECO

A *pâte-de-cristal* vase by François Décorchemont, with the impressed stamp *Décorchemont*, the underside engraved *0684*, *circa* 1910, height 10in
London £3,000 ($7,200). 5.VII.74

A Tiffany Favrile glass peacock paperweight vase, engraved *L.C. Tiffany Favrile, 9778D, circa* 1909, height 7in
New York $5,500 (£2,291). 11.I.74

The Bugattis

By Malcolm Haslam

Today, in the house of a connoisseur one might come across a piece of furniture which defies stylistic categorisation. The signature 'Bugatti' might be found either brushed *con brio* on the painted vellum stretched over the members, or written in mock Arabic characters of inlaid steel in the ebonised wood. Perhaps, in the same house, one might admire an *animalier* group in bronze, and thinking that its treatment was a little too impressionistic for Barye or Mêne, look closer to read the incised signature 'R. Bugatti'. Having admired these works of art, and about to leave, the garage's doors would open to reveal a shining motor-car, not a new model but obviously tended with loving care; and, on the enamelled disc at the head of the radiator, the visitor would read again the name 'Bugatti'.

In each instance the name indicates that the object is the work of a different member of the same family: Carlo Bugatti created the furniture, his elder son Ettore was responsible for the famous motor-cars, and his younger son Rembrandt was the sculptor. The two generations of this Italian family spanned ninety-two years, approximately a century during which, it might be argued, better furniture, better sculpture and better motor-cars were produced. But few would deny that the originality and artistry shown by each Bugatti was a notable contribution to an era that will always be highly regarded for those qualities.

Carlo Bugatti was born in Milan in 1855. His father, Luigi, was a sculptor known for his monumental chimney-pieces; but he spent most of his time and money trying to discover the secret of perpetual motion. Carlo, according to his own assertion, received no formal art-education, but his grand-daughter records that he attended the Accademia di Brera in Milan and the Académie des Beaux-Arts in Paris. He was a talented artist who applied himself to architecture before he turned to cabinet-making; he was also a painter and sculptor, and made musical instruments of his own invention. He was known among his friends as 'the young Leonardo', a sobriquet which probably alluded not only to his universal artistic genius but also to the fact that he spent much time in France as well as in Milan. Married with two young sons, he set up his home and his studio in Paris, but retained his Milanese connections.

He was acquainted with several artists and musicians who also took advantage of the new rail link between the two cities. Giacomo Puccini and his librettist Lillica were frequent visitors to the Bugattis' Paris home. Others were the sculptors Leoncavallo, De Grandi, Ercole Rosa and Prince Paul Troubetskoy. The last, whose family lived on an estate by Lake Maggiore, introduced Carlo to the ideas – and the person – of Leo Tolstoy. Another friend of the family was Giovanni Segantini the painter, who married Carlo's sister, Luigia, in 1881. It was in this milieu that Carlo's young sons grew up.

A table/cabinet by Carlo Bugatti, constructed in hard wood as four 'U' shapes, on block feet, each 'U' centring a circular fall-front shield, opening to reveal tiers of five drawers, the tabletop covered in vellum, the corners, the drawer fronts, inner shelves, legs and outer shields inlaid in formal geometric patterns in brass, white metal and ebony, the shields bordered in vellum, the insides covered by circular embossed brass panels, *circa* 1900, 27in London £4,100 ($9,840). 7.XI.73

In 1888, Carlo Bugatti first won a prize for his furniture at the Italian Exhibition in London. Before these entirely original creations of wood and painted vellum, embellished with inlaid steel, *repoussé* brass fittings, ivory and ebony, the English critics were diffident but generally congratulatory. They described the painting as 'Japanese' or 'impressionist'; one called the furniture 'quaint', and most found its style derived from Arab sources, either 'Turkish', 'Eastern', 'Algerian', or simply 'Arabian'. Some features of Bugatti furniture do suggest such sources: the arch profiles, the tassels, the uprights which terminate in minaret-like forms, and the geometrical patterns of some of the metal inlay. Bugatti had contacts with Muslim architects and supplied furniture for the palace of the mother of the Khedive in Constantinople. On the other hand, the paintings on the vellum and the naturalistic treatment of the animals, birds and fish which formed handles and hinges on some pieces represent a vigorous nod in the direction of the *japonisme* currently popular on both sides of the Channel.

The Moorish influence found in Carlo Bugatti's furniture is to be related to that passion for North Africa and the Near East which was a feature of French Romanticism. By the time the Milanese artists of Bugatti's generation reached Paris, Romanticism proper was dead, but it must have been the Paris of Hugo and Delacroix which had beckoned to them across the Alps. Other points suggest that Bugatti and his friends shared a nostalgia for the Paris they had read about, but had never known, the Paris of the years between the two revolutions of 1830 and 1848. When Carlo's second son was born with a large head, it was taken as a portent of greatness, so Ercole Rosa suggested he should be called 'Rembrandt', after the artist whose red cap of the self-portraits had become part of the aspiring Romantic artist's insignia.

Left A *sellette* by Carlo Bugatti, the wooden legs part cased in spirals of wrought copper and supporting the vellum-covered top, decorated with inlaid wood and metal shield, slung with central silk tassel. Signed *Bugatti* on the stretcher shelf, early twentieth century, 39¾in   London £1,100 ($2,640). 5.VII.74

Right A side table by Carlo Bugatti, *en suite* with the *sellette*. The vellum top signed *Bugatti*, early twentieth century, height 30in   London £3,400 ($8,160). 5.VII.74

Giacomo Puccini achieved one of his greatest successes with *La Bohème* (1896), an evocation of Henri Murger's Paris. These Italians placed a Romantic emphasis on originality. 'Of no special style' was Bugatti's description of his furniture, quoted by *The Artist* in 1888. 'In this environment', wrote Ettore Bugatti of his childhood in Paris, 'I acquired the idea that art could not be learnt, and that it was wiser not to persevere if only mediocre progress were made.'

A comparison between the illustrations of the furniture Bugatti exhibited in London in 1888 and of the rooms he furnished for the Turin Exhibition of 1902 reveals little change in style. However, two years before the latter event, Bugatti had shown his furniture at the Paris Exhibition of 1900, that apotheosis of Art Nouveau, and in the Turin ensembles the effects of that demonstration are evident. Many pieces are more organic; they curve and slide round the rooms in a way that suggests the dynamism of Guimard's or Van de Velde's suites. The furniture is no longer a collection of free-standing pieces in a room, but rather the room and its furniture have become an integrated plastic experience, in a manner which Edmond Goncourt had disparagingly labelled 'the yachting style'. Fritz Minkus, writing in *Kunst und Kunsthandwerk* in 1902, used an alternative simile from the sphere of transport, equally disparaging, in his description of the Bugatti furniture at Turin: on him it produced 'the effect

An extravagant banquette by Carlo Bugatti, constructed as two seats, of similar form to the throne armchairs illustrated on the opposite page, and flanking a central vellum table, with double horizontal back panels, one covered in vellum, the other in beaten and pierced brass, each with full fringe. The back panel signed *Bugatti*, early twentieth century, length 94in, height 58in
London £5,800 ($13,920). 5.VII.74

of a newly invented automobile, which cannot quite be comprehended at first glance, of outstanding technical refinement, together with an extremely ugly and ponderous appearance.'

The irony of Minkus' criticism must have been felt by Carlo Bugatti, if he read it. Only a few years before he had been quite unprepared for the decision of his elder son, Ettore, to become an unpaid apprentice with an engineering company in Milan which made motor-tricycles. Both Ettore (1881–1947) and his younger brother Rembrandt (1883–1916) were brought up to be artists, both having been taught painting and sculpture by their father's friend Prince Troubetskoy, who was achieving international repute for his portrait-sculpture.

'Rembrandt wanted to be an engineer and build locomotives. I wanted to be an artist, but I was no more gifted for art than he was for mechanics,' wrote Ettore Bugatti many years later. It was in deference to his younger brother's facility with the pencil and with clay, that Ettore gave up art. In 1895, he was invited by friends of his father to try out the motor-tricycle built by the Milan engineering firm of Prinetti and Stucchi. 'In a short while, just by looking at the machine, I had grasped all the intricacies of its mechanism,' Ettore recalled. With the encouragement his father had given him to work with his hands and to understand construction in wood and metal, Ettore was qualified to be an asset in any workshop and in 1898 he joined Prinetti and Stucchi.

A pair of throne armchairs by Carlo Bugatti, the flat vellum seats supported in 'U'-shaped wood frames, with vellum-covered arms, asymmetrical back props terminating in fringed discs and with circular vellum shields, slung on tasselled cords and forming the back. Each signed *Bugatti* on the vellum back, early twentieth century, height of each, 52¾in London £8,000 ($19,200). 5.VII.74

 The following decade was one of triumph for the Bugatti clan. Carlo won awards for his furniture at Paris in 1900 and Turin in 1902. Three years later he sold the right to the manufacture of his designs to the Milan firm of De Vecchi, and retired to Pierrefonds, near the forest of Compiègne, where he devoted his time to painting and sculpture. Ettore built motor-tricycles which he raced with considerable success in Italy and France until 1900 when he built his first four-wheeled car, which had four engines and was the first vehicle fitted with pneumatic tyres by Pirelli. In 1900 he aroused the interest of the Counts Gulinelli, two brothers who owned huge estates near Ferrara and who were themselves making experiments with motor-cars. Financed by them, and by his father, Ettore built his third car. It had a four-cylinder, water-cooled engine, four forward gears and one reverse, ignition by electric magneto, and overhead valves; it comfortably reached speeds of forty miles per hour. At the first International Motor Show at Milan in 1901, Bugatti won the Grand Prix with this car, for which he was also awarded a special medal by the French Automobile Club.

1933 Bugatti, type 50T, Sports two-seater

At the Milan show, Ettore Bugatti was approached by a director of the De Dietrich company of Niederbronn, Alsace, and the following year he entered into a seven-year contract with the firm to design and supervise the manufacture of his motor-cars, which would be known as De Dietrich-Bugatti. Baron de Dietrich had to send the contract to Carlo Bugatti for his approval as Ettore was under twenty-one. So began Ettore Bugatti's association with Alsace, where he remained until his death.

De Dietrich gave up the manufacture of motor-cars in 1903, but Bugatti did not have to wait long before he found his next backer, Mathis, who ran an import-export business in Strasbourg. Ernest Friderich was working for Mathis at that time and be became Bugatti's mechanic and subsequently a famous driver of his racing-cars. Together, Bugatti and Friderich built the Hermes at Graffenstanden, outside Strasbourg. This model, with an engine of nine litres capacity, was the first large car Bugatti made; it was followed by a ten-litre model in 1907 which was produced under licence by the Deutz Gasmotoren Fabrik at Cologne. In 1909, he designed another model for Deutz which had a 3.2 litre engine, but he was also building, on his own account, a light car with an 1100 cc engine. Deutz were interested only in larger cars, so Bugatti built the new model in the cellar of the house where he was living in Cologne. When it was finished, it was too big to get through the door. So with Friederich's help, Bugatti dismantled it and reassembled it in the open. He called it *Pur-Sang*. In it, he and Friderich drove to the Darmstadt Bank in Strasbourg, and finance was arranged for the establishment of workshops in an old dye-works near the village of Molsheim. Here the production of Bugatti motor-cars began in 1910, and it was here that all the great models, such as the 35, the 43 and the 57, of the next forty years were built.

Apart from the excellence of the motor-cars themselves, the methods of production at Molsheim link Ettore Bugatti to his father. The workshops, as well as the nearby house in

Bugatti's Mathis type Hermes, 60 h.p., 4-cylinder, taken at the time of the Kaiserpreis at Hamburg in 1905 in which Bugatti drove. The personalities, from left to right, are: the President of Fiat, Ernest Friderick, Ettore Bugatti (at the wheel), P. Marchal, F. Nazarro (passenger seat), V. Lancia (top left), Rembrandt Bugatti (top centre), E. C. Mathis, Wagner (top right), Agnelli.

which 'Le Patron' – as Bugatti was known – lived with his family, were kept in immaculate order. A writer in the *Journal of Decorative Art* in 1888 had commended Carlo Bugatti for the workmanship of his furniture, and saw him as a true disciple of John Ruskin. Writing forty years later in *The Autocar,* W. F. Bradley praised Ettore Bugatti and his establishment at Molsheim: 'John Ruskin's soul would have been delighted at this example of the artist-artisan; of the engineer who seeks to vent his artistic temperament in terms of mechanics . . . of the man who has happily combined an artistic home with production methods and who has succeeded in transmitting this joyous creative spirit to all those who labour with him.'

In Paris, in 1910, the name Bugatti appeared in the catalogues of three important exhibitions. At the Salon de la Société Nationale, Carlo exhibited a painting and Rembrandt sculpture. At the motor show in the Grand Palais, Ettore exhibited his new motor-car. At the Salon d'Automne, Rembrandt again exhibited sculpture. Rembrandt had started working in Paris in 1900, after exhibiting his work in Turin and Venice. Through Prince Troubetskoy, he was introduced to A. A. Hébrard, the *fondeur* whose casting is one of the glories of French sculpture at the turn of the century. Rembrandt first exhibited at the Salon de la Société Nationale in 1904; the following year his work was favourably noticed in the French artistic journals, and was the subject of a full-length article by M. Horteloup in *The Studio*. Horteloup points out the influence of Troubetskoy, and attributes the young sculptor's manual dexterity to his early training in the decorative arts which he received in his father's furniture workshops.

Rembrandt Bugatti's reputation as an *animalier* continued to grow. He was made a Chevalier of the Légion d'Honneur. He worked in plasticine directly from his models at the Jardin des Plantes in Paris and, after he moved to Antwerp, at the zoological gardens there. Horteloup mentioned that Bugatti knew 'nothing of animal anatomy . . . he relies solely on

REMBRANDT BUGATTI
L'oiseau secrétaire
Bronze, signed and numbered A2, stamped with the foundry mark *A. A. Hébrard, cire perdue*
London £650 ($1,820). 26.IV.67

REMBRANDT BUGATTI
La panthère
Signed and stamped *cire perdue A. A. Hébrard*, 8½in
London £700 ($1,750). 2.XII.71

his eye to remain faithful to the truth'. This power of observation, together with craftsmanship and technical perfection, is characteristic of the work of all the Bugattis. 'It is by observation that one can penetrate into the nature of things'; that was written by Ettore, not Rembrandt, Bugatti, who although never trained as an engineer had an intuitive understanding of machines, so much so, for instance, that he knew that inlet valves should be larger than outlet valves and not *vice versa* as had always been believed previously. Rembrandt understood that it was not anatomical exactitude which would make his sculptures look like real animals. It is the animal's pose which he selected, or the movement which he managed to suggest, that make his sculptures so real. By grouping animals together, he somehow conveys, in a way reminiscent of paintings by Franz Marc, the world of those animals as they experience it. Like Marc too, he became increasingly conscious of the animal's role as victim, and he expressed this pathos in works bearing titles such as *Antwerp Horse-Fair*, *Sick horses coming up from the mine*, and *The wounded hind*. Rembrandt left his studio in Antwerp when the Germans invaded Belgium in 1914, and returned to Paris where he committed suicide in 1916. If the reason for this act was ever known, it seems never to have been published; but, considering the Tolstoyan ethics which he must have imbibed from his father and from his teacher, both the pathos of his later sculptures and his suicide may be seen as an understandable reaction to a world where aggression and murder had become the norm.

After the Great War, Carlo Bugatti went to live with Ettore and his family at Molsheim. There he died in 1940, having survived his elder grandson Jean, who was killed when he crashed during a speed trial in 1939. Some of the car bodies Jean had designed during the 30s show that the flair for elegance and originality had passed to a third generation of Bugattis. Ettore died in 1947.

456   JEWELLERY

From left to right: Above
A cabochon emerald of octagonal shape, weighing 71.43 carats SF600,000 (£79,576; $190,981)
A hexagonal-shaped emerald, weighing 49.36 carats SF250,000 (£33,156; $79,576)
Centre
An antique octagonal emerald pendant mounted in gold. Gross weight 33.66 carats SF170,000 (£22,546; $54,111)
Below
An antique pendant, the hexagonal-shaped emerald cut *en cabochon* on the reverse. Gross weight 74.28 carats SF300,000 (£39,788; $79,576)
An antique emerald pendant of hexagonal shape. Gross weight 66.12 carats SF220,000 (£29,178; $70,027)
Sold in Zürich on 15th November 1973

Jewellery

An antique emerald pendant, the large pear-shaped emerald carved on one side and partly faceted on the other, the reversible gold mount enamelled in typical Jaipur palette of crimson, green and lilac, the border applied with twenty-two diamonds cut to simulate flower petals
SF1,350,000 (£179,046; $429,711)

A pair of pendent earrings in emeralds and diamonds, the two pear-shaped emeralds weighing respectively 24.99 carats and 21.76 carats
SF520,000 (£68,966; $165,517)
Sold in Zürich on 15th November 1973

458　JEWELLERY

A mid-nineteenth-century rajah's silver double-seated covered state howdah, length 7ft 3in
Zürich SF50,000 (£6,631; $15,915). 15.XI.73
Reputed to be from the Indumati Palace at Baroda

A mid-nineteenth-century Indian silver and silver gilt royal throne, height 4ft 5½in
SF80,000 (£10,610; $25,464)
An Indian silver and silver gilt tripod table, last quarter of the nineteenth century, diameter 3ft 4½in
SF35,000 (£4,642; $11,141)
Sold in Zürich on 15th November 1973
The only person who seems to have given any serious consideration to the difficult subject of dating Indian silver furniture was the Marquis of Curzon in *British Government in India* (London, 1925). Discussing similar Vice Regal thrones he states that they are said to have been made by Messrs Hamilton of Calcutta for Lord Northbrook, Viceroy and Governor-General of India from 1872-75. Hamiltons were probably the largest silversmiths in India, and are known to have been producing silver as early as 1815, though most of their marked products are in English style

A pair of earrings in rubies and diamonds SF85,000 (£12,057; $28,936)
A necklace in rubies and diamonds SF280,000 (£39,716; $95,319)
Sold in Zürich on 9th May 1974

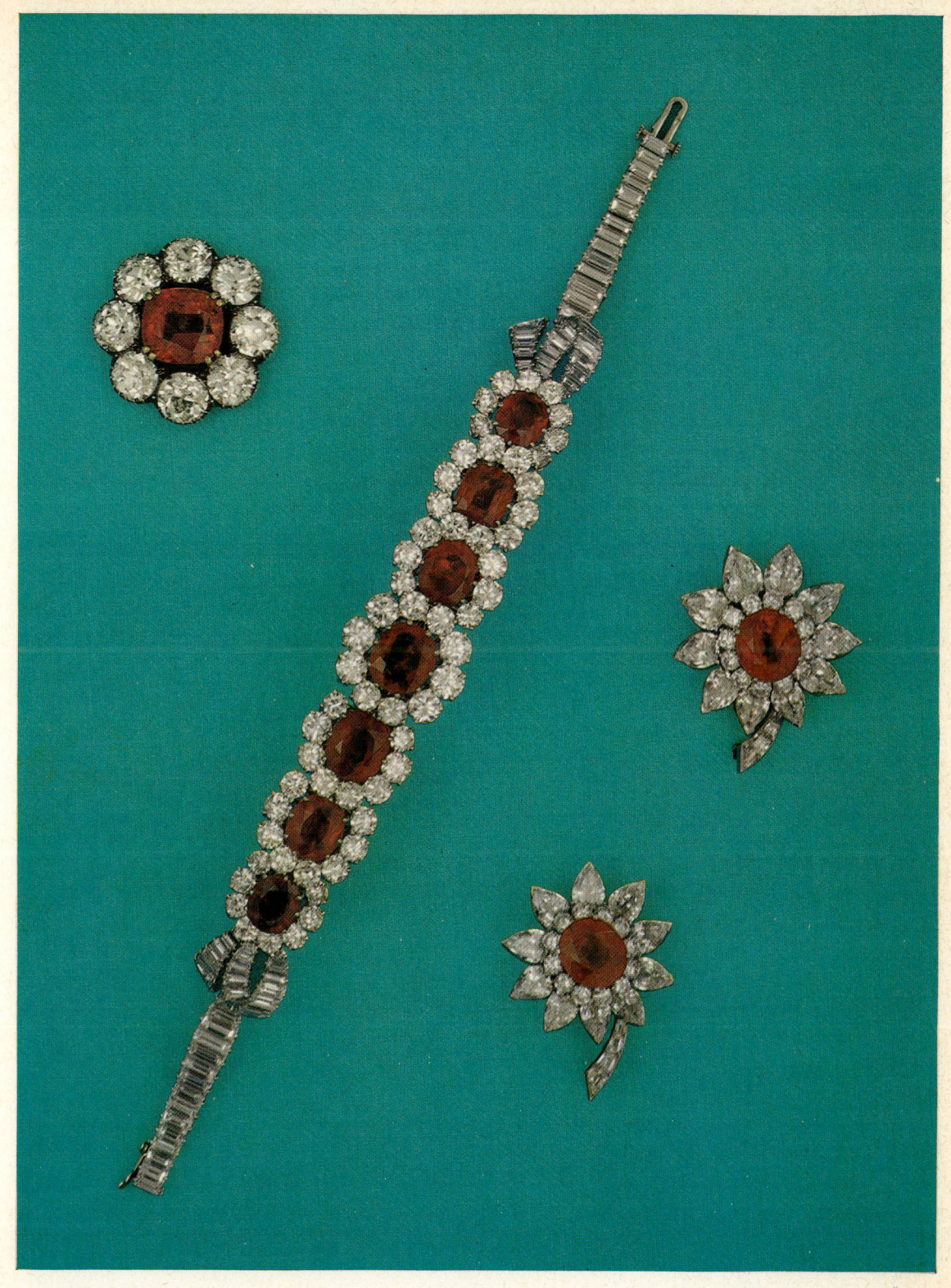

A ruby and diamond cluster brooch, the ruby weighing 13.10 carats SF210,000 (£27,851; $66,843)
A bracelet in rubies and diamonds, the centre ruby weighing 6.22 carats SF440,000 (£58,355; $140,053)
A pair of brooches in rubies and diamonds, the two rubies weighing 14.17 carats SF290,000 (£38,462; $92,308)
Sold in Zürich on 15th November 1973

A diamond brooch mounted by Boucheron, Paris. The two pear-shaped diamonds weigh 23.46 carats
Zürich SF850,000 (£120,567; $289,362). 9.v.74

A diamond necklace of variously cut stones
Zürich SF240,000 (£31,830; $76,393). 15.XI.73

464 JEWELLERY

1. An emerald and diamond ring by Harry Winston, the emerald weighing 10.25 carats, the diamonds 12.75 carats New York $77,500 (£32,292) 7.XI.73. 2. An oblong-shaped emerald mounted between two diamond baguettes as a ring, the emerald weighing 8.67 carats Zürich SF550,000 (£78,014; $187,234) 9.V.74. 3. An emerald ring weighing 16.32 carats Zürich SF700,000 (£99,219; $238,298) 9.V.74. 4. An emerald and diamond ring by Van Cleef & Arpels, the diamonds weighing 3.90 carats, the emerald 9 carats New York $75,000 (£31,250) 5.XII.73. 5. A diamond ring weighing 9.10 carats New York $115,000 (£47,917) 11.IV.74. 6. A diamond ring, weighing 8.10 carats Los Angeles $57,500 (£23,958) 12.XI.73. 7. A 'canary' diamond weighing 11.53 carats New York $115,000 (£47,917) 11.IV.74.

8. An emerald-cut diamond ring weighing 29.72 carats Zürich SF550,000 (£78,014; $187,234) 9.V.74. 9. An elongated cushion-shaped sapphire set in a heavy gold mount as a ring Zürich SF200,000 (£28,369; $68,085) 9.V.74. 10. A sapphire ring weighing 10.50 carats New York $46,000 (£19,167) 11.IV.74. 11. A ruby and diamond ring by Van Cleef & Arpels, the 44 round diamonds weighing 5 carats, the pear-shaped diamonds 7.75 carats, the ruby 18.74 carats New York $20,000 (£8,333) 7.XI.73. 12. An alexandrite ring weighing 10.65 carats New York $80,000 (£33,333) 7.XI.73. 13. A pair of ruby and diamond earclips by Van Cleef & Arpels, the 104 baguette diamonds weighing 21 carats, the 70 round diamonds 10 carats, the 4 rubies 26 carats New York $70,000 (£29,167) 7.XI.73

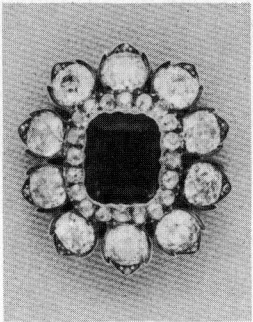

JEWELLERY 465

From left to right
A nineteenth-century gold brooch/pendant in Renaissance taste, probably German
London £1,950 ($4,680). 24.I.74
From the collection of Mrs E. P. Smith
A Victorian emerald and diamond brooch/pendant
London £9,000 ($21,600). 1.XI.73
An emerald and diamond brooch/pendant
London £13,500 ($32,400). 24.I.74
From the collection of M. F. H. Farquhar Esq
A gold, enamel, ruby, sapphire and pearl pendant by Giuliano
London £2,600 ($6,240). 21.II.74
From the collection of Mrs L. P. Spikins

An emerald and diamond pendant/brooch, the central emerald weighing 5.25 carats
New York $60,000 (£25,000). 11.IV.74

A gold, enamel and diamond brooch/hair ornament in the form of a tropical butterfly
London £3,800 ($9,120). 29.XI.73
From the collection of Mrs E. A. West

A Victorian diamond necklace/tiara
London £32,000 ($76,800). 4.x.73
From the collection of His Grace the Duke of Hamilton and Brandon

Sir William Dobell at the Sydney Opera House

Sotheby's first sale in Australia proved an immense success with one of the largest attendances in our firm's history. One thousand five hundred people packed the controversial Opera House to bid and thereby help Dobell's wish that the contents of his studio should be sold and the proceeds used for the promotion of Australian art. A generous thought and one that perhaps will be followed by other artists.

Sir William Dobell was born in 1899, the son of a building contractor. Having worked as an apprentice to an architect and studied in the evenings at the Julian Ashton School, he won, in 1929, the Society of Arts Travelling Scholarship. He came to London and studied at the Slade under Henry Tonks, remaining here for ten years with trips to Holland, Belgium and France. On returning to Sydney, he worked as a teacher, a labourer and finally as an official war artist. In 1944 he became a household name in Australia by winning the Archibald Prize for portraiture, which was unsuccessfully contested in the courts by two other entrants who claimed his entry was not a portrait but a caricature. He won this prize again in 1948, and was knighted for his contribution to Australian Art in 1959.

Left: The water skier
Oil on hardboard, *circa* 1969, 6½in by 13½in
$A16,000 (£9,836; $23,606)

Right: Six studies of a New Guinea girl (detail)
Pencil, 1950, 10⅛in by 7¾in
$A1,650 (£1,014; $2,437)

468 SIR WILLIAM DOBELL AT THE SYDNEY OPERA HOUSE

The sale consisted of paintings, gouaches and drawings and covered the whole range of his artistic development. As only one small non-commercial exhibition of Dobell's work had ever taken place outside Australia, it was decided to fly the whole collection around the world. Opening at the Aldeburgh Festival in Suffolk, it travelled to London, New York, Los Angeles and Melbourne, coming to rest finally in Sydney. The publicity ensuing from this produced a good response from collectors with many postal and telegraphed bids providing competition for the Australian collectors, the most important ingredient for a successful sale. The result was $387,650 instead of the estimated $250,000.

The drawing reproduced on the previous page gives some idea of Dobell's ability in sketching a rapid study from life. This elegant *New Guinea girl* was drawn during a trip there in 1949 or 50. The early portrait of *Bob* painted in 1932 while at the Slade makes an interesting starting point for the famous portraits that followed. The *Water Skier* painted a year before his death in 1970 depicts the view from his house at Wangi overlooking Lake Macquarie. Finally, the *Sailor and girl* drawn between 1939 and 1943 while he lived in the Kings Cross district of Sydney shows one of those character studies so typical of his work and of which he was so fond.

Bob
Oil on panel, signed 1932, 16in by 12¾in
$A10,000 (£6,148; $14,755)

Recto: Sailor and girl (illustrated)
Verso: Various studies
Pen and red ink wash over pencil, 8¾in by 6⅛in
$A2,400 (£1,475; $3,540)

From the sale of paintings and drawings by Sir William Dobell held in Sydney Opera House on 19th November 1973

Wine Auctions

The Wine Department has conducted sixteen sales in London, against ten last season and for the first time sent abroad to Zurich for an additional sale. Total sales were £525,324.

Prices of wine at auction have fallen during the season to the benefit of the private buyer. It is likely that a low level of prices will be maintained for at least two years, while there are large stocks of fine wine remaining unconsumed. The most marked changes have been for Claret, down 45%–60%, with the most expensive Châteaux leading the plunge. Red Burgundy has maintained almost the same levels as last season, with even a record bid of £400 ($1,000) for a case of 1969 Romanée Conti. Rhine and Moselle from the finest estates and of outstanding vintages seldom achieved the prices that their superlative quality deserves. Vintage Port has undergone a slight reversal with prices down about 20%–30%. This trend is likely to change, because there are relatively insignificant stocks of mature wine ready for drinking and total stocks cannot be sufficient if greater interest is shown by North American buyers.

In general it is the immature vintages of any wine, which at present are the least attractive to the Trade or private buyer, with interest rates at such a high level. Prices of 1962, 1964 and 1966 vintage wines, Clarets in particular, have ceased falling, because stocks are limited, and are unlikely to remain for very long below the opening price of the 1973 Vintage.

The most interesting items sold during this last season have been twelve bottles of Château Lafite 1875, the property of His Grace The Duke of Wellington, which had been laid down at

From left to right
Château Pichon Longueville 1905.
Glass prunt on shoulder of bottle embossed *Château Pichon Longueville, 1905 1er Grand Vin*
London £9 a bottle ($21.60)
12.XII.73
One bottle Tokay Essence
pre-1790
18th Century hand-blown Tokay bottle.
Glass prunt embossed *J.R.* on shoulder of bottle. Wax capsule.
London £120 ($288). 3.X.73
Fockink, Witte Dubbele
Anisette believed pre-1919
Wax capsule. Branded cork.
London £5 ($12) 13.III.74
Blanckenhagen Allasch Kummel
Bottle embossed *Blanckenhagen, Estate of Allasch (Russia)*
Paper neck seal printed in Russian.
London £6 ($14.40) 13.III.74

Apsley House. In the same sale two bottles of Tokay Essence, pre-1790, the property of H.R.H. Princess Elizabeth of Yugoslavia were sold. These bottles bore the initials 'J.R.' embossed in glass prunts on each shoulder and were originally in the cellars of Joseph, King of Hungary, the brother of Marie-Antoinette. Another interesting cellar offered was shipped specially from Switzerland and included Château Latour 1908 and another important Swiss cellar included wines from the Imperial Cellars of Austria which were auctioned at the end of the First World War. Among these wines were Tokay Essence 1904 and 1907 Vintage Châteaux Lafite, Latour and Margaux.

Next season, wine of good quality will continue to sell at reasonable prices. Apart from the growing interest in fine wine, there are keen collectors of items related to wine and we have added antique corkscrews and bottles to some of our sales.

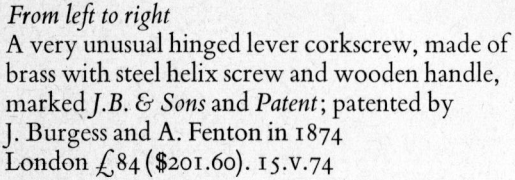

From left to right
A very unusual hinged lever corkscrew, made of brass with steel helix screw and wooden handle, marked *J.B. & Sons* and *Patent*; patented by J. Burgess and A. Fenton in 1874
London £84 ($201.60). 15.V.74

Rare Lund corkscrew with steel bottle grips, patented 1838, cylindrical barrel enclosing shaft with raising ratchet and unusually threaded inner shank
London £105 ($252). 15.V.74

One magnum Napoléon, Grande Fine Champagne Impériale Cognac 1811
Glass prunt embossed *N* with crown above
London £115 ($276). 3.X.73

Château Lafite 1865. Rare handblown double magnum. Wax seal.
London £500 ($1200). 12.XII.73
Originally the property of the Right Honourable the Earl of Rosebery
KT, PC, DSO, MC

Natural History

Above left
A gold nugget, in solid form, with traces of matrix, found in the 1930 Gold Strike, Atlantic City, Wyoming, weight 34 ounces, 2½in by 3½in
Los Angeles $10,000 (£4,160). 13.II.74
From the Ross Cook Collection.
Now in the Los Angeles Natural History Museum

Above right
A large specimen of arsenopyrite crystals, with wolframite and minor apatite, with free standing quartz crystals, the largest 6in long, from Panasqueira, Portugal
London £210 ($504). 30.XI.73

Left
A pair, male and female, of the almost certainly extinct huias, *Heteralocha acutirostris*, from the forests of North Island, New Zealand
London £360 ($864). 30.XI.73

Acknowledgements

Messrs Sotheby Parke Bernet are indebted to the following who have allowed their names to be published as the purchasers of the works of art illustrated in the preceding pages.

A. Abrahams, Esher, Surrey
Acquavella Galleries Inc, New York
Norman Adams Ltd, London
Thos Agnew & Sons Ltd, London
A. F. Allbrook, London
American Foreign Trade Development Co, New York
Albert Amor Ltd, London
The Antique Porcelain Company, London & New York
J. Apthorpe, Radlett, Hertfordshire
Peter A. Aron, New York
Asprey & Co Ltd, London
Associated American Artists, New York
M. Atallah, Beirut
Australian National Gallery, Canberra

Herman Baer, London
J. N. Bartfield Books Inc, New York
Baskett & Day, London
Kenneth Battye, Baltimore, Maryland
Robin Bellamy Antiques, Witney, Oxfordshire
Bentley & Co, London
Lester H. Berry, Philadelphia, Pennsylvania
N. Bloom & Son Ltd, London
Birmingham City Museums and Art Gallery
C. G. Boerner, Düsseldorf
Martin Breslauer, London
T. C. S. Brooke Antiques, Wroxham, Norfolk
Amiel Brown, Tel Aviv
W. E. Browne Decorating Co, Atlanta, Georgia

C. K. Chan, Hong Kong
T. Y. Chao, Hong Kong
Carlo Alberto Chiesa, Milan
Ciancimino Ltd, London
Clark & Lee & Harris Antiques, London
P. & D. Colnaghi & Co Ltd, London
Compass Antique Company, New York
Andrew Crispo Gallery, New York

Bon G. Dale, London
Peter Dale Ltd, London
William Darby, London
Dawson's Bookshop, Los Angeles

Dawson's of Pall Mall, London
Dayton's Gallery, Minneapolis
Mrs Hanita E. Dechter, Los Angeles
Brimo de Laroussilhe, Paris
Delomosne & Son Ltd, London
Marisa del Re Gallery, New York
Richard Dennis, London
M. Deutscher, Victoria, Australia
Dr A. C. R. Dreesmann, Amsterdam
Hugh M. Dunphy, Bolivar Gallery, Kingston, Jamaica

Jim Earle, Timber College, Texas
Andrew Edmunds, London
Dr W. Eichenberger, Beinwilam See, Switzerland
H. Terry-Engell Gallery, London
Marvin P. Epstein, Montclair, New Jersey
Eskenazi Ltd, London
Douglas C. Ewing Inc, New York

R. A. Farrington, Preston, Lancashire
Faustus Galleries Ltd, London
Fernandez & Marché, London
The Fine Art Society Ltd, London
Gus Fisher, Auckland
John F. Fleming Inc, New York
Dr Jean Folschveiller, Strasbourg
Kate Foster Ltd, London
Louis Franck, Gstaad, Switzerland
Mrs I. A. Fraser, Heswall, Merseyside
French & Co, New York
Alan Friedlander, Northwood, Middlesex
H. Fröhlich, St Gallen, Switzerland
Jack Frost, Santa Monica, California

Il Gabinetto delle Stampe, Milan
Peter Galbraith, Cambridge, Massachusetts
Galerie Belarte, Zürich
Galerie Beyeler, Basle
Galerie Siegfried Brumme, Frankfurt-am-Main
Galerie Jan Krugier, Geneva
Galerie des Monnaies S.A., Lausanne
Garrard & Co Ltd, London
Gay Antiques, London

ACKNOWLEDGEMENTS

The J. Paul Getty Museum, Malibu, California
Christopher Gibbs Ltd, London
Jean Rousseau-Girard, Paris
Helen Glatz, London
Byron Goldman, New York
Graham Gallery, New York
Richard Green, London
Charles A. Greenfield, New York

Hadley & Co, Philadelphia, Pennsylvania
The Hallsborough Gallery, London
W. F. Hammond, Lymington, Hampshire
Hartman Rare Art, New York
Hartnoll & Eyre Ltd, London
Hazlitt, Gooden & Fox Ltd, London
Major Anthony Heathcote, London
Ben Heller Inc, New York
Blum Helman Gallery, New York
Malcolm Henderson Gallery, London
Hendrick Imports Ltd, New York
Dean Heyde, Los Angeles
Geoffrey Heywood, Liverpool
Joseph H. Hirshhorn, New York
D. F. Brooke-Hitching, London
Ron Hodgson, Parramatta, Australia
Hofmann & Freeman Ltd, Shoreham, Sevenoaks, Kent
Hollander Gallery Inc, St Louis, Missouri
Th. Horovitz & Cie, Geneva
House of El Dieff Inc, New York
How of Edinburgh, London
John Howell Book Store, San Francisco, California
Howes Bookshop Ltd, Hastings, Sussex
Armin Huber, Zürich
Heide Hübner, Würzburg, Germany
G. S. Hunt, Brixton, Devon
Mitchell Hutchins Inc, Chicago, Illinois

Sidney Janis Gallery, New York
Jellinek & Sampson, London
Jeremy Ltd, London
Oscar & Peter Johnson Ltd, London
E. Joseph, London
Annely Juda Fine Art, London
A. Julian, London

Paul Kantor, Malibu Beach, California
Daniel Katz, London
Kilmarnoc Inc, Geneva
Joan & Larry Kindler Antiques, Whitestone, New York
The Provost & Fellows of King's College, Cambridge
James H. Kirkman, London
Walter Klinkhoff Gallery Inc, Montreal
M. Koblitz, London
E. & C. T. Koopman & Son, Ltd, London
H. P. Kraus Inc, New York

G. Blair-Laing, Toronto
Bengt-dov Lapidus, Vevey, Switzerland

Auguste Laube, Zürich
George Lazarnick, Honolulu, Hawaii
Ronald A. Lee, London
R. P. Lee, London
The Leger Galleries Ltd, London
Leggatt Brothers, London
Bernard & S. Dean Levy Inc, New York
R. E. Lewis Inc, Nicasio, California
J. H. Leyer, Heenskor, Holland
Charles S. Lichtigman, New York
Eric Lineham, London
Thomas Lumley Ltd, London
Lumley Cazalet Ltd, London

J. S. Maas & Co Ltd, London
M. McAleer, London
McCrory Corporation, New York
Maggs Bros, London
Mahoubian Gallery of Ancient Art, New York
P. Makhzani, London
Joaquin Mallo, Madrid
Mansour Gallery, London
Dr A. Queiroz Marinho, Porto, Portugal
Marlborough Fine Art (London) Ltd, London
Mrs S. E. Marshall, London
S. Matsuoka, Tokyo
Alexis Merab, San Francisco
Merseyside County Museum, Liverpool
Franz Meyer, Kunstmuseum, Basle
Roy Miles Fine Paintings, London

Michael Miller, Lindfield, Sussex
Mrs N. Richard Miller, New York
Modarco S.A., Panama, R.P.
Hugh Moss Ltd, London
Sydney L. Moss Ltd, London
Richard Mundey, London

The National Army Museum, London
Nationalmuseum Avd för konsthantverk, Stockholm
Meyrick Neilson of Tetbury Ltd, Gloucestershire
A. Neuhaus, Würzburg, Germany
Neumeister KG, Munich
David Newbon, London
New Grecian Gallery, London
Newhouse Galleries, New York
Noble Antiques, London

Oxford Fine Arts, Stratford-sub-Castle, Wiltshire

P. A. Parviz, London
David Peel & Co Ltd, London
Dwain Pelock, Bellflower, California
Perls Galleries, New York
Howard Phillips, London
S. J. Phillips Ltd, London
Physicians Planning Service Corp, New York
Dr Aldo Pironti, Benevento, Italy

William A. Pope Jnr, Mechanicsville, Virginia
S. J. Pratt Ltd, London
Premsela en Hamburger, Amsterdam
Victor Provatoroff, Hever, Kent

Bernard Quaritch Ltd, London

J. P. Raison, Walton-on-the-Hill, Surrey
R. Rayman, London
Redburn (Antiques), London
William Redford, London
Howard Ricketts, London
R. Rigamonti, Milan
J. Roberts & Son, London
C. J. Robertson, Bath, Somerset
James Robinson Inc, New York
B. Rochard, Weybridge, Surrey
Dorothy & Robert Rosenbaum, Scarsdale, New York
Rosenburg & Stiebel, New York
Bertram Rota Ltd, London

Frank T. Sabin Ltd, London
Israel Sack Inc, New York
G. Sakomoto, Tokyo
Sanders of Oxford Ltd, Oxford
J. M. E. Santo Silva, Lisbon
Chas. J. Sawyer, London
George Schoellkopf Gallery, New York
J. Schorscher, Toronto
A. C. Scott, Westerham, Kent
G. M. Segers, De Panne, Belgium
Seven Gables Bookshop Inc, New York
Beatrice Shorr, New York
S. J. Shrubsole Ltd, London & New York
E. E. Simmons, Pinner, Middlesex
Merton D. Simpson, New York
B. & G. H. Sirett & Co. London
Six Centuries Print Room, Toronto
Jan Skala, New York
H. E. Smeets, Weert, Holland
J. H. Bourdon-Smith Ltd, London
The Smithsonian Institution, Washington
John Sparks Ltd, London
Edward Speelman Ltd, London
Spindler Furniture, Germany
Spink & Son Ltd, London

Marshall Spink Ltd, London
John Starmer Antiques, London
Mrs Barbara Steinberg, New York
Allan Stone Gallery, New York
The Suaréz Fine Art Company, London
Mrs Ulla Stafford, Binfield, Berkshire
Oliver-Sutton Antiques, London
Tatton Sykes, London
R. J. Symes, London

Miss Yvonne Tan Bunzl, London
The Temple Gallery, London
Tilley & Co (Antiques) Ltd, London
Alan Tillman Antiques, London
The Time Museum, Rockford, Illinois
Charles W. Traylen, Guildford, Surrey
Trinity House, London
Tudor House (Ironbridge) Antiques, Telford, Shropshire
The University of East Anglia, Norwich, Norfolk

Geoffrey Van Ltd, London
C. J. Vander (Antiques) Ltd, London
Mr Visser, Amsterdam

George Waechter Memorial Foundation, Geneva
Jack J. Walker, London
John Walton Inc, New York
Wartski Ltd, London
Max Webber Inc, Middleton, Massachusetts
B. Weinreb Ltd, London
Robert F. Weis, Sunbury, Pennsylvania
H. Weiss, Knokke, Belgium
H. S. Wellby Ltd, London
Herner Wengraf Ltd, London
White, Boniface, Thornbury, Gloucestershire
Whitney Antiques, New York
Pieter Wenning Gallery, Johannesburg
R. J. Wigington, Stratford-on-Avon
Winifred Williams of London and Eastbourne
William E. Wiltshire III, Richmond, Virginia
Charles Woollett & Son, London

Rainer Zietz Alte Kunst Antiquitäten, Hanover
Donald S. Zinman, Boston, Massachusetts
Irving Zucker, New York

Index

Aarne, Victor 256
Adamson, Robert 192
Affleck, Thomas 352
African art, 313–316
Agafanov, Vasili 247, 254–256
Aivasovsky, Ivan 99
Akasaka, Noshu 434
Alabaster 228, 322
Alken, Henry, Snr 56
Alma Tadema, Sir Lawrence 76–84
Altdorfer, Albrecht 177
Andrejevic, Milet 137
Angell, George 288
Angell, Joseph III 287ff
Annan, Thomas 190–192
Ansdell, Richard 74
Antiquities 321–325
Apianus, Peter Bienewitz 213
Apollinaire, Guillaume 225
Archambo, Peter 285
Argy Rousseau, Gabriel 443
Armfelt, Karl Gustav 259
Arms and armour 269–276, 434
Arnd, Samuel 258
Art Nouveau and Art Deco 308, 443–446
Atget, Eugène 191
Audebert, J. B. 222
Audubon, John James Laforest 175, 222
Auguste, Henri 280
Augustin, Jean Baptiste 268
Automobiles 452, 453
Avercamp, Hendrick 23

Baccarat 441, 442
Bachman, John 222
Baines, Thomas 158
Bakst, Léon 134, 135
Ballet 134, 135
Barenger, James 56, 57
Barnard, Edward 287, 290
Barr Flight & Barr 386
Barrière, Jean-Joseph 264
Bartholomaeus, Anglicus 218
Bartholome, Georg Ludwig 393
Barye, Antoine-Louis 243, 447
Baudesson, Jordan and Daniel 261
Beauvais tapestry 363
Bedford, Francis 191
Beert, Osias the Elder 26
Behagle, Philip 363
Beneman, G. 345
Benin (see Bronzes) 314–316
Bennington stoneware 388
Bérain, Jean 363
Bersuire, Pierre 204

Bevan, Robert 87
Bianchi & Compi 360
Billinge, Thomas 385
Black, Starr & Frost 308
Blaeu, Johannes 223
Blake, William 66, 184, 225
Blanchard, Jacques 25
Blanchard, Jean-Nicolas 336
Bontecou, Lee 141
Books 212–227
Bossoli, Carlo 96
Both, Jan 24
Bottengruber, Ignaz 394
Böttger 392, 395
Bottomley, Gordon 225
Boucher, François 384
Boucheron, Frederic 462
Boudin, Eugène Louis 102
Boudin, L. 346
Boulard, Jean-Baptiste 332
Boulle, André-Charles 328
Boultbee, John 57
Bowler, Thomas W. 154
Boydell, Josiah 224
Bradburn, John 308
Brancusi, Constantin 124
Braun, Georg 223
Breguet 310
Breton, Nicholas 212
Bridge, John 289
Bridgen, Zachariah 282
Briot, François 298
Bronzes
  Benin 313–316
  Chinese 399
  Egyptian 321, 323
  Modern 93, 94, 110, 124, 128, 141, 159, 454, 455
  Nepalese 320
  Nineteenth-century 243
  Roman 322
  Russian 243
  Sino-Tibetan 320
  Sixteenth-century 238
  Seventeenth-century 238, 239
Brueghel, Pieter the Younger 9, 23
Brussels tapestry 362, 364
Bugatti, Carlo 447–455
Bugatti, Ettore 447ff
Bugatti, Luigi 447ff
Bugatti, Rembrandt 447ff
Buondelmonti, Cristoforo 206
Burne-Jones, Sir Edward 397
Burns, Robert 219
Burra, Edward 88

Burwash, William 286
B.V.R.B. (Bernard Van Risamburgh or Van Risen Borgh) 335

Cabrier 311
Caddy, J. H. 221
Caffiéri, Philippe 333
Callot, Jacques 179
Cameron, Julia Margaret 190–196
Canaletto, Giovanni Antonio Canale, called 14, 33, 37
Canton porcelain 425
Capodimonte porcelain 392
Carew, Thomas 208
Carlin, Martin 330, 331, 336, 348
Carpets 366, 367
Carr, Emily 161
Carracci, Agostino 48
Carracci, Annibale 48
Carroll, Lewis 190, 191, 211
Cassatt, Mary 187
Cassel porcelain 392
Castel Durante 390
Castiglione, Giovanni Benedetto, called Il Grechetto 183
Cellini, Benvenuto 293ff
Cendrars, Blaise 226
Ceramics
  American 388
  Chinese 399–425
  Classical 323
  Continental 360, 389, 392–396
  English 377–387
  Japanese 427, 428
  Maiolica 390, 391
  Persian 318, 319
  Victorian 397, 398
Chagall, Marc 129
Chamberlain, John 141
Chantilly porcelain 392
Chapman, Fredrich Hindrik 219
Chatard 332
Chaucer, Geoffrey 218
Chelsea porcelain 382, 383, 384, 385
Ch'êng Hua 405, 411
Chevallier, Claude 349
Chia Ching 409
Ch'ien Lung 405, 414, 420–424, 426
Chinese works of art 400, 426
Ch'ing Dynasty 404
Chippendale 350, 351, 359
Chlebnikov, Ivan 248, 250, 251
Christensen, Dan 139, 141
Church, Frederic Edwin 162
Clignancourt factory 291

INDEX

Clocks and watches 306–311
Coalport porcelain 396
Cocteau, Jean 210
Coins and medals 299–304
Collis, G. R. and Co 288
Colt revolver 276
Cooke, Edward William 71
Cooper, Samuel 266, 268
Corbett, Richard 208
Cortelazzo, Antonio 296
Costa, Giovanni 97
Cosway, Richard 267
Cotman, John Joseph 68
Cox, James 265
Cox, Stephen 297
Coxe, James 311
Cozens, John Robert 64, 65
Cressent, Charles 333, 335
Cripps, William 279
Cummings, Thomas 310
Currier and Ives 156

da Bologna, Giovanni 239
Dali, Salvador 126
dalli Sonetti, Bartolommeo 215
Dammanock, F. 326
da Montepulciano, Pietro di Domenico 10
Daumier, Honoré 105
Davidson, Jeremiah 60
De Bruyn, Michiel 278
Décorchemont, François 446
De Dietrich 452ff
Degas, Edgar 107
de Heem, Jan Davidsz. 27
de Kooning, Willem 136, 138, 139, 141
De Lamerie, Paul 284
Delaunay, Sonia 226
della Torre, Giuseppe 392
Delftware 379, 380
Deloney, Thomas 212
Del Piombo, Sebastiano 44
de Maria, Walter 139
De Morgan, William 397
Dennis, Thomas, school of 350
Dent 310
De Staël, Nicolas 130
Devis, Arthur William 52, 54, 62
Dietz, Adam Ferdinand 233
di Paolo, Giovanni 11
Dixon, Nicholas 266
Dobell, Sir William 467–468
Dodgson, C. L. (see Carroll, Lewis)
Dolep, Andrew 274
Doulton porcelain 397
Doyle, Sir Arthur Conan 210
Drawings and Watercolours
 Ballet 134, 135
 Contemporary 146
 English 64–68, 88, 89
 Impressionist and Modern 100, 101, 104–107, 111, 112, 118, 119, 121, 122
 Old Master 44–49
 Russian 132, 133
 Topographical 154, 157

Drayton, Michael 212
Dubuffet, Jean 131
Ducrollay, Jean 263
Du Ferrier, Le Sieur 312
du Monceau, H. L. Duhamel 222
Du Paquier porcelain 392
Dürer, Albrecht 176
Dutemps 336
Dyer, Lawrence 297

Eberlein, J. F. 384
Edwards, Edward 328
Edy, J. W. 224
Eliot, T. S. 211
Elkington, Mason & Co 290
Elliott, William 292
Enderlein, Caspar 298
English School 16, 19
Erlin, Elizabeth 360
Ermilov, Vassily 132
Ernst, Max 121, 123
Evans, Walker 195
Exter, Alexandra 133
Fabergé 253, 254, 256, 258–260
Faenza 391
Faïence 389
Falconet, Pierre 335
Farrell, Edward Cornelius 292, 294
Farren, Thomas 285
Fenton, R. 191
Ferneley, John Snr 52, 53, 57
Fiorentino, Niccoló Spinelli, called 299, 301
Flaxman, John 294
Flight Barr & Barr 386
Foliot, Toussaint-François 336
Fontainebleau School 237
Fontana, Lucio 148
Forestier, Etienne 335
Fox, Charles 295
Fraktur 360
Freud, Lucian 90
Frith, Francis 191
Fulda porcelain 393
Furniture 326–368, 448–451
Fuseli, Henry 224

Garbe, Richard 397
Garrard, R. & S., & Co 290
Garrard, Robert 290
Gautherot, Pierre 96
Gazuet, Jeremie 309
Gebart, Henry 311
Gelb, Melchior 278
Gertler, Mark 88
Gessner, Abraham 295–296
Gheeraerts, Marcus the Younger 18, 21
Giacometti, Alberto 127
Gibson, D. 266
Giuliano 465
Glass 319, 439–442, 443, 445, 446
Glienitz faïence 389
Gobelins tapestry 336
Goddard-Townsend School 350
Goltzius, Hendrik 178

Gorky, Arshile 146
Gould, John 217
Gouthière, Pierre 329
Goya y Lucientes, Francisco José de 45
Graham, George 306
Gratchev, G. P. 250–252
Greco, Domenikos Theotokopoulos, called El 29
Greenwood, Frans 439
Grohé 329
Grosser, Georg 274
Guardi, Antonio 38
Guardi, Francesco 32, 34–43
Guardi, Giacomo 37–39
Guardi, Nicolò 38
Guarneri del Jesu, Joseph 371
Guggenbichler, Meinrad 232
Guthrie, James 225

Haas, Andreas 298
Hackaert, Jacob Philippe 97
Hackwood, William 381
Hagedorn, H. C. 156
Han Dynasty 400
Harache, Pierre 283
Hardivillier, Noël 263
Haritsu, Ogawa called Ritsuo 437
Harnett, William M. 164, 165
Hassam, Childe 171
Heade, Martin Johnson 171
Henderson, Cooper 56
Henkels, Jan 309
Hennell, Robert IV 287
Hereke carpets 367
Herring, John Frederick Snr 52, 55, 57
Hetling, Francis 190, 192
Heywood, Thomas 208, 212
Hicks, Edward 174
Hill, David Octavius 192
Hine, Lewis 192
Hisataka 434
Hockney, David 151
Hogarth, William 424
Hogenberg, F. 223
Hokusai, Katsushika 432, 437
Holbein, Hans 17
Homer, Winslow 172
Honnami, Koetsu 437, 438
Hopper, Edward 187
Höroldt, Johann Gregor 392
Hoyte, John Barr Clarke 157
Hsüan Tê 404
Hudson, Thomas 61
Huggins of Liverpool, William 75
Hunt, William Holman 185

Icons 244–247
Imari 428
Ingres, Jean-Auguste-Dominique 46
Inness, George 170
Inro 435–438
Ivory 228, 316

Jade 426
James I, King of England 214

INDEX

Japanese works of art 429, 434–438
Jefferson, Thomas 209
Jeffreys & Gilbert 308
Jennewein, Carl Paul 243
Jewellery
    Hellenistic 324
    Renaissance 227, 236
    Roman 324
    Victorian and modern 456–466
John, Augustus 88
Johns, Jasper 138–143
Johnson, Ben 208
Johnson, Eastman 168–169
Johnson, Frank Tenney 167
Johnson, Richard 208
Johnson, Thomas 355
Jones, Howard E. 220
Jongkind, Johan Barthold 102
Joseph (Joseph Baumhauer) 336
Juvet, Edouard 311

Kaendler, J. J. 393
Kakiemon 393, 428
Kane, Paul 160
Kaneshige 434
K'ang Hsi 360, 395, 416, 418, 419
Kano School 436, 437
Kansai, Koma 436
King, Henry 208
Klee, Paul 120
Kline, Franz 138, 141
Klingert, Gustav 255, 256
Kliun, Ivan 133
Knibb, John 307
Knibb, Joseph 308
Koekkoek, Hermanus Snr 99
Kogetsu 435
Ko-Kutani 427
Koma School 435–437
Koppernik, Nikolaus, called
    Copernicus 197
Korin, Hokkyo 436, 437
Krieghoff, Cornelius 160
Kuzmitchev, Anton 248, 252, 253
Kwan 438
Kyoto School 435

Lambert & Rawlings 294–295
Lambeth delft 380
Lanceray, Eugène 243
Lawrence, D. H. 210
Le Bastier, Charles 264
Léger, Fernand 115
Le Page, Moutier 275
Leschandel, Antoine 262
Leslie, Alfred 137
Leutze, Emanuel (after) 142, 168–169
Lewis, Kensington 292, 294
Limoges enamel 228
Lincoln, Abraham 209
Lindner, Richard 153
Linke, F. 358
Lissitzky, Lazar (El) 132
Livy 204
Longton Hall porcelain 385

Lorrain, Claude Gelée called Claude
    15, 22
Louvet, Hubert 263
Lowestoft porcelain 385

McCabe, James 308
MacPherson, Robert 191
Mairet, Sylvan 310
Maler, Hans 12
Malevich, Kasimir 133
Manne, Thomas 208
Manuscripts
    Oriental 198–201
    Western 202–207
Manwaring, Arthur 283
Marc, Franz 455
Marini, Marino 128
Marlow, William 60
Marriott, Frederick 444
Marshall, Ben 53, 56, 61
Martin, Paul 192
Master of the Mansi Magdalen 28
Matisse, Henri 110
Maville, Charles 191
Medals, orders and decorations 302, 304
Medici porcelain 373–376
Meissen porcelain 360, 392, 393, 395, 396
Meissonnier, Juste-Aurèle 263
Melrose, Andrew 170
Mêne, Pierre-Jules 447
Mettlach stoneware 397
Meyer, J. J. 394
Milhouse, William 372
Mills, Nathaniel and Sons 287
Milton, John 214
Ming Dynasty 404–407, 411–413
Miniatures
    Oriental 198–201
    Portrait 266–268
Minton porcelain 397, 398
Miró, Joan 125
Mitsuhiro, Ohara 435
Moillon, Louise 27
Monbro, Georges (aîné) 329
Mondon, François Antoine 348
Monti, Emilio 273
Moore, Albert Joseph 72
Moore, Henry 89, 93, 94
Moore, John & Sons 309
Mor, Antonis 20
Moran, Thomas 163
More, Sir Thomas 214
Morel, Gabriel Raoul 264
Morel, Jean Valentin 296
Moringer, Veit 279
Morrice, James Wilson 161
Moscow School 246, 247
Moynat, Jean 262
Munnings, Sir Alfred 85, 86
Musical instruments 369–372

Nadar 192, 195
Naganobu, Fujiwara 434
Nahl, Charles C. 167
Nash, Paul 89

Natural history 471
Netsuke 435
Nevalainen, Anders Johan 260
Newman, Barnett 138, 139, 141, 143
Nicholson, Ben 92
Nigg, Joseph 98
Nolde, Emil 119
Norman, Barak 369
Norton, J. and E. 388
Nottingham alabaster 228
Novgorod School 247

Okatori 435
O'Keeffe, Georgia 142
Oldenburg, Claes 143
Oliver, Isaac 268
O'Neale, Jeffryes Hammett 386
Orr, P. and Sons 288
Ouwater, Isaak 95
Ovchinnikov, Pavel 248–253, 260

Pages, Juan 370
Palmer, Samuel 185
Paperweights 442
Patch, Thomas 66
Peacock, H. 192
Peeters, Clara 26
Peffenhauser, Anton 272
Pellatt, Apsley 441
Pennsylvania redware 388
Perchin, Michael 259, 260
Petzolt, Hans 277
Pewter 297–298
Phillips, Ammi 164, 165
Photography 189–196
Phyfe, Duncan 352
Picabia, Francis 122
Picasso, Pablo 111–113, 116, 117
Pictures
    American 162–174
    Canadian 160–161
    Contemporary 146–153
    English 60–75
    European 95–99
    Impressionist and modern 100–131
    Old Masters 9–15, 22–33
    Topographical 154–159
    Russian 132–133
Pierneef, Jacob Hendrik 159
Pierre, J. B. 365
Pigalle 335
Pissarro, Camille 103, 106
Platt, Sir Hugh 214
Pollard, James 53, 56, 58, 59
Poons, Larry 141
Pop Art 136ff
Pottery, see Ceramics
Prendergast, Maurice 173, 187
Preston, Benjamin 292
Prevost, F. L. 216
Prévost, Jean-Jacques 263, 264
Primitive art
    American Indian 317
    Maori 317
    Mexican 317

Prints 175–188
    Japanese 430, 431, 433
Prior, George 311
Prout, John Skinner 154
Prujean, John 312
Puccini, Giacomo 447ff
Purdey, J. and Sons 276

Quesnil, François 47

Rāmāyana 200
Randolph, Benjamin 352
Rascalon, Antoine 336
Rauschenberg, Robert 139, 141, 142, 147
Reinagle, Ramsey Richard 56
Reinicke, Peter 393
Rejlander, Oscar Gustav 195
Rembrandt, Harmensz. van Rijn 46, 180–182
Renoir, Pierre-Auguste 109
Revere, Paul 282
Reynolds, Sir Joshua 61
Riccio workshop 238
Riccoboni, Luigi 393
Richmond, George 185
Riesener, Jean Henri 328, 332, 334, 335, 337
Riss, Jacob 192
Rivers, Larry 138
Riza-i'Abbasi 200
Robertson, James 191
Robley, Maj-Gen Horatio Gordon 157
Roccatagliata, Niccoló 238
Rochard, Simon Jacques 268
Rosa, Ercole 447
Rosenquist, James 141, 144
Rossetti, Dante Gabriel 73
Rothko, Mark 138
Rouse, James 396
Roussel, Pierre 346
Rowlandson, Thomas 68
Rubens, Sir Peter Paul 48
Rückert, Feodor 253–257, 260
Rundell, Bridge & Rundell 285, 289, 291, 294
Ruskin, John 453

St Bridget 215
St Louis glass 442
Sadler, James 385
Saltglaze 377
Saltykov, Ivan 248, 251, 252
Samaras, Lucas 141, 145
Sanders, Auguste 195
Sansho, Kokeisai 435
Saracchi workshop 235
Sassoon, Siegfried 210
Satsuma ware 428
Sawyer, Lyddell 191
Schade, E. 397
Schedel, Hartmann 215
Schiele, Egon 118
Schirmer 275
Schmeiser 270
Schmidt, Nicholas 294

Schneider, Christian Gottfried 440
Schouman, Aert 439
Schrezheim faïence 389
Schumann 330, 332
Scientific instruments 6, 305, 312
Scioli, Stefano 271, 274
Scot, Reginald 215
Scott, Samuel 69
Sculpture
    Classical 321–323, 325
    Modern 93, 94, 110, 124, 128, 141, 159, 454, 455
    Nineteenth-century 243
    Primitive 313–317
    Seventeenth-century 238, 239
    Sixteenth-century 238
    Tibetan and Nepalese 320
Segal, George 137
Segar, William 21
Sellers, Robert 308
Semenova, Maria 248, 254, 256
Séné, Jean-Baptiste-Claude 338
Severini, Gino 114
Sèvres porcelain 327–336, 346, 396
Seymour, James 57
Shang Dynasty 399
Sharaku, Toshusai 431, 432
Shaw, George Bernard 425
Siberechts, Jan 25
Sickert, Walter Richard 91
Siervent, Samuel 285
Silver 277–296
    Indian 458–459
Sisley, Alfred 108
Skinner, Col. James 199
Slipware 378
Smart, John 267
Smith, Adolph 190
Smith, Benjamin 285
Smith, D. and Sharp, R. 286
Smith, Captain Robert 155
Snelling, Mathew 266
Snuffboxes 260-264
Sosen, Mori 437
Spence, John Allison 190
Spinelli, Niccoló, see Fiorentino
Staffordshire pottery 377
Stanley, John Mix 166
Steer, Philip Wilson 88
Stella, Frank 149
Stevens, J. and Co 276
Still, Clyfford 138
Stollewerck 329
Storr, Paul 289, 291
Stothard, Thomas 224
Stradanus, Jan van der Straet called 49
Stradivari, Antonio 371
Strasbourg faïence 389
Strudwick, John Melhuish 70
Stubbs, George 37, 50, 51

Tabriz carpet 366
Tametaka 435
T'ang Dynasty 400–403
Tapestries 362–365

Tebo 384
Temminch, C. J. 216
Teniers 264, 364
Textiles 360, 368
Thielemann, Alfred 258
Thomson, John 190, 192
Thouverez 305
Thuret, André 443
Tiepolo, Giovanni Battista 183
Tiffany & Co 252, 253, 445
Tiffany, Louis Comfort 443, 446
Tiffany Studios, 377, 380, 396
Toft, Ralph 378
Tomohide, Maizuru 434
Tompion, Thomas 307, 308
Topino, Charles 328, 346
Toulouse-Lautrec, Henri de 100, 104, 186, 188
Towne, Charles 56
Toyonobu, Ishikawa 430
Tracy, Ebenezer 359
Troschel, Hans 312
Troubetzkoy, Prince Paul 243, 447ff
Tsuneiye, Bishu Osafune 434
'Tulip Painter' 385
T'ung Chih 405
Turner, Joseph William Mallord 67
Twombly, Cy 141, 145, 150

Utamaro, Kitagawa 433

Valadier, Luigi 281
Valen, Ioannes 312
Vallois, Nicolas 332
van Bloemen, Jan Frans, called Orizonte 22
Van Cleef & Arpels 464
van Cleve, Joos 13
Van der Auwera, Johann Wolfgang 233
Van der Toorn, Gregorius 281
Van Dyck, Sir Anthony 17ff
Van Gogh, Vincent 101
Van Ruysdael, Salomon 24
Van Vianen, Adam 278
Van Wouw, Anton 159
Veronese, Paolo Caliari, called Paolo 30, 31
Vertu, objects of 261–265
Viellot, J. P. 222
Vienna porcelain 394, 397
Vile, William 354
Villon, Jacques 186
von Kloeber, August-Karl-Friedrich 397
Vulliamy, Justin 308
Vyse, Charles and Nell 397

Waldmüller, Ferdinand Georg 98
Wan Li 412
Ward, James 56
Warhol, Andy 137, 139, 142
Warth, C. 397
Washington, George 219
Waterloo, Antoine 49
Watteau, Jean-Antoine 330
Webb glass 441

Webb & Sons, Thomas 441
Webster, William 308
Wedgwood 397
Wedgwood and Bentley 381
Weiditz, Christoph 241
Weisweiler, Adam 329, 330
Wesselmann, Tom 152
West, Benjamin 224
Western Chou Dynasty 399
Whieldon 380
Whistler, James Abbott McNeill 186
Whitcombe, Thomas 69
Whitehurst 308
Wigström, Henrik 258–260
Willard, Simon 308, 309
Willems, Joseph 384
Wimar, Charles 166

Wine 469–470
Winston, Harry 464
Wise, John 309
Wood, Ralph 377
Woodall, George 441
Woolf, Virginia and Leonard 211
Worcester porcelain 384, 385, 386, 387
Wordsworth, William 211
Works of Art
  Baroque 232, 233
  Classical 321–325
  eighteenth-century 242
  Gothic 230, 231
  Medieval and Renaissance 227–229, 234–239
  Middle Eastern 318, 319
  nineteenth-century 242, 243

  Primitive 317
  Russian 244–260
  seventeenth-century 238–241
  sixteenth-century 241, 316
  Tibetan and Nepalese 320

Xhrouet, Mademoiselle 346

Yasutake, Kobayashi 436
Young, Peter 139
Yung Chêng 416, 417
Yung Lo 406, 407

Zeshin, Shibata 438
Zuloaga, Placido 242
Zürich porcelain 394

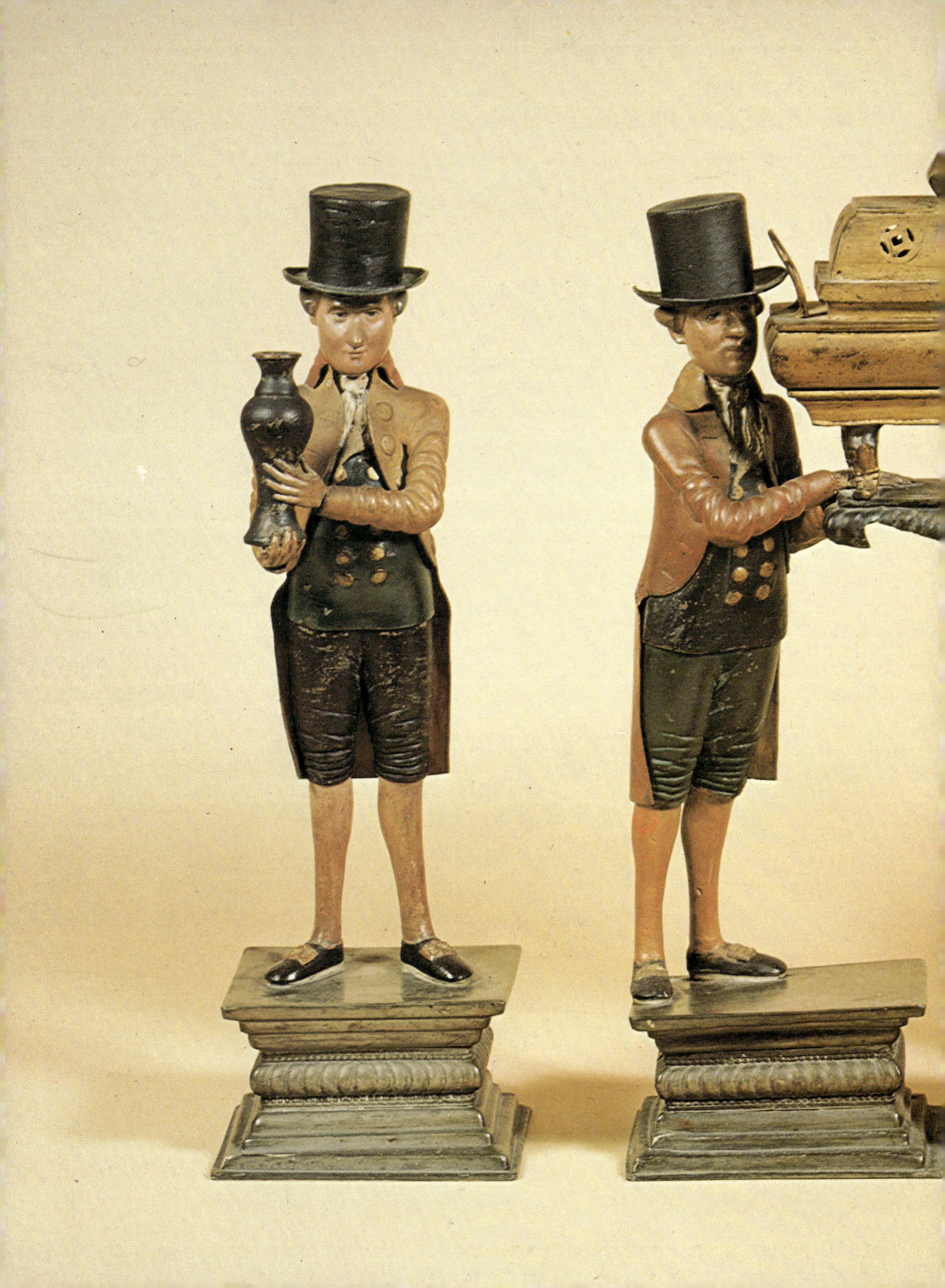